A Self-Diagnostic Approach
to Understanding Organizational
and Personal Stressors

A Self-Diagnostic Approach to Understanding Organizational and Personal Stressors

The C-O-P-E Model for Stress Reduction

Bernadette H. Schell

QUORUM BOOKS
Westport, Connecticut • London

Library of Congress Cataloging-in-Publication Data

Schell, Bernadette H. (Bernadette Hlubik), 1952–
    A self-diagnostic approach to understanding organizational and
personal stressors : the C-O-P-E model for stress reduction /
Bernadette H. Schell.
        p.   cm.
    Includes bibliographical references and index.
    ISBN 0–89930–938–0 (alk. paper)
    1. Stress (Psychology)   2. Stress management.   3. Work—
Psychological aspects.   I. Title.
BF575.S75S327   1997
158.7—dc20   96–9048

British Library Cataloguing in Publication Data is available.

Library of Congress Catalog Card Number: 96–9048
ISBN: 0–89930–938–0

First published in 1997

Quorum Books, 88 Post Road West, Westport, CT 06881
An imprint of Greenwood Publishing Group, Inc.

Printed in the United States of America

The paper used in this book complies with the
Permanent Paper Standard issued by the National
Information Standards Organization (Z39.48–1984).

10 9 8 7 6 5 4 3 2 1

To Andy, Jenny, Mandy, Brendan, and Ryan

A special "thank you" to the following people, who understand and practice being supportive: Nellie Lanteigne, Robert Gillis, Paul Cappon, Larry Denomme, Gisele Bonin, Lionel Bonin, Lou Zanibbi, Joan Mount, J. Austin Davey, Laurie Gregg, Jean Hyland, Paul Giustizia, Susan Cahoon, Warren Holmes, Stan Pasierowski, Karen DeBenedet, Stewart Tait, Marcy Weiner, and Jim Ice.

Contents

Preface

Stress is a natural part of living. Organizational members at all levels of the organization experience personal and organizational stress, but many individuals are not sure what stress is or how best to cope with excessive amounts of it.

BOOK'S AUDIENCE

This book, *A Self-Diagnostic Approach to Understanding Organizational and Personal Stressors*, was written to help anyone who works in an organization to better understand and to cope with the many stressors that are present both on and off the job. The primary aim of this book is employee survival through awareness and enhancement of one's own and other organizational members' stress-coping potentials.

BOOK'S APPROACH

The thesis of this book is rather simple: While moderate amounts of stress are constructive (and even necessary) for a fulfilling life, too much or too little stress can be destructive and distressing. The key to long-term survival, then, is for organizational members, managers, and executives to become adept at managing stress demands and opportunities in order to maintain a lifelong level of stress moderation. This book's approach emphasizes that stress moderation is effective stress-coping.

While relying heavily on psychological theories and inventories to assist the reader in discovering his or her own stress-coping potential, this book's approach attempts to be both reader-friendly and practical. That is, to help increase the reader's ease of understanding, this book is filled with inter-esting stress-related case studies from government documents, newspapers, and the author's organizational clinical files. Furthermore, practical stress-coping summary points are placed at the end of each chapter.

Beyond the introductory section, which presents the international orga-nizational stress–reduction challenge and the basic terminology associated with the stress-coping process (Part I), the remainder of the book is reader-focused and is packaged in four main parts. Each part evolves from a four-step stress management model called "C-O-P-E." The C-O-P-E model was developed by the author for use by individuals in high-stress industries.

C-O-P-E is an abbreviation that stands for the four key types of self and organizational analyses that the author (and her alter ego, William Bartell) believes are essential for understanding and developing organizational members' stress-coping potentials:

• C: the *Control* that organizational members perceive they have over personal and organizational stressors (Part II);
• O: the *Outward Signs* of distress presenting personally and organizationally (Part III);
• P: the *Personality Predispositions* and conditioned behavioral patterns contrib-uting to organizational members' overall stress levels (Part IV); and
• E: the *Energy Expenditures and Energy Returns* of organizational members as a matter of stress buffering or stress disability (Part V).

Put simply, the C-O-P-E approach is one of self-diagnosis and self-prescription. By the book's end, the reader should not only be able to diagnose his or her own ability to manage personal and organizational stress but be able to make appropriate changes (as recommended) in his or her work and home life to bring about a better-adjusted self and a de-stressing lifestyle.

BOOK'S RETURN

A Self-Diagnostic Approach to Understanding Organizational and Per-sonal Stressors attempts to share the wisdom of stress management profes-sionals at a fraction of the cost that would normally be required for stress management counseling for all individuals within the organization.

Furthermore, unlike other marketed stress management techniques that are doomed to failure because of their inherent complexity, the C-O-P-E method, as outlined here, is not only easy to remember but brings positive results to those who commit themselves to this four-step strategy. Because of its already recognized return to those who have attended the author's C-O-P-E seminars in high-stress industries, several North American companies have incorporated the C-O-P-E methodology into their leadership development and organizational member empowerment programs.

Since the primary objective of this book is to help organizational members at all levels of the organization to reach their optimal stress-coping potential, it is hoped that readers, like previous C-O-P-E seminar attendees, will have, by this book's end, a clearer understanding of the degree to which their

- Conditioned methods of stress-coping are effective in helping them to maintain control over their lives;
- Symptoms of distress are nearer the "normal" or the "danger" end of the stress continuum;
- Personality predispositions and established behavioral routines are "self-healing" or "self-destructive" as a matter of stress impairment over the longer term; and
- Established lifestyles are energy-refueling (and thus stress buffering) or energy-draining (and thus stress disabling).

Finally, this book has returns for organizations as well as for organizational members. By giving organizational members the opportunity to complete the inventories and to follow the stress-coping pointers suggested within these pages, human resource managers can provide their organizational members with vital stress reduction information and techniques without the hefty expenses associated with individualized counseling for stress-coping awareness. Today, when work-related stress illness is, by law, compensable, human resource managers need to provide their organizational members with the tools needed for surviving even the most stressful of times. This book provides one means of meeting this key company objective.

The reason that the C-O-P-E strategy has been so well received by human resource professionals is that the basic premise underlying this model is that organizational members themselves are accountable for their own stress-coping activity. Since this book commits to this philosophy of stress-empowerment—essentially a stress-awareness and behavioral modification regimen—this approach is a lot more pragmatic than other stress management approaches on the market. In short, it demands continual efforts by *both* organizational members and managers if workplaces are to become stress-safe zones.

Furthermore, some human resource professionals have commented that unlike other costly stress management approaches that give only "blanket cures" to those who purchase the seminar or book, the C-O-P-E strategy provides a custom-designed stress management awareness-and-improvement package for each participant. And since stress-coping is, theoretically, a very individualized phenomenon, one's approach for dealing with it must also be individualized rather than generalized. Like its C-O-P-E organizational seminar counterpart, *A Self-Diagnostic Approach to Understanding Organizational and Personal Stressors* helps organizational members to meet this key objective.

In the follow-up to the three-day C-O-P-E sessions that are commonly offered to organizational members in high-stress industries, many managers and human resource professionals have confided that returns on the C-O-P-E strategy are readily apparent. First, participants are given "bottom-line" information about whether or not they are effective stress-copers. Second, organizational members who believe in their own stress-coping potential and who employ the C-O-P-E strategy over the longer term talk quite freely about feeling more in control of their lives. And when organizational members feel more "in control," suggest these managers, the company gains—in terms of reduced absenteeism and accident rates and in terms of improved morale and productivity.

Part I

The Organizational Stress–
Reduction Issue

Chapter 1

Understanding the Organizational Stress–Reduction Challenge

A CASE IN POINT

William Bartell, Human Resource Manager for Wyler [Whitler] Industries Limited (*Procter v. Whitler Industries Ltd.*, 1992), sat at his desk feeling rather concerned about the way that his company had handled the incidents leading up to the job stress claim of Warren Potts. He knew that the OLRB's (Ontario Labour Relations Board's) latest findings on the Warren Potts case would be reviewed by top management shortly. From what he observed about management's behavior during the months leading up to the stress claim hearing and during the hearing itself, William was convinced that Wyler Industries could have been more effective in recognizing and in reducing stress in the workplace. There was no doubt in his mind that the stress claim of Warren Potts could have been avoided altogether, had Wyler's management team been more aware of the outward signs of job stress and better skilled at handling organizational conflicts.

He ran through the chronology of events around the case. In January 1991, Warren Potts, an organizational member with Wyler Industries Limited for only four months, lost the end of the small finger on his right hand while cleaning a dust collector at his work site. Potts was placed on workers' compensation benefits during his four-week recovery period. Immediately on his return to work one month after the accident, Warren Potts went to his foreman complaining that his work site was in the "same unsafe state" as when he had injured his finger. In his own words, Mr. Potts's reaction to the stressful incident was to lose his temper and start hollering and screaming at his foreman. Top management's reaction to the stress incident was to terminate Potts later that same day—calling his dismissal "a layoff."

Believing that his dismissal was unlawful, Mr. Potts pursued two avenues of redress. Under the Occupational Health and Safey Act, he filed a complaint with the OLRB, asking for reinstatement and compensation for personal losses following the dismissal. He also filed a claim with the WCB (Workers' Compensation Board) for mental stress compensation caused by excessive, unrelenting stress on his job, provoked, in large part, by poor relations with Wyler's management team and with Mr. Pikes, "the top man," in particular.

THE "DOWN-SIDE" TO THE JOB-STRESS CHALLENGE

The organizational stress incident of Warren Potts is not an isolated Canadian stress episode or a one-industry event. It represents, rather, an increasingly commonplace event and a job-stress challenge that organizations around the world have recently faced or are beginning to face. In 1991, the International Labour Office (ILO) in Geneva cited excessive, pathological (i.e., disease-producing) job stress as the end-of-the-century affliction from which no country or job stratum is spared (ILO, 1991).

Pathological job stress seems to strike especially hard in industrialized countries. In Japan, for example, 60% of the approximately 120 million adults employed there say they are adversely affected by excessive job stress. Elsewhere around the globe, organizational members with supervisory duties report being hard hit. In the United States, for example, 45% of organizational members employed in posts of responsibility self-report as being highly job-stressed, and 15% self-report repeat bouts of chronic depression caused by excessive and unrelenting job demands. But supervisors in developing countries are not spared from pathological job stress either. A recent poll in Morocco, for example, revealed that 40% of the company executives working there reported living under constant work pressure and suffering its wrath (ILO, 1991).

Moreover, contrary to what many believe, organizational managers and executives are not the sole victims of excessive job stress. Organizational members employed in blue-collar and pink-collar jobs around the world seem to be particularly vulnerable to pathological stress, oftentimes brought on by their inability to control both the number of organizational demands placed on them and the resources needed to accomplish these task and interpersonal demands. Research in several countries, including Germany, the United States, Canada, the United Kingdom, and Sweden, has shown that the incidence of stress-related cardiovascular disease, in particular, is significantly higher among blue-collar (ILO, 1991) and middle-management organizational members (Moss, 1981) than it is among those in the top strata.

Cardiovascular disease and chronic bouts of depression are two of the main ways that pathological job stress presents, but these are only part of a range of discomforts and illnesses that have been attributed to excessive stress levels in organizational members. The most frequent stress-related disorders studied by experts range from short-term depression, chronic fatigue, anxiety, insomnia, migraine headaches, stomach ulcers, asthma, arthritis, and substance abuse to long-term disabilities and potentially terminal disorders such as cardiovascular disease, traumatic accidents, suicide, and cancer.

Without question, widespread pathological job stress—left unchecked—is costly to individuals and to organizations. This outcome represents the "down-side" of the job-stress reduction challenge. For individual members, unchecked chronic stress can result in life-threatening disabilities. For organizations, unchecked chronic stress can result in a de-motivated workforce, work-related accidents, frequent or prolonged sick leaves, resource-draining stress claims, decreased productivity, sabotage, and even bankruptcy.

For example, there have been recent estimates that chronic job stress costs the U.S. economy approximately $150 billion a year for stress-related presentations—including absenteeism, accidents, disability claims, and replacement costs for stress-disabled organizational members (Bale, 1990). Other estimates regarding U.S. job stress suggest that over $700 million annually is spent by employers to replace 200,000 middle-aged organizational members afflicted by cardiovascular disease alone; and personnel managers at Xerox estimate that it costs their company, on average, $600,000 annually just to replace one executive stricken with stress-related illness (Cooper, 1986).

Furthermore, stress-related illnesses such as alcoholism, coronary disease, and mental ill health are costing European industry a fortune. The Centre for Health Economics estimates that over £1.3 billion alone is lost each year in the United Kingdom due to alcohol abuse by organizational members. And within the last decade, the World Health Organization published figures indicating that not only is the United Kingdom near the top of the world league table in terms of mortality caused by cardiovascular disease, but that substantial yearly increases in this type of mortality have been noted for the United Kingdom by experts studying health trends. In contrast, countries whose industries have taken steps to reduce job- and lifestyle stress by introducing health promotion and stress management programs for their organizational members are showing declines in cardiovascular disease for the first time this century (Cooper, 1986).

Besides stress-related illness costs, there is a secondary source of growing stress-related costs to industry. Like Mr. Potts in the earlier case, organizational members around the world, and particularly in North America, are increasingly filing job-stress claims against their employers through worker compensation regulations and job-applicable stress laws.

For example, since the California Supreme Court upheld its first stress-disability case in the early 1970s, the stress-related compensation claims for psychiatric injury in this U.S. state now total over 3,000 a year. The California Labor Code now stipulates specifically that workers' compensation is allowable for disability or illness caused by repetitive mental or physical traumatic activities extending over a period of time, the combined effect of which causes any disability or need for medical treatment (Cooper, 1986). Evidence collected by various insurance bodies in the United States indicates that stressed-out organizational members in other states are following suit. There have been recent reports that workers' compensation claims related to job stress have tripled in the United States since 1980. In 1989, for example, stress claims accounted for 15% of all occupational disease claims, up from less than 5% in 1980 (Levan, Katz, & Hochwarter, 1990).

In North America, most stress claims have thus far been litigated within the workers' compensation system, and in the United States the average payment made to successful claimants has been about $15,000 (Levan, Katz, & Hochwarter, 1990). This award average is expected to rise as stress-claim allegations by organizational members are carried to other court and arbitration arenas—a shift caused mainly by an over-burdened WCB system suffering from a tremendous case backlog.

In Canada, a rise in average award level for job-stress claims has not yet been observed. In fact, successful job-stress awards in Canadian hearing settings have been considerably lower than those stemming from the U.S. workers' compensation system. Although Canadian courts have allowed by law compensation ranging from $500 to $25,000 on this head of damages, the majority of successful awards to date have fallen near the low end.

Although job pressures and harassment are the most frequently cited causes of job-related stress in the North American litigation arenas, additional sources of job-imparted distress have included unrealistic workload and time pressures, poor managerial attitudes and interpersonal skill development, negative workplace relationships, unpleasant client contacts, and job insecurity (Levan, Katz, & Hochwarter, 1990).

Compared to North America, stress claims in European countries have been somewhat delayed. In the United Kingdom, for example, several unions began supporting stress claims by individual organizational members during the mid-1980s. Despite this relative delay, stress experts in the United Kingdom suggest that the industry trend is certainly in the direction of future disability claims and general damages being awarded on the basis of cumulative trauma in the workplace (Cooper, 1986).

Predictions are that distressed organizational members in up-to-now "dormant" countries will soon mimic their North American and European counterparts who have decided to proact against chronic and unrelenting job stress. Some stress experts suggest that both the stress-claim dollar settlement amounts and the number of claims around the world are likely to increase dramatically to the point that job-related stress claims will dominate the occupational disease field.

Several demographic changes in the workforce are likely to contribute to this increase. For example, those classes who have not yet filed large numbers of stress claims—namely, the white-collar, female, and neophyte organizational member segments—are expected to file in greater numbers. Organizational factors likely fueling this rise in stress claims include an increase in mergers, plant closings, and relocations caused by difficult economic times; job growth in the highly stressful service industries; and positive decisions from courtroom arbitrators and judges who are likely to be more sympathetic to claimants' arguments than overworked WCB committee members (Levan, Katz, & Hochwarter, 1990). In support of the latter point, the Massachusetts Supreme Court recently ruled that a terminated employee could collect workers' compensation for the mental stress that she suffered when she was laid off.

But what about job-dismissed Warren Potts? How did he fare with his two stress claims in the OLRB and the WCB arenas? What was Potts's basic stress claim? What types of evidence did the parties to the dispute bring before the hearers of the case? What criteria did the hearers use to arrive at their decisions? Based on cases already heard in North America, what are the probabilities that organizational members will be successful at winning their claims? The remainder of this chapter addresses these very important questions. However, before these questions can be attended to effectively, the positive side of the job-stress challenge needs to be examined.

THE "UP-SIDE" TO THE JOB-STRESS CHALLENGE

Until now, this chapter has focused on the negative side of the stress equation, particularly organizational or job stress. Often, members at all levels of the organizational hierarchy conceptualize the stress process—whether it be triggered by one's job or by one's personal life—as a negative event and as something to be avoided. But how realistic is this approach to stress?

Let's face it, there is no such thing as a stress-free life. In fact, the only time that humans are truly stress-free is when they are six feet underground and not moving. Some degree of stress is good. A certain degree of stress makes life interesting and helps human beings to self-actualize (i.e., to become everything that they are capable of becoming). It is now time to look at the positive side of the stress equation and, further, the positive side of the international job-stress challenge.

Understanding the Positive Side of the Stress Process

To begin, each human being is born with a finite set of life energy for accomplishing all that needs to be accomplished during one's lifetime. Given that most individuals are programmed by nature to live well into their seventies and beyond, individuals' resourceful spending of their finite life energy is critical for long-term survival and biologically appropriate aging.

Sometimes in life, machines and humans alike need extra bursts of energy to accomplish an extraordinary life demand or an extraordinary set of life demands. As a case in point, take an airplane that is required to fly an extended distance to deal with an unscheduled emergency pickup; the pilot may, through necessity, have to tap into the plane's emergency fuel reserves to meet this special demand. Similarly, humans may need an extra energy supply to meet special demands, such as the boss's request to work an overtime shift or the spouse's request to paint the entire living room in a three-hour period.

Knowing that humans would occasionally need extra fuel for demanding life situations (ranging from self-preservation to self-esteem building and self-actualization), nature supplied all human beings with a kind of emergency fuel pack called "the stress mechanism." By definition, the "stress mechanism" is a mind-body process that enables humans to draw on their energy reserves when required, in response to some special demand (a stress stimulus) or to a series of special demands (stress stimuli).

By convention, stress stimuli are called "stressors." Stressors can be real or imagined. They can be perceived by the emotional portion of the mind to be undesirable and anger producing (the "distressors") or to be desirable and pleasure producing (the "eustressors"). By convention, stressors emanating from the organizational environment are called "job stressors" or "organizational stressors," whereas those emanating from the home and nonwork environment are called "personal stressors."

Although the physiological stress mechanism is very complex, it works something like this: When the mind perceives that the body's "normal" fuel supplies are not adequate for a stressor or set of stressors, it emits an "alert message" to the body, advising it that extra energy is required. Once alerted, the body instantaneously responds by releasing energy from its body stores through a complex set of biochemical reactions and through the coordination of the sympathetic nervous system and the endocrine system.

Just as few things in life are free, there is a cost associated with stress mechanism usage. Every time that the physiological stress mechanism is called on, some degree of strain is placed on the human system. By definition, "strain" is the degree of physiological, psychological, or behavioral deviation from the human system's "normal" life pattern that results from a stressful life event or a series of stressful life events. The degree of energy consumed both in meeting the demand and in returning the human system to its "normal" state determines the amount of overall strain—and thus the amount of potential destruction—experienced by the human system at any given point in time.

Research evidence has shown dramatic premature aging of human systems placed under excessive, unrelenting periods of strain (called "chronic strain"). By its very nature, aging places the human system at risk for a range of physiological, psychological, and behavioral complications, including reduced immunity to disease and an inability to recuperate rapidly after disease onset.

Short-term stress and strain present in humans through a variety of symptoms or outward signs, including elevated blood pressure (a physiological manifestation), anxiety or depression (psychological manifestations), and work obsession or work avoidance (behavioral manifestations).

Chronic stress and strain generally present much more forcefully and dramatically, through disorders such as cardiovascular disease (a physiological manifestation), clinical depression or panic attacks (psychological manifestations), and alcoholism or workaholism (behavioral manifestations). Table 1.1 summarizes the common human system symptoms of stress and strain.

To reduce humans' risk for excessive stress and strain, nature seems to have stamped on the brain at birth a kind of invisible warning label that reads "FOR LONG-TERM SURVIVAL, USE THE STRESS-MECHANISM SPARINGLY AS WELL AS CRITICALLY AND INTELLIGENTLY." In short, although the physiological stress mechanism is a very positive and critically essential means of coping with (i.e., dealing with) life's special demands, it should not be overused or misused. When put on "overdrive" for too long, the constructive physiological stress mechanism actually becomes destructive. Thus, it should not be called into use by the mind for noncritical life events. Critically intelligent, conscious use of the stress mechanism is not only good stress management but sound finite life-energy management.

With time, this kind of warning label seems to fade, and humans' patterned attitudes and behaviors (i.e., their personality predispositions) then set the stage for the amount of stress and strain experienced by them, along with the stressful life situations that present but are outside humans' conscious control (such as the death of a relative or the employer's filing for bankruptcy). Given this reality, stress experts suggest that the appropriate means for assessing stress and strain for any human system is to understand that human's stress-predisposing factors—physiologically, psychologically, and behaviorally—as well the events (both on and off the job) that the human perceives are stressful but outside his or her conscious control.

Although everyone in life experiences distressing life events, not everyone

Table 1.1
Individual Symptoms of Stress

1.	Physiological	
	Short term:	Heart rate, GSR, respiration, headache
	Long term:	Ulcer, blood pressure, heart attack
	Nonspecific:	Adrenaline, noradrenaline, thymus deduction, lympth deduction, gastric acid production, ACTH production
2.	Psychological responses (affective and cognitive)	
	Flight or withdrawal	
	Apathy, resignation, boredom	
	Regression	
	Projection	
	Negativism	
	Fantasy	
	Expression of boredom with much of everything	
	Forgetfulness	
	Tendency to misjudge people	
	Uncertainty about whom to trust	
	Inability to organize self	
	Inner confusion about duties or roles	
	Dissatisfaction	
	High intolerance for ambiguity, do not deal well with new or strange situations	
	Tunnel vision	
	Tendency to begin vacillating in decision making	

Tendency to become distraught with trifles
Inattentiveness: loss of power to concentrate
Irritability
Procrastination
Feelings of persecution
Gut-level feelings or unexplainable dissatisfaction

3. Behavior
   A. Individual consequences
      Loss of appetite
      Sudden, noticeable loss or gain of weight
      Sudden change or appearance; decline/improvement in dress
      Sudden change of complexion (sallow, reddened, acne)
      Sudden change in hair style or length
      Difficult breathing
      Sudden change of smoking habits
      Sudden change in use of alcohol
   B. Organizational consequences
      Low performance-quality/quantity
      Low job involvement
      Loss of responsibility
      Lack of concern for organization
      Lack of concern for colleagues
      Loss of creativity
      Absenteeism
      Voluntary turnover
      Accident proneness

Source: Schuler, R. S. (1980). Definition and conceptualization of stress in organizations. *Organizational Behavior and Human Performance, 25,* 186.

self-destructs physiologically, psychologically, or behaviorally. Recently, researchers have made great inroads into understanding why some personalities seem to be "self-healing"—even in highly stressful work and home situations—whereas other personalities seem to be "self-destructive"—even in relatively nonstressful life environments. What these researchers have found is that it is not people who have healthy ways of expressing the anger that results from distressing life situations who generally suffer from stress-related disorders. Rather, it is people who suffer from chronic misplaced anger who generally suffer such fates. These "disease-prone" individuals tend to repress anger rather than consciously deal with it; turn the anger onto themselves and become depressed; or project it, unreasonably, onto others.

Thus, life-energy efficiency and mind-body preservation equate to good stress management. Good stress management means using nature's built-in stress-survival mechanism to its full advantage for the purpose it was intended. Poor stress management means misusing or overusing this mechanism. Energy mismanagement results in excessive draining of one's finite life resources, premature aging, and stress-disabling responses. In short, stress "self-healers" are good stress managers, while stress "disease-prone" individuals are poor stress managers.

This book on personal and organizational stress reiterates this key point throughout its chapters: *That while moderate amounts of stress stimulation are constructive and even necessary for a fulfilling life, too much or too little stress stimulation can be anger producing and, thus, potentially self-destructive.*

Transferring this learning to the organizational environment, members at all levels of the organization need to become adept at managing their personal and organizational stress demands in order to maintain a lifelong level of moderate stress and an adequate supply of finite life energy for accomplishing what needs to be accomplished both on and off the job.

Understanding How Organizations Can Better Meet the Job-Stress Challenge

Recent evidence from around the world suggests that organizations who have discovered the principle of stress moderation and have committed themselves to it in the workplace have benefited immensely. As two cases in point, the United States and Finland seem to be showing declines in their levels of stress-related illness on two fronts—cardiovascular disease and alcoholism. In contrast, as noted, within the last decade, the United Kingdom has been facing spiraling mortality rates caused by cardiovascular disease.

Experts in countries who have not fared so well on the stress front are asking, Why the success in the United States and Finland? Do these two countries have privileged health information that other countries do not have? Is it the case that U.S. and Finnish employers are significantly more caring about organizational members and significantly less "bottom-line fixated" than their colleagues around the world?

In response to the first question, it seems inappropriate to argue that the United States and Finland are more health information privileged than other developed countries. In recent years, developed countries around the world have pumped billions of research dollars into determining the causes of stress-related disease and the means for rehabilitating individuals who are afflicted by various stress-and-strain presentations. But the many positive findings that have flowed from these studies are readily available in academic journals that circulate around the globe. Thus, in response to the first suggestion, it is unlikely that privileged health information in the United States and in Finland is the secret to these countries' stress-reduction successes.

In response to the second question, U.K. stress expert Cary Cooper suggests that U.S. employers are no more altruistic or caring about their organizational members than employers in other countries; if there is a difference in orientation, it is probably that the U.S. employers are becoming more accountable when it comes to stress reduction in the workplace (Cooper, 1986), as compared to some of their colleagues around the world. Dr. Cooper maintains that two trends in the United States have likely forced companies to become more accountable. First, American industry is facing an enormous and ever-spiraling organizational member health-care bill. While individual insurance costs have risen by 50% over the past twenty years, employers' contributions have risen by over 140%. Second, because more and more organizational members are filing stress claims, U.S. employers are left with one viable option: either PROACT against pathological levels of stress in the workplace or REACT to the stress claims that "stressed-out" organizational members file (and be prepared to face the distress and hefty financial losses that accompany such claims).

Dr. Cooper further maintains that many employers in the United Kingdom are under the false impression that their organizational members can live under intolerable stress and strain conditions because the taxpayer is there to pick up the health rehabilitation bill through the National Health Service. There is no direct accountability or incentive for U.K. firms to maintain the health of their employees. Even though the indirect costs of stress-related disease are enormous to industry, rarely do companies with this "external-locus" (i.e., "other-responsible") type of attitude attempt to estimate this cost. Instead, they simply treat absenteeism, labor turnover, substance abuse, low morale, and low productivity as an intrinsic part of doing business (Cooper, 1986). Thus, it is probably not a lack of information or an exaggerated sense of altruism that differentiates job-stress-reducing countries from job-stress-inducing countries—but rather individuals and organizations that are stress-accountable.

What, specifically, have job-stress-accountable companies done to tackle excessive levels of job stress? For starters, there is a pervasive positive and "internal-locus" (i.e., "self-responsible") attitude toward stress recognition and stress management in the workplace. Further, this positive attitude exists at all levels of the organizational hierarchy, starting at the top. Two key understandings seem to comprise this reality, consistent with points raised earlier and consistent with this book's theme:

1. There is a recognition by organizational members at all levels that stressors need not be totally abolished, because in moderate amounts stress stimuli can be healthful and self-actualizing; and

2. There is a recognition by organizational members that pathological levels of organizational and personal stress are destructive and extremely costly from both an organizational member and an organizational survival perspective.

There also seems to be an ongoing behavioral commitment to stress reduction in the workplace by organizational members and management alike. More and more job-stress-accountable unions and company management are jointly providing stress management seminars to help organizational members at all levels of the hierarchy to recognize the outward signs of excessive stress and strain and the means for preventing such excesses; stress counseling for organizational members who want professional assistance in bringing about a better-adjusted self and a stress-reduced lifestyle; keep-fit and wellness programs to help organizational members maintain a healthy physical regimen; and comprehensive Employee Assistance Programs to help organizational members get professional advice/assistance on areas required for personal health and productivity, including but not limited to alcoholism treatment, smoking cessation, assertiveness training, cue-induced muscle-relaxation training, and family counseling.

U.S. managers who have proacted against pathological stress in the workplace have raved about the returns on their investments. For example, the New York Telephone Company reported that their wellness program, which has a comprehensive cardiovascular fitness program, saves the organization at least $2.7 million in absence and health treatment costs annually. Moreover, after Kennecott (the giant copper corporation) introduced a counseling program for organizational members in distress, management discovered that the absenteeism rates of organizational members dropped by nearly 60% in a year, and medical costs were reduced by a significant 55% (Cooper, 1986). Other organizational experts have reported the benefits of ongoing stress abatement programs in significantly reducing organizational accident rates and the enormous personal and organizational costs associated with them (Steffy et al., 1986).

In contrast, asserts Dr. Cooper, only a few companies in Europe have attempted to proact in such a manner against job stress—and the United Kingdom's cardiovascular disease record speaks to this problem. In addition, suggests Dr. Cooper, many European human resource personnel or company executives who have noted problems of stress excesses in their organizational members have found it difficult to implement stress management programs because senior managers often feel that "stress is none of our business" or that "they [organizational members] should be able to cope on their own" or that "our responsibility is to make profits for our shareholders, not to mollycoddle our employees" (Cooper, 1986).

It is this kind of negative, external-locus attitude about stress reduction by company managers that feeds stress-claim allegations by organizational members. Moreover, it is an ignorance of the stress process by organizational members at all levels of the organization that promotes self-destruction and low productivity rather than self-healing and high productivity.

Dr. George Coppee of the Medical Section of the ILO's Occupational Safety and Health Branch notes a particular void in the knowledge base of organizational members, particularly managers. Briefly, asserts Dr. Coppee, there is ignorance of the "stress bridge" between organizational members' physical, mental, and social well-being. An attack on one aspect of the human being by work and personal stressors means an attack on the other aspects. "Thus, a cut in the hand is a physical wound but at the same time it affects the mind, provoking distress or anxiety, and can cause functional disability and incapacity to work. Similarly, the loss of one's job has an impact on the mind and on the physical health of the individual" (ILO, 1991, pp. 1–2).

Dr. Coppee concludes, "As long as one continues to compartmentalize man and his health, one will be unable to understand either fatigue or stress. . . . Thus, for example, in the case of an accident, workplace health services should not simply administer first aid and send the victim to hospital but should also be actively concerned with minimising the psychological and social consequences of the accident and ensuring a follow-up until the injured person returns to work" (ILO, 1991, p. 2).

But was the latter stress-reduction prescription the case with Wyler Industries and Warren Potts? Did Wyler's management team practice sound job-stress management when "stressed-out" Warren Potts went to his foreman complaining about the unsafe state of his workplace? Did either the OLRB or the WCB conclude that Wyler Industries was successfully meeting the job-stress challenge?

Before answering these specific questions on the Warren Potts case, it is wise that we return, first, to an earlier set of questions raised around the factors known to affect the success of job-stress claims.

FACTORS RELATED TO THE SUCCESS OF JOB-STRESS CLAIMS

The odds of an organizational member's winning his or her job-stress claim seems to rest on some key factors. Based on the North American cases that have been heard to date, these can generally be summarized as follows:

- The grounds on which the job-stress claim is filed;
- The criterion hearers of the case use to arrive at their decisions;
- The types of evidence brought by the parties to the hearers of the case; and
- The probability of organizational members' winning their stress-claim cases, based on available award data.

The Grounds for Job-Stress Claims

Notwithstanding a range in allowances made and limitations imposed by stress laws existing in various geographic jurisdictions, organizational members in North America have commonly filed their job-stress claims on one of the following three grounds:

1. Physical-mental claims, whereby a physical-injury stressor leads to a mental disability (e.g., a loss of one's finger tip leads to chronic depression);
2. Mental-physical claims, whereby a mental stressor leads to a physical disability (e.g., observing one's coworker die on the job brings on an immediate heart attack); and
3. Mental-mental claims, whereby a mental stressor leads to a mental disability (e.g., a period of continuous harassment by management leads to disabling anxiety attacks and a fear of work).

Organizational members and employers need to be clear about which ground the stress claim is filed on, for some grounds seem easier for the claimant "to prove" in court than others. As a rule of thumb, the more "visible" the pathology presenting, the easier the court battle is for the claimant.

The Criterion Hearers Use to Arrive at Their Decisions

As suggested already, hearers of the job-stress claim generally focus on the degree of stress-related disability that presents in the claimant. By definition, "stress-related disability" refers to the ill-health conditions that the organizational member may experience as a result of the stress response to the job stressor(s) in question.

If the hearers' conclusion is that a sizable stress disability exists, then the size of an appropriate award for the claimant is determined. The purpose of a compensation award is to return the claimant as nearly as possible to the situation that he or she would have been in if the job stressor(s) in question had not presented. In other words, the objective in making an award is to make the claimant "whole" again, avoiding under- or over-compensation on the loss the complainant suffered. The award amount is based, in large part, on the degree of disability presenting. Thus, employers need to ascertain early on the extent of the disability being claimed so that they can budget properly.

The Types of Evidence Brought by the Parties to the Hearers of the Case

In the 1970s, many of the stress claims taken to North American litigation arenas were the "visible" cases, characterized by the physical-mental and the mental-physical claims. Then, in the early 1980s the less visible but severe mental-mental cases began to appear in litigation arenas. Since that time, the trend has been for the courts and the WCBs to be the most willing to grant stress-claim awards to organizational members presenting acute traumatic neuroses, commonly called "nervous shock." Although *The Diagnostic and Statistical Manual of Mental Disorders*, or "DSM-III-R" (1987)—the recognized authority on the diagnosis of mental and psychological illnesses—does not recognize "nervous shock" as a disorder, since 1986, it has recognized a stress-related disability called "post-traumatic stress disorder," or PTSD.

Briefly, PTSD may be suffered by a person who experiences an event (1) that is outside the "normal range" of human experience and (2) that would be markedly distressing to almost anyone experiencing it. Thus, a serious threat to one's life or physical integrity, such as a threatening workplace accident, would qualify as a markedly distressing event. A real or perceived threat to one's children, spouse, or other relatives would also qualify. Sudden destruction of one's home or community, and seeing someone be physically injured or killed as a result of an accident or physical violence would also qualify as stressors likely inducing PTSD (DSM-III-R, 1987, p. 250).

PTSD is important for employers to recognize and to respond to quickly for the following award and damage-apportionment reasons (Hewitt, 1982):

1. PTSD can only be directly attributed to a severe, life-threatening situation involving the claimant or one which he or she has witnessed. Therefore, if PTSD is correctly diagnosed by a psychiatrist or other recognized mental health professional as having been caused by the "situation" for which the employer is liable, the employer's defense strategy of

looking to a preexisting personality disorder in the organizational member for an apportionment of damages is, indeed, limited.

2. Although PTSD is generally receptive to psychotherapy treatment, left undiagnosed and untreated, PTSD can worsen—particularly when the claimant is involved in litigation hearings that encourage him or her to ruminate about the traumatic event. Thus, employers facing legitimate PTSD cases are well advised by their defense lawyers to settle the case early rather than later in order that the claimant can receive the necessary psychological treatment.

3. Because the diagnostic criteria for PTSD have been around only since 1986, it is not uncommon for errors to be made in the diagnosis of this disorder. Employers should be cautioned that because the hallmark of PTSD is that it is triggered by a traumatic environmental event, the hearers are more likely to attribute the PTSD disability to the alleged work event than to a preexisting personality disorder in the organizational member. To date, the failure of the employer's defense counsel to challenge the diagnosis of PTSD in the appropriate case and to educate the hearers of the case on the definition of this disorder often prejudices the defense.

Although all 50 U.S. states and most Canadian provinces recognize that such "visibly traumatic" PTSD claims are compensable and stand a good chance of winning in the courts, the compensability of less visible mental-mental disabilities is still new and problematic for the claimant to win for a number of reasons (Levan, Katz, & Hochwarter, 1990). First, since there is no physical corroboration for either the stressor or the disability, it is hard for the claimant's legal officer to prove that the disability was caused by work. The employer's legal officer will often argue, in defense, that other factors such as distressing personal relationships at home, preexisting personality disorders, and financial difficulties are the real reasons for the mental disability's presenting.

Second, uncertainties surrounding the field of psychiatry and the patient's timing in terms of entry into the medical system for psychological treatment make it difficult for the hearers of the case to determine whether the claimant was mentally disabled before the entry of the alleged work distressor, or after. The employer's legal officer will argue, most often, that the claimant had a predisposing psychiatric disability prior to the onset of the alleged work distressor.

Third, there is often concern by hearers of the case about whether the work-related stressor aggravated a preexisting psychiatric condition, and if so, whether it should be compensable. The employer's legal officer will make argument, most often, that if a preexisting psychiatric condition did exist, the onus should be on the claimant to receive appropriate treatment for his or her disabling condition. The employer should not have to pay for a work situation (albeit distressing) that most other organizational members who are normally predisposed could likely manage.

To prevent the frivolous or vexatious filing of stress claims by organizational members against their employers, in recent years a number of U.S. states and Canadian provinces have begun to set some limits on allowable stress-claim grounds, with some jurisdictions being more restrictive than others (Levan, Katz, & Hochwarter, 1990). For example, as of 1990, six U.S. states had passed restrictive legislation stating that a nonphysical stressor causing a mental disability must be sudden, and in ten states, there was legislation stating that the stressor must be unusual if it is gradual. In another ten U.S. states, there was rather nonrestrictive legislation allowing the granting of compensation for gradual psychological injury resulting in mental disability, regardless of whether the stressor was unusual.

In 1989, only the Canadian provinces of Saskatchewan and Quebec allowed chronic mental-mental stress claims. The remaining provinces allowed acute physical-mental and mental-physical claims.

The Probability of Organizational Members' Winning Their Stress-Claim Cases

The probability of a claimant's winning his or her case depends as well on hearing factors, including the effectiveness of expert witnesses' arguments and the argued degree of mental disability presenting in the claimant.

As is probably already evident, both parties to a stress-claim dispute are likely to place on the expert witness stand one or more psychiatrists (i.e., medical doctors with a specialty in mental health). The polarized nature of claimant- and defense-procured psychiatric reports (both oral and written) is obvious in light of each party's objectives. Commonly, claimant-secured psychiatric evaluations maximize both the severity and length of psychiatric disability and impairment (Marcus, 1986). The cause of the mental disability is imputed to the organizational "situation" at issue. Suggested psychiatric treatments commonly consist of one or more of the following: biofeedback sessions to help the clients relax; counseling sessions by a trained professional to help clients reestablish mental health; and antidepressant/tranquilizing medications (such as amitriptyline, buspirone, Limbitrol, prazepam, and Triavil) to help reestablish a positive emotional framework.

In contrast, defense-secured psychiatric evaluations commonly minimize the severity of disability and vehemently question its presence (Marcus, 1986). Mental disabilities, if they exist at all, are generally argued to be temporary, minimally disabling, and not in need of professional assistance. If a mental disability presents, it is argued to be preexisting, caused by a personality dysfunction or by distressing life circumstances. If the claimant did receive psychiatric treatment for a preexisting mental disability, the defense-secured psychiatric assessment might argue that the treatment received was "overtreatment"—caused, in part, by the treating psychiatrist's promotion of dependency in his or her clients.

After submissions, the hearers of the case must decide if there is a sizable degree of mental disability presenting that was caused by the alleged job stressor or set of job stressors.

Often, the degree of disability is assessed in terms of psychiatric impairment criteria, such as those listed in the U.S. Social Security guidelines. These guidelines include the following specifics (Marcus, 1986):

1. Estimated degree of impairment of the claimant's ability to relate to other people (both on and off the job).

2. Estimated degree or restriction of daily activities, such as the claimant's ability to go to church, to work around the house, to leave the house, and so on.

3. Estimated degree of deterioration in the claimant's personal habits.

4. Estimated degree of constriction of the claimant's interests.

5. Estimated degree of limitations on the claimant's ability to do the following, on a sustained basis, in a routine work setting: understand, carry out, and remember instructions; respond appropriately to supervision; respond appropriately to coworkers; respond to customary work pressures; perform simple tasks; perform complex tasks; perform repetitive tasks; and perform varied tasks.

Considering both the ability of the parties to present convincing evidence and the degree of disability presenting in the claimant, stress experts estimate that, across most job families, the probability that the claimant will be successful in a job-stress claim is about 30%. Claimants in high-stress occupations such as police work, air-traffic control, and psychiatry fare considerably better, with success probabilities falling closer to the 40% mark (Oregon Department of Insurance and Finance, 1987).

THE CONCLUSION TO THE WARREN POTTS CASE

It is time now to return to the Warren Potts case, which introduced this chapter and the job-stress reduction challenge. How did Warren Potts fare in his attempts to seek redress for the alleged wrongful job dismissal and the alleged mental disability that ensued? Recall that Potts, believing that his dismissal was unlawful, filed a complaint with the OLRB, asking for reinstatement and compensation for his losses. He also filed a complaint with the WCB for compensation for mental stress.

The WCB rejected Potts's claim for job-stress compensation, a decision he then appealed. By a decision dated May 3, 1991, the OLRB allowed Mr. Potts's complaint for wrongful dismissal and recommended that he be reinstated in his job at Wyler Industries Limited. The OLRB further ordered that the parties settle on the quantum of compensation owing to Mr. Potts for his wrongful dismissal—and remained seized in case the parties could not agree on the amount owing.

While this summary may appear to provide a quick ending to a job-stress claim story, like many job-stress situations, the Potts-Wyler Industries stress challenge got worse before it got better.

In accordance with the OLRB May 3, 1991, order, Mr. Potts was offered reinstatement by Wyler Industries on May 23, 1991. However, Mr. Potts did not return to work on this stipulated date because he maintained that he could not perform his work duties. Mr. Potts told management that because of his finger-tip injury and an additional condition known as "carpal tunnel syndrome" (a wrist condition often affecting finger mobility), he needed to stay off work. Accepting this argument temporarily, Mr. Pikes placed Mr. Potts on Workers' Compensation Benefits.

In August 1991, Mr. Pikes wrote to the WCB, questioning the relatedness of Mr. Potts's carpal tunnel syndrome to his January 1991, workplace finger injury. The WCB reviewed Mr. Potts's case and concluded that his carpal tunnel condition was not related to his compensable injury. Mr. Potts was then notified that his compensation benefits would be terminated, effective November 1991. Dissatisfied with the outcome, Mr. Potts appealed the WCB decision. He remained off work, arguing that he could not complete the work duties required of him.

In late November 1991, the dispute between Mr. Potts and Mr. Pikes intensified. Since the parties had not been able to agree on an amount of compensation owing, an OLRB hearing to deal with the matter was scheduled for December 9, 1991. But on November 20, 1991, Mr. Potts's counsel requested that the OLRB adjourn the December hearing date because her client, Warren Potts, was undergoing surgery—an event, she argued, that required a six-week recovery period (as documented by a physician).

On November 21, 1991, the OLRB received a letter from Mr. Pikes, requesting that there be no hearing on December 9, or thereafter, because, in Mr. Pikes's words, he did not feel that any hearing was necessary on the issue of damages. Then in a November 27, 1991, follow-up letter to the request for consent for hearing adjournment, Mr. Pikes wrote to the OLRB, saying that he not only believed that a hearing on the issue of damages was unnecessary but that an adjournment for six weeks was unreasonable and exaggerated by the claimant's physician.

In the end, the OLRB granted the adjournment on medical grounds, saying that there was adequate medical documentation to show that Mr. Potts's request was reasonable and made in sufficient time to reschedule the matter. The compensation hearing was rescheduled for January 16, 1992, despite yet another letter written by Mr. Pikes to the OLRB objecting to any hearing at all.

Mr. Potts's Grounds for His Job-Stress Claim

The particulars of Mr. Potts's claim before the OLRB on January 16, 1992, consisted of vacation pay and damages for mental distress caused by the unlawful layoff in February 1991. The claim was also for damages caused by the loss of dental plan coverage in the months following his wrongful dismissal.

The Types of Evidence Brought by the Parties to the OLRB Hearing

At the January 16, 1992, hearing, Mr. Potts testified that since the time of the loss of part of his finger at work in January 1991, he suffered nightmares and had frequent headaches and stress. His layoff a month after his injury, he maintained, made his stress worse. He also expressed feelings of fear, saying that any contact with Wyler Industries, especially with Mr. Pikes, caused him great stress.

Relating to the period around his discharge, Mr. Potts specifically mentioned being disturbed by his insensitive treatment by management when trying to get his separation papers. He testified that Mr. Pikes had him return twice before filling out a separation slip, making remarks such as, "I want to fire you, but I can't get away with it, so I am laying you off." He went on to say that he had a number of other stressful contacts with Mr. Pikes since his discharge around his reinstatement and other matters.

Concerning Mr. Potts's claim that his finger accident and his discharge one month later caused him great mental distress, the Board admitted, over the objection of Wyler Industries, two medical reports—one written by a psychiatrist who had assessed Mr. Potts in the Spring of 1991 (Dr. Olive) and one written by Mr. Potts's family physician (Dr. Sly).

According to Dr. Olive, on April 18, 1991, Mr. Potts presented stress symptoms consisting of "headaches up to five times a day, anger, nightmares about the accident, and repeated memories, with emotional content, of the incident." Accordingly, he described Mr. Potts as having a mild post-traumatic stress disorder. Dr. Olive suggested that "Given the somewhat horrific nature of the circumstances surrounding the injury it is not surprising that he [Mr. Potts] had developed a mild post-traumatic stress disorder which seems to be perpetuated by the unresolved work situation and the rage he feels."

The June 11, 1991, opinion of Dr. Sly, whom Mr. Potts had seen weekly since the time of his finger injury, mirrored that of the psychiatrist. He spoke of Mr. Potts's high degree of psychological strain resulting from work. Emphasizing his client's three-week bout of depression, Dr. Sly wrote:

Contributing to his [Mr. Potts's] ongoing struggle was the termination of his job this winter. For a three week interval immediately following this event, he felt quite depressed. He expresses to me the anger, humiliation and frustration over the inconsistent and contradictory dealings he had with his employer.

Mr. Potts has suffered a stress reaction that resulted in nightmares, loss of self-esteem and a phobia towards his former work site. This stems from his injury and has been reinforced by his job termination.

The OLRB was also informed during the hearing that Mr. Potts sought further psychiatric assistance from Dr. Olive for his stress-related discomforts in August and in December 1991.

As to his claim for dental benefits, Mr. Potts testified that he had an abcessed tooth that required extraction in July 1991, a procedure that cost him $300. During the tooth extraction, his dentist told him that he needed further root canal work (costing about $700) and seven fillings (costing another $700). Even though this type of dental work was covered by the Wyler Industries' dental plan, Mr. Potts was removed from coverage by Mr. Pikes when the claimant had not returned to work in May 1991. Thus, Mr. Potts testified that he did not have any other dental work completed besides the one tooth extraction because he simply could not afford to have it done.

In closing their submission, Mr. Potts's counsel argued that the OLRB's jurisdiction to award mental distress damages was established in a 1987 case, *Jacmorr Manufacturing Limited*. In the latter case, the OLRB declined to award damages for mental distress because the claim had not been raised in a timely manner. However, the OLRB clearly found that its broad remedial jurisdiction included the possibility of such damages and saw no reason why the Board should be less sensitive than the courts or other tribunals to the possibility that illegal conduct might give rise to this form of damages.

As to the amount of damages for mental distress claimed, Mr. Potts's counsel said that the courts had ordered damages from $500 to $25,000 on this head of damages, and she left the matter in the Board's hands. On the subject of dental benefits, counsel argued that had her client not been unlawfully dismissed in February 1991, he would have been covered for the dental work he needed. He, thus, should be awarded the full cost of the dental work that he already had or still required (i.e., $1,700).

Mr. Pikes responded for Wyler Industries. No expert testimony by a psychiatrist was presented before the Board on behalf of Wyler Industries Ltd. As Mr. Pikes began his testimony, he did not deny making remarks to Mr. Potts such as, "I want to fire you, but I can't get away with it, so I am laying you off." His major line of defense throughout his submission was that if damages for mental distress were to be awarded in Mr. Potts's case, they would be warranted every time an employee did not like his or her employer. He also argued that based on the 1987 case precedent cited, this was not a proper case for mental-distress damages because there was no mention of the damages in the initial OLRB hearing on the merits of the complaint. Mr. Pikes questioned the validity of the family doctor's opinion on stress disability. As before, Mr. Pikes was adamant that no damages should be awarded to Mr. Potts. In his closing statement, Mr. Pikes suggested that Mr. Potts was actually better off financially on WCB benefits than he would have been working for Wyler Industries because of the differential tax treatment of WCB benefits. He urged the Board to take the latter point into account when coming to a decision.

Mr. Pikes's position on the dental benefits was that if Mr. Potts was subject to reinstatement during the period in which dental work was needed, he would be entitled to the benefits. However, since Mr. Potts did not return to work—for reasons beyond the control of Wyler Industries— he should not be entitled to such.

The Board's Decision and Reasoning

In response to the critical question of "Has the complainant Warren Potts shown that he suffered a mental-distress loss caused by the unlawful discharge?" the majority of the Board found that

There is uncontradicted medical evidence that he suffered mental stress as a result of the termination, and that it aggravated the level of stress he was experiencing after his serious occupational injury. Although Mr. Pikes questioned the validity of the family doctor's opinion in a psychiatric matter, the family doctor's opinion is consistent with the psychiatrist's. It remains uncontradicted, and not inherently lacking in credibility. Therefore, we have no legal basis to ignore it. The evidence does not establish any reason to conclude that the additional stress outlined in the medical reports probably resulted from something other than the unlawful discharge.

Regarding Wyler Industries' accountability, both attitudinally and behaviorally, on the job-stress reduction challenge issue, the Board concluded:

It is reasonable to conclude from Mr. Potts's testimony and all the circumstances of the case that a successful return to work after the loss of part of his finger might have alleviated some of the stress he was experiencing at that point. Instead, his abrupt termination within hours of his return to work, for complaining about safety conditions related to his injury, had an exacerbating effect on his symptoms of stress. His family doctor mentions a period of three weeks of depression. In April, three months after the discharge, the psychiatrist found both the unresolved employment situation and the unresolved health issues to be perpetuating factors in the mild post-traumatic stress disorder he diagnosed. Thus, the unlawful discharge caused increased symptoms of stress and a loss of peace of mind in the form of depression and perpetuation of a stress disorder.

We are satisfied that these facts fall within the category of mental distress, rather than more common forms of stress and aggravation. Although the evidence did not establish that the effect on Mr. Potts's mental state was part of Mr. Pikes's considerations when he fired him, it was foreseeable that an abrupt, unlawful discharge, related as it was to a safety concern that had earlier resulted in the loss of part of Mr. Potts's finger, would cause mental distress to Mr. Potts. Thus, the damages are not too remote in the chain of causation to be recognized. . . . The evidence before us is persuasive that there was a mental distress loss due to layoff.

Concerning the award, the OLRB ordered Wyler Industries Limited to compensate Mr. Potts as follows:

1. An amount of $500 (with interest since February 17, 1991) for mental distress, set at this level because of the evidence, which indicated that the stress that followed Mr. Potts's injury and the unresolved health issues that ensued were the major components of his mental distress; the discharge was an exacerbating factor.

2. An amount of $1,700 for dental work or arrangement for coverage by the carrier (with interest on portions Mr. Potts paid from the dates that he paid them), set at this level because of the evidence, which indicated that the plan in place at Wyler Industries covered the type of dental work that Mr. Potts needed. Further, given that the only specific evidence of a disentitling event was the unlawful discharge itself, and given that there was no evidence that sick leave or absence on workers' compensation would have disentitled Mr. Potts from the receipt of dental benefits, Mr. Potts was found to be entitled to their receipt.

3. Vacation pay, calculated at 4% of whatever Mr. Potts earned between September 1990 and February 16, 1991.

A minority Board report, also submitted, agreed with the majority panel that although the OLRB has the jurisdiction to award damages for mental distress, there was dissent from that portion which awarded damages for mental distress. Though not raised by Mr. Pikes in the hearing, "a preexisting psychiatric disorder argument" was suggested in the minority report, based on excerpts from the psychiatrist's opinion that revealed that Mr. Potts was a recovered alcoholic who was reportedly sober since November 1990—just two months after his being hired at Wyler Industries. The minority report argued that Mr. Potts's preexisting stress disorder and alcoholism were the major causes of his mental distress, not the work situation. This argument is illustrated in the following minority-report excerpt:

The picture I perceive is a recovered alcoholic claiming to have been sobered since November 1990—some two months after his employment by Whitler Industries in September 1990. No doubt a stressful situation for Mr. Potts.

In January 1991 Mr. Potts lost the end of the small finger on his right hand while cleaning an exhaust system at work. No doubt a stressful situation for Mr. Potts.

On his return to work in February 1991 he found the situation . . . "unsafe." No doubt a stressful situation for Mr. Potts. However, instead of refusing to work and lodging a complaint under the Occupational Health and Safety Act, Mr. Potts' reaction, in his own words, was to lose his temper and start hollering and screaming. I would suggest Mr. Potts was already in a highly stressed state of mind before he was terminated.

CONCLUSION

This chapter focused on the horrendous costs associated with pathological levels of job stress. The "down-side" of the job-stress challenge is that pathological levels of job stress are not isolated events, but are becoming increasingly apparent in industries throughout the world. The "up-side" of the job-stress challenge is that with critical and intelligent management of personal and organizational stressors, the destructive side of stress can be minimized.

This chapter's theme was: While moderate amounts of stress stimulation are constructive and even necessary for a fulfilling life, too much or too little stress stimulation can be anger producing and, thus, potentially self-destructive. Stress symptomology, brought on by the misuse or abuse of the stress mechanism by organizational members, commonly presents on three fronts: physiologically, psychologically, and behaviorally. Therefore, good stress management is necessary for long-term health maintenance and productivity.

Stress symptomology also presents in organizations—primarily because of management's use of stress-avoidance and stress-escalation strategies. Organizational symptomology presents in terms of decreased morale, lowered productivity, and high absenteeism and accident rates among organizational members. Companies in the United States and Finland who have proacted against pathological job stress by owning stress-accountable attitudes and by practicing stress-accountable behaviors on a regular basis have reaped many benefits—including turnarounds in stress-disabling outcomes. Companies that have chosen a stress-avoidance or stress-escalation strategy have been hard hit, at times, with stress-disability claims from organizational members. When this happens, the organizations' managers have little option but to pay the tremendous bills that usually accompany such claims.

STRESS-COPING SUMMARY POINTS

1. Good stress management means appreciating the benefits accruing from the stress mechanism but recognizing the costs assumed when the stress mechanism is misused or overused.

2. Having a "self-healing" life profile instead of a "stress-destructive"

one means adopting a stress-accountable attitude and stress-accountable behavioral patterns both on and off the job.

3. Good job-stress management includes cooperating with organizational members at all levels of the organization to maintain a "stress-safe" zone.

4. When management fails to cooperate in setting and maintaining a "stress-safe" zone, organizational members may have to proact against excessive levels of job stress by filing job-stress claims. Although this objective should be saved for later (rather than sooner), sometimes it is the only "straw" that can break the organizational stress pathology cycle.

5. If job-stress claims present, both employers and claimants need to prepare themselves well in order to optimize their chances of winning their positions.

REFERENCES

Bale, A. (1990). Medicolegal stress at work. *Behavioral Sciences and the Law*, 8, 399–420.

Case based on factual data in 3248–90–OH Wade Dennis Procter, Complainant, v. Whitler Industries Limited, Respondent: *Procter v. Whitler Industries Ltd.* [1992], O.L.R.B. Rep. 875 (*sub. nom.* Whitler Industries Ltd. v. Procter) 17 C.L.R.B.R. (2d) 102.

Cooper, C. L. (1986). Job distress: Recent research and the emerging role of the clinical occupational psychologist. *Bulletin of the British Psychological Society*, 39, 325–331.

The Diagnostic and Statistical Manual of Mental Disorders (DSM-III-R). (1987). Rev. 3d ed. Washington, DC: American Psychiatric Association.

Hewitt, T. D. (1982). Legal principles governing the apportionment of damages in cases of psychological injury. *Canadian Insurance Law Review*, 2, 355–366.

International Labour Office (ILO). (1991). Coming to terms with stress. *ILO Information*, 27 (February), 1–2.

Levan, H., Katz, M., & Hochwarter, W. (1990). *Personnel* (May), 61–64.

Marcus, E. H. (1986). Psychiatric disability evaluations: Plaintiff and defense perspectives. *American Journal of Forensic Psychiatry*, 7, 11–19.

Moss, L. (1981). *Management Stress*. Reading, MA: Addison-Wesley.

Oregon Department of Insurance and Finance. (1987). *Mental Stress Claims in Oregon, 1980–1986*, 21.

Schuler, R. S. (1980). Definition and conceptualization of stress in organizations. *Organizational Behavior and Human Performance*, 25, 186.

Steffy, B. D., Jones, J. W., Murphy, L. R., & Kunz, L. (1986). A demonstration of the impact of stress abatement programs on reducing employees' accidents and their costs. *American Journal of Health Promotion* (Fall), 25–32.

Chapter 2

Understanding Basic Stress-Process Terminology

A CASE IN POINT

William Bartell, Human Resource Manager for Wyler Industries Limited, was beginning to panic. He was asked to prepare a plan for management about how they could more effectively deal with stress in the workplace, and the initial meeting to hear William's thoughts on the matter was scheduled in two hours' time. Although William had read a lot about stress and stress-coping to prepare for the hearing of Warren Potts, he had a lot of difficulty deciding how to explain the complexity of the stress process to a group of managers who were "technically" rather than "people" trained. After all, no one on the management team had a Ph.D. in psychology or in physiology, and the slides he had prepared for the meeting now seemed a bit too complex for the audience he was about to address. He needed to simplify his approach.

Nevertheless, William was optimistic. Wyler's management team was presently showing some interest in the topic of workplace stress. A year ago, most of the managers at Wyler Industries seemed to be very uninterested in and, if anything, very smug about their avoidance of the subject of job stress. Then when Warren Potts was dismissed for not wanting to work in an "unsafe" work site, their sarcasm around the subject seemed to grow even stronger. More than one manager was heard muttering words like, "Stress is none of our business; making profits for our shareholders is!" and "Keep 'scared' Potts around when there are several thousand other people around who'd love to have his job? No way! Pikes was right telling him to 'ship-out!' "

Job-stress attitudes started to soften, however, with the OLRB decision on Warren Potts. It wasn't the size of the award that "stirred the pot" as much as the fact that Potts won his job-stress claim.

Now, some managers seemed more willing to hear about stress-accountability in the workplace. And probably the most surprising outcome of the stress-claim matter was the fact that Mr. Pikes himself was now guardedly interested in the topic of job stress. Although Mr. Pikes had not committed himself, as of yet, to a stress-reduction strategy for Wyler Industries Limited, he did admit in conversation that the incidents with Warren Potts and the OLRB hearing were very stressful, even for him.

Despite some recent progress on the job-stress-reduction front, William admitted to himself that most of Wyler's managers were still quite job-stress paranoid. He heard many predict that the filing and winning of one stress claim means that many more will follow.

How, then, to thwart management's stress-claim paranoia and, more importantly, the stress claims themselves? William knew that unless Wyler Industries Limited sent a strong message to its organizational members that management is ready to PROACT against excessive job-stress rather than REACT to it, the company could, indeed, be facing more of the same type of claim. But how could Wyler's managers know where to begin with "proaction" on the job-stress front when many of them were not particularly well versed on the topics of stress-management and stress-coping?

THE OPENING ADDRESS: STRESS-MODERATION "EMPOWERMENT"

In two hours' time, William began his speech to management:

Many of you here this afternoon probably think that Wyler Industries' safety-conscious image has been shattered with the recent events around Warren Potts's workplace accident. Many of you probably fear that with the award given to Mr. Potts on his job-stress claim, Wyler Industries Limited is now at risk for being viewed by the public and by the trade unions as "a stressful enterprise."

You are not alone. A similar attitude of fear about stress in the workplace was verbalized by Mr. Pikes at the OLRB hearing when he shared with the hearers of the case the message that a win for Potts would mean a win for any employee who does not like his or her employer. It was, in fact, a multidimensional fear of image tarnishing, of stress labeling, and of perceived "unfair play" that likely motivated Mr. Pikes to request, repeatedly, that Mr. Potts's OLRB hearing on damages be canceled altogether.

I am not here this afternoon to ask you to part with these fears or to apologize for them—but, rather, to confront them. I am asking you to consider what it is that we have learned from our stress-claim experience with Warren Potts.

My hope would be that most of you would respond, with sincerity,

"That, in the future, we at Wyler Industries Limited should 'err' on the side of organizational members' physical and emotional safety rather than on the side of potential image tarnishing."

How, then, might we approach this safety issue, which is multidimensional and complex? I've got two words for all of us to consider: *stress proaction.*

The answer to our dilemma on this whole safety and job-stress issue, I am sure, could be found in setting up a job-stress-reduction program for all organizational members that would incorporate the notion of STRESS PROACTION rather than STRESS REACTION.

Maybe a while back we did not see Warren Potts as a "stress-proactor," but that is what he is. When he went to his foreman and complained that his worksite was in the same "unsafe" state as when he had his finger injury one month earlier, Warren Potts was sharing a strong sense of safety ownership and of stress-accountability in his job. Unfortunately, his foreman failed to perceive Mr. Potts in this role. We managers further failed to see him as a proactor. We, in fact, punished him for his stress-empowerment efforts by dismissing him later that day.

Perhaps it is time to admit that in 1991 we managers at Wyler Industries were misdirected in our approach to safety and stress. We should have praised Mr. Potts and awarded him. But we didn't. Maybe the OLRB gave him what he truly deserved—an honorarium for helping Wyler Industries Limited move ahead on the job-stress-reduction scene rather than fall behind and suffer, even more severely, because of it.

It is not too late for us to move forward! With the Warren Potts's stress-claim case behind us, the time is right for Wyler Industries Limited to "empower" all of our organizational members in workplace safety and in stress reduction. Three requirements set out by the International Labour Office (ILO) as working toward this stress-empowerment goal include

1. Providing organizational members with a safe and healthy work environment;
2. Advocating a work environment that optimizes well-being and stress moderation for all organizational members, as well as respect for human dignity; and
3. Providing the day-to-day possibilities for organizational members to empower themselves to develop and serve society through their work. (ILO, 1991)

Now I'd like to share with you some powerful words delivered by Dr. Coppee a few years ago in an *ILO Information* brief, entitled, "Coming to terms with stress." He said:

In an overall conception of health at work, ergonomics and the different methods of work organisation play a vital role. It is essential that every worker benefit from optimal conditions so as to give the best of himself without prejudice to his health; that is, his physical, mental and social well-being. These conditions are not only material. It is necessary at the same time to be concerned with freeing the individual from certain fears such as being dismissed, of not seeing his efforts recognised, or of being the victim of his chief's sudden changes of mood. One of the major causes of stress is the fear of the unknown and a lack of control over the duties to be carried out and over the organisation of work. Under these circumstances, the treatment of stress and its prevention are not medical matters, but are "information" and "participation." (ILO, 1991, p. 2)

Like Dr. Coppee, I am asking you this afternoon to commit yourselves to receiving more "information" on stress-coping and to "participate" in Wyler Industries Limited's new stress-reduction program, called "Stress-Empowerment."

The objective behind Stress-Empowerment is to make organizational members throughout Wyler Industries Limited good stress managers. Good stress management begins with the basic recognition that although moderate amounts of stress stimulation are constructive and even necessary for a fulfilling life, too much (or too little) stress stimulation can be anger producing and, thus, potentially self-destructive. On January 16, 1992, the Ontario Labour Relations Board (OLRB) found that in 1991 Wyler Industries Limited failed to act on this critical stress-management principle by dismissing Warren Potts for presenting "job-distress signals."

But, unlike the OLRB, we are not here to assess blame for the stress situation of Warren Potts. Nor are we here, over the longer term, to self-destruct—as individuals or as an organization—because of pathological job-stress levels. Instead, we are here to remain viable and productive—as individuals and as an organization. I am, therefore, asking all of you present to seriously consider the option to "stress-empower" our organizational members so that we can meet both our personal and our organizational objectives.

The next time someone reads about Wyler Industries Limited in the newspapers or in the OLRB Reports, we want to be credited as good stress managers. We do not want to blame ourselves a second time for failing to become informed about job stress or to participate in a job-stress-reduction program when, thanks to our insights gained from the Warren Potts stress case, we had the perfect opportunity to become more proactive.

C-O-P-E-ING: A FRAMEWORK FOR UNDERSTANDING STRESS-EMPOWERMENT

Many of you in the audience may now find yourselves committed to the principles of job-stress accountability and sound stress management but are somewhat overwhelmed with all the information that exists on the stress process. Others of you might openly admit that you are perplexed about how to start the kind of stress-empowerment program that is being advocated. Still, others of you may be asking yourselves, "How can I participate in a stress-empowerment program as a 'good role model' when I don't even know if I am a good 'stress-coper'?"

I can understand your uneasiness both with the vast amount of information published on the topic of stress and with your lack of feedback about your own stress-coping capabilities. I was in the same position you are in today when I started preparing for the Warren Potts stress-claim hearing—overwhelmed and confused.

But after a while, the more reading that I did on the stress process and on stress management, the less overwhelmed and confused I became. I started to see "stress themes" emerge in the readings. Then, in my final stages of hearing preparation, I felt that I had a "good handle" on these stress topics. Perhaps more important to me as an individual, I began to have a clearer understanding of my own stress-coping capabilities.

At each preparation session, I organized my readings around a four-letter "theme model" that I called C-O-P-E. C-O-P-E stands for "stress-coping," and particularly, "what it takes to become a good stress-coper." I'd like to share my model with you this afternoon, but before I do, I'd like to depart for a moment to discuss what it means "to cope" with stress and what the relationship is between stress and coping.

What It Means "to Cope" with Stress

"Coping" in the stress literature refers to an individual's efforts to master life conditions or life demands that tax or exceed one's "adaptive resources" (Monat & Lazarus, 1977). Taxing life demands—whether they emanate from work or from the home—are labeled as "stressors" in the literature. An individual's "adaptive resources," described more fully in a few minutes, are multidimensional and are integrally related to one's stress-management capabilities.

Simply stated, because taxing life demands, or stressors, draw on an individual's FINITE life-energy supplies, each individual needs to develop his or her own repertoire of "adaptive resources" in order to use one's energy supplies efficiently and effectively. Efficient and effective use of energy is good stress management.

A major part of stress-coping and stress management involves the individual's unique ability to optimize his or her "returns" on life-energy expenditures. Thus, whenever an individual's mind perceives "a taxing demand," it alerts the body to release "emergency energy" from its stores. Concurrently, the mind does a quick assessment of the "projected returns on the energy-expenditure investment."

In general, energy expenditures on taxing life demands are projected by the individual as resulting in (1) some desirable, positive returns; (2) some undesirable, negative returns; or (3) mixed returns. By convention, experts classify the positive-return projections (and eventual outcomes) as "eustressing." They classify the negative-return and mixed-return projections (and eventual outcomes) as "distressing."

Recent research findings have shown that distressors are particularly destructive for individuals—physiologically, psychologically, and behaviorally—because they are anger producing as well as life energy draining. Further research evidence has shown that whereas unchecked, misplaced anger in the short term can be unpleasant and uncomfortable, unchecked, misplaced anger over the long term destroys—individuals, work groups, and organizations.

An individual's "stress-coping potential," then, is a kind of measurement of both the extent of and the effectiveness of one's adaptive resources repertoire. This repertoire, as noted, is multidimensional and includes such physiological, psychological, and behavioral components as

Physiological:

- The overall amount of finite life energy that the individual was born with and is able to manage throughout his or her life;
- The capacity one has developed to moderate one's life-distressing events and to optimize one's life-eustressing events, in order to buffer oneself against stress-related disease and energy burnout.

Psychological:

- The strategy insights that one has gained from past life experiences about coping with taxing personal and organizational life demands;
- The flexible thinking ability that one has developed to work through alternative strategies for dealing with taxing life demands rather than just impulsively "shooting from the hip"—and regretting having done so later on;
- The self-awareness that one has developed around one's own needs for life-fulfillment and the other-awareness that one has honed about other individuals' needs for life-fulfillment.

Behavioral:

- The intimate people vents (on and off the job) that one has developed and can use to talk through the frustrations (and opportunities) presented by taxing life demands;
- The interpersonal skills that one has developed to not only assert oneself regarding one's needs and ability to remain productive, but to resolve any conflicts that might threaten these needs or ability to remain productive.

What the Relationship Is between Stressors and Coping

The relationship between stressors and stress-coping is best viewed as a dynamic, compounding process, rather than as a static, noncompounding one. Thus, determining an individual's ability to cope with stressors requires an understanding of both the composite and the compounding of returns uniquely assigned by that individual to environmental and self-induced stressors in the short term (i.e., in one-day, one-week, one-month periods) and over the longer term (i.e., over one's lifetime). This "composite of returns" at any point in time, called "one's life-stress situation," can be predominantly positive and eustressing or predominantly negative and distressing.

Engineers know that a building with a solid foundation designed to survive earthquakes can tolerate more drastic geophysical activity "strains" than a building with a weak foundation not designed to survive earthquakes. Similarly, stress experts know that an individual with a predominantly positive life-stress situation and a solid self-esteem foundation at any point in time can tolerate considerably more "bruising" from distressors than an individual with a predominantly negative life-stress situation and a low self-esteem foundation. It is for this critical reason that nature "designed" human beings to not only be energy efficient but also energy refueling. That is, humans were designed to optimize their positive returns on their energy investments as a sort of life-energy refueling mechanism and as a foundation-stabilizer for self-esteem maintenance. These positive returns on energy investments can be physiological (i.e., keeping physically fit), psychological (i.e., keeping emotionally satisfied and cognitively self-actualized), or behavioral (i.e., maintaining a reasonable pace of productivity at work and at home).

Because of the dynamism of the stressor/stress-coping relationship, even a positively life-situated individual can suffer intense strains with "traumatic" life situations. That is, even a predominantly positive individual is apt to feel intense pain and depression with the death of a beloved friend or relative. It is important to realize, therefore, that an individual's life-stress situation on Friday can be vastly different from that on Monday. Similarly, an individual's life-stress situation in the morning of any given day can be vastly different from that at the end of the day.

Mr. Potts's changing and continually deteriorating life-stress situation from January 1991 through January 16, 1992, illustrates

1. The dynamic, compounding relationship between the number and intensity of "distressing" personal and job events appraised by Warren Potts during one year and his decreasing ability to "cope";
2. The escalating, "misplaced" anger arising from these distressing events; and
3. The compounding strain and eventual deterioration of Warren Potts's personal system—physiologically, psychologically, and behaviorally.

Mr. Potts's outward signs of strain and mental disability included his suffering of frequent headaches, his developing an intense fear of his job at Wyler Industries Limited, and his having recurrent nightmares. By his own admission, Warren Potts was not stress-coping well over the twelve months in question. Therefore, he sought professional help from both a physician and a psychiatrist to rehabilitate and stabilize his bruised psychological foundation.

Now I'd like to describe the C-O-P-E model mentioned earlier. It helps to put into focus why it was that Warren Potts was not stress-coping over the said twelve-month period. In other words, the C-O-P-E model helps us to see that Warren Potts's life situation was predominantly negative during this period. There was no mention made by him of positive refueling.

The C-O-P-E Model

C-O-P-E is an abbreviation that stands for four key types of self and organizational analyses that stress experts believe are essential for individuals to complete so that they can understand their unique stress situations and develop their optimal stress-coping potentials. In this four-letter model:

- "C" represents the *control* that individuals perceive they have over their personal and organizational stressors at any point in time.
- "O" represents the *outward signs* of distress that present—in an individual or in the organization at any point in time.
- "P" represents the *personality predispositions* and conditioned behavioral patterns contributing to an individual's overall stress level, particularly over the longer term.
- "E" represents the projected and real *energy expenditures and energy returns* of individuals over some period of time, such that the predominance of eustressors acts as a sort of "stress buffer" and such that the predominance of distressors acts as a sort of catalyst for "stress disability."

Applying this C-O-P-E model to Warren Potts's situation during the period of January 1991 to January 1992, one can readily understand why Warren Potts felt, increasingly, "*out of control.*" The taxing life demands, or stressors, "pulling" him out of control, as detailed in his testimony before the OLRB on January 16, 1992, included his worksite finger injury in January 1991; his return to a perceived "still unsafe" worksite in February 1991; his immediate dismissal from work for complaining about the situation on the day of his return; his "disturbing" treatment from Wyler Industries Limited management when trying to get his "separation papers"; his unpleasant treatment from Mr. Pikes concerning his reinstatement as well as other matters; his perceived loss of self-esteem as a function of the job dismissal and related incidents; and his financial difficulties resulting from his job layoff.

By his own admission, Warren Potts's life-energy supplies were clearly being "taxed." To survive this energy-draining period, his mind undoubtedly and repeatedly called on his body's emergency energy reserves (by provoking his "stress mechanism") to get him through these life events.

Eventually, Warren Potts presented with multiple *outward signs* of distress and strain: He suffered frequent headaches, he feared going to his job at Wyler Industries Limited, and he had recurrent nightmares. Declaring Warren Potts to be depressed and suffering from mild posttraumatic stress disorder, or PTSD, his psychiatrist (and family physician) posited that Warren Potts's distressors and the rage that he experienced emanated primarily from his work environment, not from his personal life or from his personality predispositions.

Although in the OLRB hearing Wyler Industries Limited did not raise the issue that Mr. Potts had an apparent *"stress-predisposed personality"* and was recovering from an alcohol addiction, Mr. Pikes implied in his testimony that Warren Potts's job-stress problem likely resulted from his dislike for his boss. Mr. Pikes further argued that Warren Potts's job-stress problem was complicated by the fact that he did not return to work on his reinstatement date in May 1991. Thus, Mr. Pikes concluded, the claimant was very much the cause of his own self-induced distress. Wyler Industries Limited had, in fact, acted responsibly throughout the twelve-month period under review.

Having considered the degrees of *energy expended* by both Warren Potts and Wyler Industries Limited in an effort to reduce pathological levels of stress in the workplace (i.e., the desired positive energy return), the OLRB found for Warren Potts and his claim that his excessive distress and presenting mental disability were job-induced and not self-induced. The Board concluded in their report that "the evidence before us is persuasive that there was a mental distress loss due to the layoff." The damages were set accordingly "because of the fact that the evidence indicates that the stress which followed his injury and the unresolved health issues were the major components of the complainant's mental distress, while the discharge was an exacerbating factor."

CONCLUSION

I'd like to close this presentation this afternoon by boldly suggesting that many people—Warren Potts; Warren Potts's foreman, Mr. Pikes; organizational members throughout Wyler Industries Limited; and all of us in this room, including myself—could benefit from a detailed C-O-P-E analysis of ourselves and of our work and personal environments. That, my fellow managers, is the critical objective that we can meet with the Stress-Empowerment Program that I have introduced today and would like to develop with you in future sessions.

A good diagnosis of our life- and job-stress situations can be obtained if we and, equally as important, our organizational members are willing to collect a systematic and detailed C-O-P-E data set on themselves and on their organizational environments. This information could become the "baseline" on which to build—or maintain—a solid foundation (personally and organizationally) that is capable of withstanding life's minor and major "earthquakes." That is not to say that some personal and organizational foundations might not need some responsible intervention by medical, social, and organizational "professionals" in order to reinforce or in some way rehabilitate the foundation which exists. But the important point to remember is that we are not here to assess blame for the "stress-quake" of Warren Potts, which "shook" in February 1991. We are also not here because we fear that other "stress-quakes" might "shake" in future months or years. Nor are we here to self-destruct, as individuals or as an organization, because of pathological job-stress levels and unrelenting "job-quakes." Instead, we are here—in both the short and long term—to remain viable and productive. I am, therefore, asking all of you present to seriously consider the option to "stress-empower" our organizational members at Wyler Industries Limited so that we can meet both our personal and our organizational objectives.

STRESS-COPING SUMMARY POINTS

1. To ward off stress-claim paranoia and stress claims in organizations, managers need to send a strong message to organizational members that they want to PROACT against excessive job-stress rather than REACT to it.

2. Along with the former strategy, stress fears and phobias in organizations need to be confronted and worked through rather than avoided or excused.

3. Managers fearing potential "image tarnishing" for engaging in stress-reduction organizational programs should "err" on the side of organizational members' physical and emotional safety rather than on the side of image tarnishing.

4. "Stress-Empowering" ILO organizational goals include
    a. Providing organizational members with a safe and healthy work environment;
    b. Advocating a work environment that optimizes well-being and stress moderation for all organizational members, as well as respect for human dignity; and
    c. Providing the day-to-day possibilities for organizational members to empower themselves to develop and serve society through their work.

5. To better cope with excessive stress, organizational members need to develop their physiological, psychological, and behavioral "adaptive resource repertoires."

6. A major part of stress-coping and stress management for organiza-

tional members involves optimizing their "positive returns"—physiologically, psychologically, and behaviorally—on their life-energy expenditures.

7. Determining an organizational member's unique ability to cope with stressors requires an understanding of both the composite and the compounding of "returns" uniquely assigned by that individual to environmental and self-induced stressors in the short term and over the longer term.

8. The C-O-P-E model helps put into focus an organizational member's stress-coping capability at any point in time. In this four-letter model:

- "C" represents the *control* that individuals perceive they have over their personal and organizational stressors at any point in time.
- "O" represents the *outward signs* of distress that present—in an individual or in the organization at any point in time.
- "P" represents the *personality predispositions* and conditioned behavioral patterns contributing to an individual's overall stress level, particularly over the longer term.
- "E" represents the projected and real *energy expenditures and energy returns* of individuals over some period of time, such that the predominance of eustressors acts as a sort of "stress buffer" and such that the predominance of distressors acts as a sort of catalyst for "stress disability."

REFERENCES

International Labour Office (ILO). (1991). Coming to terms with stress. *ILO Information*, 27 (February), 1–2.

Monat, A., & Lazarus, R. S. (Eds.). (1977). *Stress and Coping: An Anthology.* New York: Columbia University Press.

Part II

The Control Issue

Chapter 3

Assessing One's Own Ability to Maintain Control

A CASE IN POINT

William Bartell, Human Resource Manager for Wyler Industries Limited, had spent the last six months working with organizational stress consultants to develop an inventory-and-theory package to deliver to organizational members as part of the approved and managerially promoted Stress-Empowerment Program.

The C-O-P-E model, introduced in William's first session, was used to organize the material for the stress-coping and stress management seminars. In all, eight seminar sessions on the C-O-P-E model were developed.

The first two sessions were designed to deal with the *control* issue—by allowing organizational members to assess their own "microsystem" ability to maintain control and their organization's "macrosystem" ability to provide for organizational members' control and empowerment. The next two sessions were designed to deal with the *outward sign* issue—by having organizational members assess their own outward signs of distress as well as the organization's role in alleviating pathological levels of stress for organizational members. The third set of sessions was designed to deal with the *personality predisposition* issue—by helping organizational members to understand the difference between "self-healing" and "disease-prone" personalities and to assess in relative detail their own stress-inducing or stress-reducing personality predispositions and behavioral patterns. The last two sessions were designed to visit the *energy expenditure and energy returns* issue—by having organizational members not only assess their own life-energy "balances" and burnout potential but understand more fully the organization's role in promoting positive returns on its organizational members' energy investments.

William was convinced that the eight inventory-and-theory sessions would go a long way to reducing excessive job stress at Wyler Industries Limited. But he sensed that a few of the managers who were expected to be stress management role models were still a bit skeptical about whether the participants would be honest in supplying the personal and organizational information requested in the stress sessions and about whether the empowerment sessions would result in more empathetic attitudes by managers toward organizational members suffering from stress disorders.

At any rate, the managers sitting in the meeting room just six months ago were scheduled to be the first group of program test cases in just one hour's time. William decided to begin his first control seminar on these two topics of expressed concern: honest inventory-responding by seminar participants and projected returns on the stress-session investment.

THE OPENING ADDRESS: HONEST RESPONDING AND POTENTIAL RETURNS ON THE STRESS-SESSIONS

William began his first stress-empowerment "personal control" session:

Just six months ago we were contemplating a Stress-Empowerment Program for the organizational members of Wyler Industries Limited. Today, we are moving forward with this program. All of you present have volunteered to be the first group of stress-reduction managerial role models. For your participation in the job-stress-reduction challenge, you are to be applauded.

However, I am not naive enough to think that all of you present are here without hesitations or concerns. Some of you are probably thinking that some participants in the room will not take this event seriously, and that a lack of sincerity on their part will result in faulty or useless stress data being generated at both the microsystem and macrosystem levels. Still others of you are probably wondering if our management team will be more empathetic toward organizational members suffering from job-related stress. I'd like to respond to these two attitudinal concerns before we get into the content issues for today.

Recall that in our first meeting, we outlined the three requirements set out by the International Labour Office (ILO) as working toward an appropriate organizational stress-empowerment goal:

1. Providing organizational members with a safe and healthy work environment;

2. Advocating a work environment that optimizes well-being and stress moderation for all organizational members, as well as respect for human dignity; and

3. Providing the day-to-day possibilities for organizational members to empower themselves to develop and serve society through their work.

I would like to go one step futher today and say that no organization can provide its organizational members with a safe and healthy work environment or with the day-to-day possibilities to have its members empower themselves if there is a lack of respect for human dignity within the organization. It is because of the respect that we have for ourselves and for our fellow workers that we should commit ourselves to this Stress-Empowerment Program as fully as we can. Otherwise, the major driving force behind this stress-reduction challenge—the maintenance of human dignity for all organizational members—becomes a nonissue; consequently, the impetus for organizational growth and change on the stress-reduction front weakens exponentially.

But what does it mean to be attitudinally committed to this Stress-Empowerment Program? First, participants should engage in honest participation and information-sharing in the sessions that are presented, or the baseline data that result from these sessions will give a false impression of the micro- and macrosystem states of "stress health" that exist. Second, managers need to walk the stress-reduction and organizational member empowerment talk, for if the managers who attend these stress management sessions do not manifest trust, honesty, and concern for human dignity in their interactions with organizational members on leaving these stress sessions, then in the minds of our organizational members, our much-touted Stress-Empowerment Program becomes just another power game by management to "milk" its members of confidential information in order to exploit them. Certainly, the latter outcome would not only spell the death of this Stress-Empowerment Program but, even more critically, deal a severe blow to our organization's delicate managerial and organizational members' trust relationships. And when there is a failing organizational trust relationship, the chances for stress claims being filed climb dramatically.

Now for the content portion of today's session, which is the maintenance of microsystem or personal control. The objective of this first control session is to allow organizational members to assess their own ability to maintain personal control and to consider what to do when they have lost it—or fear that they are about to lose it. Good stress management requires, at a minimum, that an organizational member be able to answer over time these two basic questions: "Do I feel 'in control' of my life situation at this time? If not, why not?"

All of us in this room have experienced a loss of personal control at one time or another in our lives. Some of us may even say that we experience a loss of control often—sometimes at work, sometimes at home. Most times, many of us would affirm, we are able to regain the control that we are seeking through our own sets of adaptive resources. For example, by moderating a hectic productivity schedule at work or by taking time to "energy refuel" with loved ones, we feel that we can and often do move back into feeling "in control."

Occasionally, we may need to get some help from others in order to regain control. And at no time, we firmly believe, should we be punished for getting the help that we need—whether the help comes from coworkers, our family members, our bosses, or a mental-health professional.

I'd like to share with you now the case of Kelvin Browne, an individual who felt that he had "lost control" but went to get some professional help to regain control. After I tell you a bit of Mr. Browne's plight, I'd like to visit more fully the issue of projected returns on these stress management sessions, in general, and of this personal control session, particularly.

Mr. Browne's piece appeared in one of our newspapers about a year ago. I find his stress story to be good food for thought for all stress-session participants because for Mr. Browne, as for most organizational members who appraise themselves as being somewhat or totally out of control, the causes for the loss of control are usually not all that remarkable. I find Mr. Browne's stress story to be especially meaningful to managers embarking on a Stress-Empowerment Program in their organizations, because his story raises an interesting point of organizational trust concern. Here now, is the start of Kelvin's stress story:

I have been rejected for disability insurance because I consulted a psychologist and said so on my insurance application. I am not just assuming this is why my application was declined. I have it in writing from the insurance company.

I saw Dr. X 20 or so times during the latter part of 1992 and the first few months of 1993. My psychologist received similar correspondence that quite explicitly says that, in the view of the insurance company, I am a bad risk because I sought advice about my mental health.

As you will read, it was the fact of consulting the psychologist, not the content of the therapy, that was the reason for turning down my application.

Before I get into my story, I want to state that I believe in free enterprise and I don't think any company should have to insure me if it doesn't want to.

What I am angered by is that a company, and perhaps the insurance industry, in general, has attitudes about mental health that are archaic. And if these attitudes are lurking in insurance companies, you can't help but think that despite whatever politically correct attitudes a human-resources department may recommend, Canadian corporate culture still quietly believes that only crazy people seek help for mental distress. (Browne, 1994)

Let us break into Kelvin Browne's story momentarily and reflect on his last two lines: "What I am angered by is that a company . . . has attitudes about mental health that are archaic. And . . . you can't help but think that despite whatever politically correct attitudes a human-resources department may recommend, Canadian [or, for that matter, any other country's] corporate culture still quietly believes that only crazy people seek help for mental distress."

I see all of Wyler Industries' managerial participants in our Stress-Empowerment Program as providing more than just "lip service" to the critical notions that "If a human system is 'broken,' help fix it" and "If the organization is part of the reason that the human system is 'broken,' help fix it too." By condoning these two modern-day stress management notions, we are not implying in any way that well-adjusted human systems never break or that seemingly well-adjusted organizations never need some mending. To the contrary, we are recognizing that ALL human systems can break if markedly or unrelentingly strained—even those with stable mental and physical foundations. Moreover, ALL organizations can have organizational members who become pathologically stressed as a result of taxing demands made on them—on and off the job.

Accepting that what Kelvin Browne openly fears about present-day managers is real, we DO NOT want our organizational members to think that at Wyler Industries Limited we archaically believe that only crazy people seek help for mental distress. Through our commitment to this Stress-Empowerment Program and through our ongoing stress-reduction actions in the workplace, we hope, instead, that our organizational members will come to realize that even well-adjusted people sometimes need to seek help for their distress so that they can stay well adjusted and productive over the longer term. This realization and commitment to this principle by all of our organizational members, I would submit, is the primary return that I see resulting from our Stress-Empowerment sessions. But in order to drive this critical message home and in order to have it believed by the masses, we managers at Wyler Industries Limited have to daily walk our stress management talk, for actions do speak louder than words.

We'll find out later why Kelvin Browne sought help from a mental-health professional for his exaggerated stress levels, but now I'd like to begin the content portion of our program on the issue of personal control.

So as not to bias your responses to the inventories you are about to complete, *I would ask that you please turn to the appendix for this session* (i.e., Chapter 3 Appendixes) *and complete as honestly as you can the inventory items that appear before you. Please do not score these inventory items until asked to do so. After you have finished responding, please join us for further discussions of this material.*

WHAT IT MEANS FOR INDIVIDUALS TO BE "IN CONTROL"

The psychosocial literature has many variations on the theme of "personal control." An individual who is "in control" is characterized as having the adequate physiological, psychological, and behavioral adaptive resources to cope with presenting taxing life events. Contrarily, an individual who is not in control or is moving out of control is characterized as lacking the adequate adaptive resources to cope with presenting taxing life events.

When we observe individuals at work or in social settings and comment that they look "in control," what we are suggesting is that they look well adjusted and outwardly balanced on the physiological, psychological, and behavioral dimensions. That is, there seems to be a kind of invisible "control bridge" connecting these aspects of individuals' well-being. Moreover, "in control" individuals seem to be able to cope with most presenting life stressors, whether they occur on or off the job. In short, "in control" individuals appear to others to be

- Relatively free of disease;
- Emotionally happy;
- Cognitively able to think through life's challenges and opportunities; and
- Behaviorally productive at work and at home.

In contrast, when we observe individuals and comment that they look "not in control" or "out of control," what we are suggesting is that these individuals look less well adjusted, or dimensionally off balance. Their control bridge, so to speak, seems to have one or more of the well-being components missing. Moreover, depending on the degree of the stress disability presenting (see Table 1.1 for a detailed listing of common presentations), these individuals seem to be less able, or unable, to cope with their life stressors. In short, "not-in-control" or "out-of-control" individuals appear to others to be, in varying degrees,

- Physically "uncomfortable" to physically disabled;
- Psychologically "uncomfortable" to chronically anxious, depressed, or angry;
- Cognitively less able or unable to think through life's challenges and opportunities; and
- Behaviorally less productive or nonproductive, at work and at home.

The Mind-Behavior "Control" Link: Manifestations of Competence and Aspiration

When we describe "personal control" in terms of a microsystem mind-behavior relationship, as in commenting that "not-in-control people think, feel, and behave 'differently,'" we are essentially linking their outside observable behaviors with their internal unobservable information-processing and feeling capabilities. But are we correct in making this mind-behavior link?

According to U.K. mental-health expert Peter Warr, associations between individuals' behavior and their mental well-being are likely to be observed in practice, even though behaviors are conceptually quite distinct from the feelings and information-processing that are involved in psychological, or mental, well-being. When individuals really are "in control" psychologically, they illustrate this reality to observers through two behavioral expressions, in particular (1) competence, or mastery, and (2) aspiration, or self-actualization (Warr, 1990). In contrast, when individuals are "not in control" or are moving "out of control" psychologically, they illustrate this reality to observers by lacking competent and/or aspiring behaviors.

Competence, or mastery, has been widely discussed in the life-coping literature in the last 50 years under a number of labels (Jahoda, 1958; Bradburn, 1969; Bandura, 1977; Pearlin et al., 1981). For example, in the 1950s, Jahoda described "competent" individuals as having mastery over their environment. In the 1970s, Bradburn and Bandura described "competent" individuals as continually building a repertoire of rich adaptive resources to enable them to cope with and transcend their difficulties in living; moreover, these individuals not only believe that they are self-efficacious (i.e., they have the energy to produce desired life effects), but, throughout their various life stages, they maintain realistic expectations about their ability to accomplish this mastery. In the 1980s, Pearlin, Menaghan, Lieberman, and Mullan explicitly linked "mastery" with "control" in "competent" individuals, suggesting that "mastery" refers to the extent to which competent people see themselves as being "in control" of the forces that importantly affect their lives.

A similarly positive picture has been painted of individuals displaying "high aspiration," or a need for self-actualization (Herzberg, 1966; Maslow, 1973; Warr, 1990). By definition, individuals who display "high life aspiration" are not only mentally well adjusted but are continually interested in and engaged in "positive-return" behaviors with people, things, and events in their personal and work environments. Moreover, high-aspiration individuals tend to establish life goals, including both work and home life goal subsets. They tend not to live life purposelessly. Because of their strong commitment to self-established life goals, high-aspiration individuals consciously attempt to expend their finite life energy on events that will move them closer to their goals rather than waste it on events that seem contrary to a positively returning purpose. In short, high-aspiration individuals are generally good energy managers.

Moreover, high-aspiration individuals seem to be able to adapt to changing environmental circumstances and to move successfully ahead through later life stages because they are able to maintain a sense of cognitive, or thinking, flexibility. They seem to be constantly on the alert for new life opportunities that might result in further cognitive or emotional growth.

Finally, high-aspiration individuals not only make intensive efforts to survive unpreventable life crises but they tend to convert these life crises into "positive life events," if possible, and thus become "eustressed" rather than "distressed" by these events. In short, high-aspiration individuals are generally good stress managers.

The Mind-Behavior "Control" Link: Carryover Effects from Work to Home

Despite the often verbalized belief that "organizational members should leave their home problems at home and their work problems at work," researchers have found that such a notion is rather naive, if not impossible, from a mind-behavior-link perspective. Put simply, individuals who self-report as being "in control" at work also tend to self-report as being "in control" at home because of a mind-behavior control link that remains consistent and in tact in various settings. Generally speaking, the high-competence, high-aspiration characteristics of "in control" individuals can be noted in both work and home settings.

By extension, the diminished competence and aspiration characteristics of "not-in-control" individuals at work tend to carry over into their personal lives. That is, individuals who self-report as being "not in control" on the job often report negative consequences on their family member interactions and on their leisure-time enjoyment (Piotrkowski, 1978; Evans & Bartolome, 1980; Near, Rice, and Hunt, 1980; Warr, 1990). Furthermore, individuals who self-report being "not in control" at home often report negative consequences on their task productivity and on their ablity to stay accident-free (Piotrkowski, 1978; Evans & Bartolome, 1980; Near, Rice, and Hunt, 1980; Warr, 1990) in the workplace.

The Mind-Behavior "Control" Link: Manifestations of Competence and Aspiration from Early Life Stages Onward

Also, there is a self-perceived competence and aspiration carryover effect from one life stage to the next, starting in early childhood. That is, as a result of early childhood patterning and conditioning, individuals become motivated throughout their life stages to obtain control or to remain in control. Thus, the psychology literature consistently notes that children and adults with a high need for being "in control" have an "internal locus of control" orientation; that is, they feel that they themselves—and not someone else—are responsible for their various life-event "wins" as well as "losses."

Because of this self-accountability, internal-locus trait that seems to reside in "in control" individuals throughout their life stages, they tend to make their own decisions and solve their own problems rather than rely extensively on others; they take feasible and reasonable personal actions to avoid a loss of psychological control; they moderate their energy expenditures to accomplish their established life goals without infringing on others' abilities to do the same; and they assume "task- and people-balanced" leadership roles in various work and personal life settings.

Furthermore, aspiring individuals with a high need for control generally like themselves. That is, they reflect in their attitudes and behaviors a positive self-esteem. Because of the respect that they have for their own human dignity as well as for that of others, these seemingly balanced individuals have life situations that look, cyclically, like this:

1. From early childhood onward, in times of moderated stress, high-need-for-control individuals' aspirations for performance remain relatively high, realistic, and consistent with the individuals' cognitive and behavioral potential;

2. From early childhood onward, even when environmental circumstances become "taxing," not only do high-need-for-control individuals decide when and how to appropriately expend their life energy so that they can maintain personal control but they remain concurrently aware of other individuals' needs to also maintain control;

3. From early childhood onward, as long as "taxing" life events remain, these high-need-for-control individuals are not only highly motivated to avoid failure but they try to resolve the presenting problem or oversee an opportunity by themselves before seeking help from others or giving up altogether; and

4. From early childhood onward, as the "taxing" life events pass or reach some sort of steady state, these high-need-for-control individuals not only credit themselves with their positive life-event outcomes but they attribute their negative life-event outcomes to some combination of a lack of personal effort, a lack of personal skills, a lack of luck, or a lack of personal knowledge. In the end, these individuals actively work on improving their odds of success over the longer term and through later life stages. (Burger & Cooper, 1979; Burger, 1984)

When high-need-for-control individuals face a chronic series of negative life events or a disastrous life event, it is not uncommon for their roots of competence and self-aspiration to become temporarily bruised or, in severe cases, permanently damaged. Stress experts currently believe that the bruising or damaging of these "control" roots is caused by misplaced or inappropriately dealt-with pain or anger accompanying appraised distressing life events. Thus, depending on the individual's willingness and ability to appropriately deal with the presenting pain or anger—which does not include the rationalization or suppression of such "real" emotions—three mind-behavior outcomes can result. The high-need-for-control individual can:

1. *Healthily and appropriately confront the pain or anger experienced, with or without assistance from others.*Through healthful confrontation, the bruised competence and aspiration roots are able to eventually heal and the high-need-for-control individual can go on to mature—mentally and

behaviorally—through later life stages, maintaining a positive sense of self along the way; or

2. *Avoid confronting the pain or anger experienced by rationalizing it away, projecting it onto others in the work or home environment, or suppressing it.*Through these pain and anger "escape" tactics, the bruised roots may appear to heal but they actually develop various degrees of "scar tissue"; thus, depending on the severity of scarring, minor or major problems in the individual's future life-stage adjustment can result. In severe cases of scarring, the individual can become attitudinally and/or behaviorally "fixated" (i.e., stuck) in a given life stage as well as develop a negative sense of self; or

3. *Not only avoid constructive confrontation of the pain/anger but also ruminate on the negative life event(s) and, by doing so, escalate the amount of anger, pain, and distress experienced over time.*With the escalating pain/anger levels, the damaged roots of competence and aspiration tend to atrophy. Thus, the formerly "fulfilled" high-need-for-control individual is often seen to become increasingly depressed with increasingly unmet personal expectations. The individual may even regress attitudinally and behaviorally to earlier life stages which were emotionally less threatening than the present painful or anger-producing life stage.

In severe cases of competence and aspiration root atrophy, a high-need-for-control individual can develop not only a strong negative sense of self but a jealousy of and cynical resentment toward others who seem to be more well adjusted, competent, and aspiring. Research has shown that besides jealousy and cynicism, chronically unfulfilled high-need-for-control individuals report becoming clinically depressed and/or substance-addicted (Burger & Arkin, 1980; Burger, 1984).

PERSONAL FEEDBACK: HOW "IN CONTROL" HAVE YOU FELT RECENTLY? DO YOU SEE YOURSELF AS BEING CLOSER TO A NON-SELF-ACTUALIZING "1" OR A SELF-ACTUALIZING "9"?

Now it is time for participants to receive feedback on how "in control," competent, and aspiring they appraised themselves to be in the past few weeks.

Appendix 3.1 includes an inventory designed and developed by mental health expert Peter Warr (1990). It gives participants a measure of their recent mind-behavior well-being and provides them with information on nine critical competence and aspiration dimensions related to their jobs and personal lives. *Please complete the scoring for appendix 3.1 now.*

All participants should now have nine mind-behavior well-being "final" scores. Given these scores, participants should be able to answer "yes" or "no" to the following nine personal control questions:

- Has your job recently made you feel out of control ("anxious") or in control ("contented")? (See your Appendix 3.1.A.1 final score.)
- Has your job recently made you feel out of control ("depressed") or in control ("enthusiastic")? (See your Appendix 3.1.A.2 final score.)
- Has your personal life recently made you feel out of control ("anxious") or in control ("contented")? (See your Appendix 3.1.C.3 final score.)
- Has your personal life recently made you feel out of control ("depressed") or in control ("enthusiastic")? (See your Appendix 3.1.C.4 final score.)
- Have you recently felt in control ("competent") in your job? (See your Appendix 3.1.B.5 final score.)
- Have you recently felt in control ("aspired") in your job? (See your Appendix 3.1.B.6 final score.)
- Have you recently felt there to be a not-in-control "negative carry-over" from your job to your personal life? (See your Appendix 3.1.B.7 final score.)
- Have you recently felt in control ("competent") in your personal life? (See your Appendix 3.1.D.8 final score.)
- Have you recently felt in control ("aspired") in your personal life? (See your Appendix 3.1.D.9 final score.)

Participants might now be wondering how their nine well-being scores place relative to those of other working adults. To provide such normative information, Peter Warr obtained data from 1,686 employed men and women in the United Kingdom, all of whom worked in their jobs for more than 30 hours a week. His study sample was drawn with approximately equal numbers of men (839) and women (847). Gender was balanced within occupational level and age, and three occupational levels were specified: higher professional and managerial positions; lower professional or supervisory or skilled nonsupervisory positions; and manual positions. Mean scores and standard deviations on these nine well-being measures were then computed by Warr for the study sample, with differences in gender, occupational level, and age accounted for.

Table 3.1 summarizes Warr's normative data results. The overall pattern of mind-behavior well-being for working adults is summarized in the first column of Table 3.1. The comparison groups' scores follow in the remaining columns of the table.

To give themselves feedback on a 1–9 "personal control" scale, participants might want to now compare their nine "mean" well-being scores with those listed in the first column of Table 3.1. With the exception of number 7 on negative carryover, participants should give themselves 1 mark for each mean score that meets or exceeds the "normative mean" listed in the first column of Table 3.1. For number 7 only, participants should give themselves 1 mark if their mean score was equal to or less than that listed in the first column.

Table 3.1
Mean Mind-Behavior Well-Being Scores (Standard Deviations in Parentheses)

	Full Sample	Gender		Occupational Level			Age		
		Men	Women	Higher Professional/ Managerial	Lower Professional/ Supervisory/ Skilled Non- Supervisory	Manual Positions	18 to 34	35 to 49	50 and above
Affective Well-Being									
1. Job anxiety-contentment	4.17(.81)	4.12(.82)	4.22(.80)	3.96(.77)*	4.20(.82)*	4.35(.80)*	4.06(.80)*	4.12(.82)*	4.34(.82)*
2. Job depression-enthusiasm	4.55(.79)	4.48(.81)*	4.62(.76)*	4.61(.70)*	4.58(.82)*	4.46(.83)*	4.48(.78)*	4.51(.81)*	4.68(.76)*
3. Personal anxiety-contentment	4.41(.76)	4.43(.75)	4.39(.78)	4.31(.74)*	4.43(.77)*	4.48(.77)*	4.36(.75)*	4.36(.79)*	4.52(.73)*
4. Personal depression-enthusiasm	4.62(.72)	4.63(.70)	4.62(.73)	4.66(.69)	4.65(.70)*	4.56(.75)	4.60(.67)	4.57(.76)	4.71(.71)
Other aspects of mind-body health									
5. Reported job competence	3.88(.54)	3.94(.54)*	3.82(.53)*	3.78(.56)*	3.93(.53)*	3.93(.50)*	3.77(.53)*	3.91(.53)*	3.98(.54)*
6. Reported job aspiration	4.06(.50)	4.03(.53)	4.09(.48)	4.22(.42)*	4.07(.50)*	3.90(.53)*	4.04(.50)	4.07(.52)	4.09(.49)
7. Negative carry-over	2.73(.91)	2.68(.91)	2.77(.92)	3.03(.95)*	2.65(.90)*	2.53(.82)*	2.75(.88)	2.77(.91)	2.65(.95)
8. Reported personal competence	3.76(.53)	3.79(.50)	3.74(.56)	3.78(.54)	3.79(.53)	3.72(.53)*	3.75(.52)	3.76(.55)	3.79(.53)
9. Reported personal aspiration	3.92(.48)	3.90(.48)	3.95(.50)	3.99(.47)*	3.93(.48)*	3.84(.50)*	3.97(.46)	3.91(.51)	3.88(.49)
Number of Cases	1686	839	847	516	649	521	578	576	532

[a]Statistically significant differences in comparisons between groups found (p < .001).
Source: Warr, P. (1990). The measurement of well-being and other aspects of mental health. *Journal of Occupational Psychology, 63,* 202.

Considering a maximum "in control" score of 9, how high was your score for recent weeks? Are you a totally "in control," competent and self-actualizing "9"? Or are you closer to the "out-of-control," non-self-actualizing "1" end? Each participant should now be able to conclude:

- If, in recent weeks, he or she was "in-control" and able to remain competent and aspiring—both on and off the job;
- If, in recent weeks, his or her "negative" and energy-draining life events seemed to be emanating from the work environment, the home environment, or a combination of the two; and
- If, in recent weeks, his or her "positive" and energy-refueling life events seemed to be emanating from the work environment, the home environment, or a combination of the two.

The following differences in mean scores were noted for Warr's (1990) comparison groups, as outlined in the results in Table 3.1:

1. Women exhibited significantly greater job-enthusiasm than men but reported significantly greater difficulty in coping with their work (i.e., they had lower mean scores on job-competence).

2. Organizational members in high-level professional and managerial jobs reported significantly more job-related enthusiasm and job-related aspiration than their other-level counterparts. However, those in the high occupational levels also reported being more job-anxious, more energy-drained by a high negative carryover from work to home, and less job-competent than their other-level counterparts.

3. Significant age differences in mind-behavior well-being were noted, with older organizational members having higher job-related contentment, job-related enthusiasm, job-related competence, and personal-related contentment than their younger counterparts. Such age differences might be associated, in large part, with greater adaptive resource development and better stress-coping attitudes and behaviors in older organizational members.

THE RELATIONSHIP BETWEEN "CONTROL" AND "LIFE STRESS"

The Dynamic Nature of "Control" and "Life Stress"

It is common for individuals who perceive themselves to be "in control" to also feel "appropriately stressed" or even "positively stressed" (i.e., eustressed). It is also common for individuals who perceive themselves to be "not in control" to feel "distressed." But why does there exist a link between individuals' perceived "control" and their perceived "stress and strain"?

There exists a relationship between control and stress (and strain) because *what* allows individuals to stay in control, to become energy-refueled, and to feel appropriately stressed or eustressed is *what* also causes individuals to move out of control, to become energy-drained, and to feel distressed. The *what* is individuals' life events, or more correctly, their appraisals of past and prevailing life events.

Since the landmark work of Lazarus (1966), stress experts have accepted, with little debate, that individuals' unique cognitive and emotional appraisals of their life events determine whether they feel "in control" and "appropriately stressed" or "out of control" and "distressed."

Lazarus emphasized that uniqueness in programming and variability in response, rather than sameness in programming and variability in response, is the theme to individuals' informational appraisals of their life events, particularly when these appraisals of life events are being made between individuals or within individuals over the short term (usually defined as a period of minutes, days, or weeks).

Because of interindividual "programming differences" in information processing and life conditioning, it can happen that individuals who are thought to be undergoing a very distressing life event by so-called "objective" populationwide standards—such as being fired from their jobs—will not think, feel, or behave out of control or show any outward signs of being distressed by such an "obviously" distressing life event. The reason for this seemingly "odd" mind-behavior outcome (by populationwide standards) for such individuals is that they are not appraising the event to be "distressing." Instead, it is likely that as a result of the individuals' unique life conditioning and recent life events, they have been "programmed" to "process" the so-called "distressing" event in a nonthreatening, appropriately stressing, or even a eustressing, frame of reference.

This theme of variability in response also applies to any individual over the short term. Because of short-term vascillations in mood, it can be and often is the case that someone who is experiencing and visibly manifesting "distress" in response to a given life event on Monday—such as being asked by the boss to work overtime—may not be feeling or showing the same degree of "distress" to the same (or similar) request from the boss on Friday. Because of the "mood swing" phenomenon that influences an individual's information processing in the short term, if one's mood is predominantly "negative" on Monday, then any life event that is appraised by the individual during that time period may be processed in a prevailing "negative" frame of reference. Similarly, if one's mood is predominantly "positive" on Friday, then any event that is appraised by the individual during that time period may be processed in a prevailing "positive" frame of reference.

What causes this uniqueness in life-event "programming" and variability in life-event "response" for individuals in the short term? Most experts agree that individuals appraise their life events by a dynamic but past-linked "standard" that is mood-responsive. Thus, the uniqueness in programming and variability in life-event responding are a function of this complex past-present "mind-behavior" control link. At any point in time, individuals' appraisals and responses to presenting stimuli—be they real or imagined—are a function of many short-term and long-term variables, including but not limited to the individuals' recent moods, appraised returns resulting from recent life-events, past "positive" or "negative" meaning assigned to similar or perceived-to-be-similar life events, and patterned or conditioned responses to the same or perceived-to-be-similar life events.

Over the longer term, individuals' informational appraisals are unique but somewhat more predictable. The reason for this greater predictability of response over the longer term is that individuals tend to develop predominantly positive or predominantly negative appraisal and information-processing predispositions. Simply stated, individuals have a sort of "filter" or "lens" on their information appraisal systems which results in their viewing and processing life events as predominantly "optimistic" and "likely eustressing," or as predominantly "pessimistic" and "likely depressing." By recent convention (since about 1982; Watson & Clark, 1984; Chen & Spector, 1991; Burke, Brief, & George, 1993), the former set of individuals are generally called "positive-affective" types, or PAs, and the latter are generally called "negative-affective" types, or NAs.

In the psychosocial literature, high-NA individuals, as contrasted with low-NA individuals, are likely to

1. Experience distress and life dissatisfaction in the short and long term;
2. Dwell on their failures and shortcomings—at work and at home—rather than accentuate their successes and strengths;
3. Focus on the negative side of the world, in general;
4. Have a less favorable view of themselves and their lives, both in terms of their competence and their aspirations;
5. Have high absenteeism rates at work, report frequent physicians' visits, and complain about many varied physical symptoms of poor health; and
6. Respond to self-report stress (and strain) inventory assessments from a rather negatively skewed standard or reference. (Watson & Clark, 1984; Chen & Spector, 1991; Burke, Brief & George, 1993)

In recent years, stress experts have consistently found that individuals who chronically appraise life events as "distressing" tend to, by their very nature, consume large amounts of finite life energy in order to cope with presenting life events—even when such energy expenditures are not warranted. Moreover, high-NAs seem less able to effectively energy-refuel; they, therefore, are at high risk for moving out of control, for becoming stress-disabled, and for physically burning out as a result of poor energy balance.

Measuring the Impact of Life Events on Individuals' Stress Levels with the SRRS

Although stress experts have recognized since the time of Lazarus' writings that life-event appraisal is a very unique, often variable, and subjective experience, they have tended, nevertheless, over the past 30 years, to measure individuals' susceptibility to move out of control and to become stress-disabled using inventories based on homogeneous (rather than on variable) concepts and on objectively-oriented (rather than on subjectively-oriented) frames of reference.

Probably the most popular objectively-framed instrument used in clinical circles has been the Holmes and Rahe (1967) Social Readjustment Rating Scale (SRRS), consisting of 43 "objective" life events that have population-response "reference scales" for determining the degree of overall stressfulness of each event listed. Basically, the SRRS ranks 43 life events by the amount of finite life energy commonly consumed by individuals to cope with the event. According to the developers, individuals use "LCUs, or life-change units" for coping with the life events listed and returning to equilibrium (i.e., "back to normal"). The 1967 version of the SRRS is presented in Table 3.2.

The numbers in the "Mean Value" column in Table 3.2 indicate the number of LCUs associated with each life event listed. In the left-hand column of Table 3.2, the life events are ranked by number of LCUs, with the lowest rank assigned to the largest LCUs required for recovery. These units were established by assigning an arbitrary value to the life event "marriage" and then asking individuals to rate the other 42 items relative to it.

Besides clinical applications, the SRRS has been used in research studies to better understand the relationship between life events and presenting stress disability. Respondents are usually asked to state which of the 43 events listed in Table 3.2 they have experienced over the past 6 months or over the past year. The values for the respondents' stated "life events" (based on LCUs) are then totaled.

Research findings with the SRRS inventory have consistently demonstrated that about 80% of individuals with scores exceeding 300 and about 53% of individuals with scores between 150 and 300 report a significant stress disability during or shortly after the period following the stressful life event(s). Individuals with scores below 150 have a low reported incidence of stress disability.

The stress disabilities whose onset has been associated with high SRRS scores have included trauma and mental distress, sudden death, heart attacks, acute respiratory illnesses, and various musculoskeletal problems.

Table 3.2
Social Readjustment Rating Scale

Rank	Life Event	Mean Value
1	Death of spouse	100
2	Divorce	73
3	Marital separation	65
4	Jail term	63
5	Death of family member	63
6	Personal injury/illness	53
7	Marriage	50
8	Fired at work	47
9	Marital reconciliation	45
10	Retirement	45
11	Change in family member's health	44
12	Pregnancy	40
13	Sex difficulties	39
14	Gain of new family member	39
15	Business readjustment	39
16	Change in financial state	38
17	Death of close friend	37
18	Change to different line of work	36
19	Change in number of arguments with spouse	35
20	Mortgage over $10,000	31
21	Foreclosure of mortgage/loan	30
22	Change in responsibilities at work	29
23	Son or daughter leaving home	29
24	Trouble with in-laws	29
25	Outstanding personal achievement	28
26	Wife begins or stops work	26
27	Begin or end school	26
28	Change in living conditions	25
29	Revision of personal habits	24
30	Trouble with boss	23
31	Change in work hours or conditions	20
32	Change in residence	20
33	Change in schools	20
34	Change in recreation	19
35	Change in church activities	19
36	Change in social activities	18
37	Mortgage or loan less than $10,000	17
38	Change in sleeping habits	16
39	Change in number of family get-togethers	15
40	Change in eating habits	15
41	Vacation	13
42	Christmas	12
43	Minor violations of the law	11

Source: Holmes, T. H., & Rahe, R. H. (1967). The social readjustment rating scale. *Journal of Psychosomatic Research*, 11, 214.

Contrary to Lazarus's subjective approach to life-event appraisal, the "objectively-based" SRRS has been tested in a variety of settings and cultures and has been found to follow the same relative pattern of response to the

Table 3.3
Perceived Stress Scale

1. In the last month, how often have you been upset because of something that happened unexpectedly?
2. In the last month, how often have you felt that you were unable to control the important things in your life?
3. In the last month, how often have you felt nervous and "stressed"?
4. In the last month, how often have you dealt successfully with irritating life hassles?
5. In the last month, how often have you felt that you were effectively coping with important changes that were occurring in your life?
6. In the last month, how often have you felt confident about your ability to handle personal problems?
7. In the last month, how often have you felt that things were going your way?
8. In the last month, how often have you found that you could not cope with all the things that you had to do?
9. In the last month, how often have you been able to control irritations in your life?
10. In the last month, how often have you felt that you were on top of things?
11. In the last month, how often have you been angered because of things that happened that were outside of your control?
12. In the last month, how often have you found yourself thinking about things that you have to accomplish?
13. In the last month, how often have you been able to control the way you spend your time?
14. In the last month, how often have you felt difficulties were piling up so high that you could not overcome them?

Source: Cohen, S., Kamarck, T., & Mermelstein, R. (1983). A global measure of perceived stress. *Journal of Health and Social Behavior, 24,* 385–396.

43 life events by individuals of different ages and races, including white and black Americans, Danes, Swedes, and the Japanese (Rahe, 1972).

From an organizational-use perspective, the SRRS's greatest shortcoming is its disproportionately low number of life events dealing with work (i.e., there are only seven work-related events of 43 life events listed; see, for example, items 8, 10, 15, 16, 18, 22, 31 in Table 3.2).

Measuring the Impact of Life Events on Individuals' Stress Levels with the PSS

In 1983, a subjectively-framed global measure of individually-appraised life-event stress (and strain) was developed by experts Cohen, Kamarck, and Mermelstein (1983). Simply called "The Perceived Stress Scale," or (PSS), this short inventory has rapidly become popular in clinical and in industrial circles around the world as a reliable assessment tool for determining individuals' loss of control and stress-susceptibility. The fourteen items of the PSS are shown in Table 3.3.

Respondents are typically asked to respond to the 14 items shown in Table 3.3 regarding their past month of experience. They are asked to use a frequency scale ranging from 0 (never) to 4 (very often) for each of the statements presented, and the responses to the positively-worded items are then recoded in order that a measure of "overall stressfulness and moving-out-of-control propensity" is measured for each respondent. Thus, the range of response for the PSS is 0–56.

For community adult "norms" collected to date, females generally score slightly higher on the PSS (with a mean score of about 26) than males (with a mean score of 24). That is, compared to males, females generally appraise their life events as being more "stressful" in the short term. Whether females lead more stressful lives or are more honest in their reporting of stressful life-events is still under debate.

Compared to other life-event and stress-assessment instruments on the market, however, the PSS has shown in recent studies to be better able to predict individuals' onsets of depression, anxiety, and other stress disabilities. The PSS is also able to predict usage of health services for stress-related illness. The conjectured reason for its high success in prediction has been attributed to the model's being based on dynamic, subjective appraisals of global life-events rather than on objective, discrete life-events like the SRRS (Cohen, Kamarck, & Mermelstein, 1983). Moreover, unlike the SRRS, the PSS does not distinguish between stressors emanating from work and those emanating from home; rather, it assumes a cumulative buildup of stress and strain from both segments of the life environment.

PERSONAL FEEDBACK: HOW "IN CONTROL" AND "APPROPRIATELY STRESSED" OR HOW "NOT IN CONTROL" AND "DISTRESSED" HAVE YOU BEEN RECENTLY?

Participants can now receive feedback on how "in control" and how "stressed (and strained)" they became as a result of life events within the past month and within the past year. *Please now score your responses to the Social Readjustment Rating Scale* (in Appendix 3.2) *and the Perceived Stress Scale* (in Appendix 3.3).

First, we'll discuss participants' results on the PSS (Appendix 3.3). Recall that the range of response for "stressfulness" of the life events in the past month and "inability to stay in control" was 0 through 56, with higher scores indicating a higher degree of stressfulness and inability to maintain "control." Considering a community mean score of 26 for females and 24 for males, does your global PSS score meet or exceed the comparison group mean? That is, would you conclude from your PSS score that you were relatively "in control" and "appropriately stressed" in the past month or relatively "out of control" and "distressed"? Were there any significant life events in the past month that may have triggered your moving out of control or that may have allowed you to remain in control?

Now we'll discuss participants' results on the SRRS (Appendix 3.2). Considering that research studies have shown that scores approaching 300 are in the "stress disability high-risk range," how "at risk" for stress-related disability do you appear to be, given your SRRS total score for the past year? Were there any significant life events over the past year that may have triggered a major moving-out-of-control experience for you, or was there a cumulation of "minor" but stressful life events? Do you think that there is a relationship between your ability to cope with stress and to stay in control over the past month *and* your ability to cope with stressful life events and to stay in control over the past year? If so, what is this relationship?

Participants should now be able to conclude:

- If, in the past month, they appraised life events on the PSS such that they were able to stay "in control" and remain "appropriately stressed," or even "eustressed";
- If their ability to cope with life events in the past month was in any way related to the energy consumed by "taxing" life events of the previous twelve months, as indicated by their total SRRS score; and
- If their ability to cope with life events in the past month and over the past year had any impact on their ability to remain competent and aspiring at work or at home.

PERSONAL FEEDBACK: HOW HAVE YOUR "MOODS" AND YOUR LIFE-EVENT APPRAISAL "FILTERS" BEEN RECENTLY—POSITIVE OR NEGATIVE?

As noted earlier, researchers have in recent years become interested in knowing what kind of "filter" or "lens" individuals view their worlds through and appraise their life events by. Now, participants will receive assessments of their positive-affect, or PA, and negative-affect, or NA, tendencies within recent weeks and over the past year. *Please now score your responses to the PANAS items in Appendix 3.4.*

Participants should now have four PA and NA scores (i.e., PANAS) before them. But what exactly do these four affect, or mood, scores indicate?

The PANAS inventory, provided in Appendix 3.4, was developed by Watson, Clark, and Tellegen (1988) as a means of giving individuals feedback about (1) their short-term "mood," or "state," NA and PA tendencies (i.e., two of the scores) and (2) their longer-term "processing predispositions," or "trait," NA and PA tendencies (i.e., the remaining two scores).

As stated earlier, individuals can be classified as being "predominantly PA" or "predominantly NA," both in the short term and over the longer term. Although this statement is true, it is important to note that at all times, individuals have varying amounts of PA and NA "coexisting" within them. It is also interesting to note that in industrial settings, individuals perceiving themselves to be "in control," "competent," and "aspiring" tend to self-report normative or above-normative levels of PA and normative or below-normative levels of NA.

Now for the PANAS feedback that is available to participants. When the "past few weeks" time frame and set of scores are considered, "PA" reflects the extent to which an individual has recently appraised life events through an "optimistic lens" and, consequently, felt psychologically and behaviorally enthusiastic, active, and alert. "High PA," then, is a state or mood characterized by high energy, full concentration, and pleasurable engagement with people and things in one's work and/or home environments. "Low PA," on the other hand, is a state or mood of sadness and lethargy.

When the "past few weeks" time frame and set of scores are considered, "NA" reflects the extent to which an individual has recently appraised life events through a "pessimistic lens," and, consequently, felt psychologically and behaviorally distressed and unpleasurably engaged with people and things in the work and/or home environments. "High NA," then, is a state which subsumes a variety of aversive mood states, including anger, contempt, disgust, fear, and nervousness. "Low NA," on the other hand, is a state or mood characterized by calmness and serenity (Watson, Clark, & Tellegen, 1988).

When the "past year" time frame is considered, "trait PA" corresponds to the dominant personality trait of extraversion. Conversely, "trait NA" corresponds to the dominant personality trait of anxiety/neuroticism. Although more will be said about these important personality traits in later sessions, for now it is important to recognize that in the psychosocial literature, NA but not PA has been consistently related to self-reported distress and poor "coping" with taxing life events. In contrast, PA but not NA has been consistently related to good stress-coping, high social-emotional refueling, and high life satisfaction. That is, high-PA individuals seem to be good stress-copers and good energy managers, whereas high-NA individuals seem to be poor stress-copers and ineffective energy managers.

To help individuals place their PANAS scores along a "mind-behavior health" continuum, the developers of the PANAS asked thousands of university students and working adults to complete their inventory. Calculations showed no systematic differences in scores between students and working adults or between males and females.

The mean and standard deviation "normative" data on the PANAS for the various time-frame instructions typically assigned by clinicians and industrial stress consultants are presented in Table 3.4 (Watson, Clark, & Tellegen, 1988).

Participants can readily note from Table 3.4 that the study subjects reported more PA than NA, regardless of the time-frame instructions. Moreover, mean scores on both PA and NA tended to increase as the measured time period increased. Such a pattern, as earlier suggested, shows that as

Table 3.4
Descriptive Data on the PANAS

Time Instructions	Number of Subjects	PA Mean	PA Standard Deviation	NA Mean	NA Standard Deviation
Moment	660	29.7	7.9	14.8	5.4
Today	657	29.1	8.3	16.3	6.4
Past few days	1002	33.3	7.2	17.4	6.2
Past few weeks	586	32.0	7.0	19.5	7.0
Past Year	649	36.2	6.3	22.1	6.4
General	663	35.0	6.4	18.1	5.9

Source: Watson, D., Clark, L. A., & Tellegen, A. (1988). Development and validation of brief measures of positive and negative affect: The PANAS scales. *Journal of Personality and Social Psychology, 54,* 1065.

the rated time-period increases, the probability that an individual will have experienced a significant amount of a given affect, or affect conditioning, (i.e., PA or NA) also increases.

Now, participants should be able to compare their PA and NA scores— in both the short term (i.e., over the "past few weeks") and the over the longer term (i.e., over the "past year") with the entries displayed in the "PA Mean" and the "NA Mean" columns in Table 3.4.

Considering that the short-term PA mean was 32 for 586 subjects tested, over the past few weeks, did you find that your PA mood score "healthily" met or exceeded this value of 32? Considering that the short-term NA mean was 19.5 for 586 subjects tested, over the past few weeks, did you find that your NA mood score "healthily" met or fell below this value of 19.5? Considering that the "Past few weeks" PA/NA ratio was 1.64 for the 586 subjects, did your PA/NA "self-healing/disease-prone" ratio healthily meet or exceed 1.64?

Considering that the longer-term PA mean was 36.2 for 649 subjects tested, over the past year, did you find that your PA predisposition score "healthily" met or exceeded this value of 36.2? Considering the longer-term NA mean was 22.1 for 649 subjects tested, over the past year, did you find that your NA predisposition score "healthily" met or fell below this value of 22.1? Considering that the "Past Year" PA/NA ratio was 1.64 for the 649 subjects, did your PA/NA "self-healing/disease-prone" ratio "healthily" meet or exceed 1.64?

Having done this comparison, participants should be able to conclude:

• If they have a mood or "state" tendency that indicates mind-behavior "health" or "stress-disabling risk";
• If they have a personality predisposition or "trait" tendency that indicates mind-behavior "health" or "stress-disabling risk"; and
• If their prevailing life-event appraisal tendencies have in any way "filtered" their earlier self-appraised levels of competence and aspiration, both on and off the job.

THE PROGNOSIS FOR HIGH-NEED-FOR-CONTROL INDIVIDUALS WHO ARE IN A "NA RUT" BUT WHO DO NOTHING TO GET OUT OF IT

Industrial clinicians and researchers, alike, have noted that the prognosis for "chronically" stifled high-need-for-control individuals is not good IF these individuals fail to do something constructive about the anger and pain that often accompany distressing, unrelenting, energy-draining life events.

As noted earlier, when high-need-for-control individuals misplace their anger or pain rather than deal constructively with it, they commonly experience and manifest to the outside world, NA "behavior"—which includes a range of aversive mood presentations, including unprovoked anger, contempt, disgust, fear, and nervousness. NA behavior in the short term is unpleasant but "normal." NA behavior in the long term can be and often is destructive—psychologically and behaviorally.

When high-need-for-control individuals stay in a "unfulfilled" life situation for relatively long periods of time, they develop patterns of seemingly "underreactive" or "overreactive" behavior to environmental stimuli. What their rather unpredictable or "inappropriate" behavior relates to the outside world is a reflection of the pain and anger that is being processed over and over again within these stressed individuals' minds. Namely,

I am experiencing repeat bouts of helplessness and hopelessness. I perceive no reasonable means of alleviating this pain and anger that I have. Therefore, I have little hope of regaining control. I am angry at the world and at myself. I am affectively NA. With each passing day in this NA rut, I feel, increasingly, energy-drained and depressed. Even more frightening, there are days when I feel uncontrollably angry, ready to lash out at myself or others with minimal provocation.

Expert Jerry Burger explains that persons high in need for control prototypically react to life's challenges or to taxing life demands with increased effort when all is going well and when they appraise themselves to be eustressfully refueled and generally "in control." But at some point in their lives, Burger warns, these high-need-for-control individuals may fall into a NA rut when the projected "returns" are not appraised to follow from their energy investments or when things are generally appraised by them as "not going well." Thus, they tend to develop prototypically NA "performance-inhibiting reactions" (Burger & Arkin, 1980; Burger, 1984; Burger, 1985) during chronic phases of low refueling. If these individuals stay in a NA rut for extended periods of time, they dig themselves deeply into a pit of depression and inaction—a pit that escalates the amount of distress experienced by them the longer they remain in it.

Stress experts suggest that the "psychological noise" and stress escalate for unfulfilled high-need-for-control types because inhibited performance over time leads to self-appraised reductions in competence and self-actualization. Self-appraised reductions in competence and self-actualization result in low- ered self-esteem, which further fuels performance-inhibiting responses.

In other words, when chronically stifled, once in-control PA individuals become chronically distressed, demotivated, and energy-depleted, they suc- cumb to the mind-behavior costs of lingering NA moods. Their life becomes characterized by intense feelings of negativity, hopelessness, and helpless- ness rather than positiveness, competence, and aspiration. When high-need- for-control individuals develop an overwhelming sense of hopelessness and helplessness, they have a tendency to avoid getting the professional help that they need to turn around their faltering mental health and their de- creased productivity.

The important point being made here is not that in-control, high-PA types are inevitably doomed to move out of control and manifest high-NA characteristics. Rather, the significant point being made is that if high-need- for-control individuals are receiving feedback about themselves through inventories, or through individuals in the workplace or at home, that they might be in a "performance-inhibiting state," they should recognize this assertion, accept it as a likely problem that needs attending to, and attend to it. Attending to the distress state should come sooner rather than later. Avoiding the performance-inhibiting state situation or allowing the pre- vailing NA mind-behavior state to escalate only leads to higher levels of distress and more severe mind-behavior disabilities with the passage of time.

PERSONAL FEEDBACK: DO YOUR INVENTORY RESULTS INDICATE THAT YOU ARE POSSIBLY IN A NA RUT?

Participants should now do some reflection on their inventory results compiled thus far. To how many of the following questions do your in- ventory results suggest that you should answer "yes"?

1. Looking first at your well-being results on the nine indices of Warr's inventory, out of a possible overall rating of 9, was your rating on the nine well-being indices considerably below 9?
2. Looking next at your score on the SRRS, was your overall distress score for the past year over 150 and approaching 300?
3. Looking next at your score on the PSS, did your overall score on the fourteen items for the past month exceed the distress "norm" for your gender?
4. Looking finally at your PA and NA scores on the PANAS for the short term and over the longer term, was your PA/NA score in either the short term or over the longer term below the 1.64 norm?
5. Was your NA score in either the short term or over the longer term above the "healthy" norm?

Participants should now be able to conclude after looking at the number of "yes" responses that they had to the preceding five questions:

- If they are in an overall energy-refueling and eustressful phase, or if they are in an overall energy-draining and distressing phase (and possibly in a NA rut); and
- If they are in a possible NA rut, whether they should seek the help of a professional or an organizational manager in order to move more readily back into control.

SUGGESTIONS FOR BREAKING A SHORT-TERM "NA CYCLE"

Individuals who do not feel that professional assistance is needed to get out of a NA rut but who want to cope better with "NA" events might want to engage in some short-term cognitive "reprogramming" or "reappraisals" the next time appraised "negative" life events present. Three of the most common cognitive reappraisal strategies suggested by stress experts as being effective in this regard are as follows (Pearlin et al., 1981):

1. *Comparative Frame of Reference Cognitive Reappraisals*, whereby the distressed individual survives a "painful" life event by telling himself or herself that "other persons or groups who have experienced similar stressors are worse off, or at least no better off, than me in the present set of life circumstances." Thus, in selectively contrasting one's own standing with that of others who may be engaged in more severe life-event struggles, the distressed individual can arrive at a positive (rather than at a negative) appraisal of his or her own life event.

2. *Devaluation of a Particular Success Outcome*, whereby the distressed individual tries to reduce the hardship around an event of appraised importance by lowering in his or her mind the priority of the particular success outcome or reward in question. For example, a distressed individual might devalue the importance of a "sale not had" or a "widget not produced" by telling himself or herself that "money is nice but it doesn't buy happiness." Such "self-talk" often reduces anxiety around events that fall short of projected targets. In short, by demeaning the importance of a particular success outcome or the rewards that it can bring, the distressed individual may effectively shield himself or herself from some of the anger and frustration linked to "lack of success" on this particular life-event dimension.

3. *Characterological (Self-Blame) Attribution Reformulation*, whereby the distressed individual tries to reduce a cycle of self-blame and learned helplessness for negative life events by attributing "the situational negative outcome" not to an internal, stable, global personality trait (i.e., "I'm always bad at anything I do") but to a less-fixed and more readily changeable behavior (i.e., "I've been late often; this behavior needs to be addressed by me").

There are a number of useful behavioral strategies for on-the-spot coping with negative life events. Two of the most popular are the "count-to-ten-and-then-respond" strategy and the cue-induced muscle relaxation strategy. More details on these strategies will be given in future sessions.

If, after some reasonable length of time, an individual has tried these suggested cognitive reappraisal and behavior strategies but no significant NA relief is perceived, then this individual should seriously consider receiving NA-intervention assistance from a mental-health or stress-reduction expert. After all, even high-need-for-control individuals sometimes need to seek help from others in order to stay mentally healthy and behaviorally productive.

CONCLUSION

I'd like to close this "Control" session by suggesting that all participants now have the start of a personal data base to ascertain how they have been C-O-P-E-ing in recent weeks and over the past year. Over our next sets of sessions, we will continue to build on this base. This session allowed participants to introspect about whether or not they have recently been "in control," and if not, why not.

But continued stress management and improved stress-coping require an ongoing assessment of one's ability to remain "in control." For, as we have noted in this session, the stress process is a dynamic process. Thus, stress management must be a dynamic, not a static as process. Moreover, stress management commonly requires more than an ongoing self-diagnostic process. If the individual who appraises himself or herself as "not coping well" wants to improve his or her stress-disability prognosis, then stress management must also become an action-taking process, which is, by its very nature, self-directed and sometimes also other-assisted.

Some of you participants may be leaving this session relieved to find that you have been "in control" in recent weeks and perhaps even over the past year. Others of you may be leaving somewhat disturbed with the feedback that you have received thus far. Given your feedback, you may already be prepared to see a mental-health or stress expert for some distress relief. Others of you may be thinking about seeking assistance but are waiting for more feedback from future sessions before you act on these thoughts. Regardless of what option you eventually choose, the important point is that you have honestly begun to look at your life events and your stress-C-O-P-E-ing capabilities. And for this, all of you need to be commended.

Some of you may be wondering what happened to Kelvin Browne. You may even want to know if he ever got disability insurance.

I'd like to return now to the case of Kelvin Browne. First, I'll read you the balance of his piece in the newspaper. Then, I'd like to share my thoughts with you on the relevance of his case from a stress management perspective.

Here is how Kelvin continued his story about losing personal control and trying to regain it:

So why did I see a psychologist? I saw a psychologist because I couldn't see a psychiatrist. Every psychiatrist I called had a three-to-ten-month waiting list. Aside from consideration of who could work with me best, I also would have preferred to see a psychiatrist because OHIP [government-funded, Ontario Health Insurance Plan] would have paid for it. Since I was interested not in a historical analysis of my problem but help in resolving it, a friend recommended a psychologist who had an opening. I took it. As it turned out, it was an excellent recommendation, as she was an ideal therapist for me.

I think I was a good patient. I went to see her to resolve some specific problems, and we terminated therapy when we agreed we had dealt with them. I was not seeking to change my life nor was I a narcissistic personality indulging myself in an hour a week of attention from someone paid to be fascinated by my problems. I wasn't non-functional either. My difficulties at the time could hardly be considered a medical emergency.

My then-employer's group-insurance plan paid for three visits a year to a psychologist. My therapy spanned two calendar years, so I was lucky to have six of the sessions paid for. At the rate of about $100 an hour, I paid for the remainder myself. I was lucky that I was in a financial situation that enabled me to buy the psychological help I wanted when it wasn't otherwise available to me. I know others are not so fortunate. I also came to realize that paying for most sessions made me concentrate diligently during each one. I was responsible for getting my money's worth. I certainly didn't want to continue therapy any longer than I felt I had to, since I was paying for it.

But I sound like I'm avoiding telling why I needed help. I could say it is a private matter. I could also claim that this information is not relevant to the point I want to make. If I did, though, you might think that I went to see a therapist for some reason that did make me a bad risk for any company to consider insuring. The facts are quite unremarkable.

During the time I was talking to Dr. X, I left a relationship of 15 years, began living with someone else, commuted from Toronto to Vancouver to visit with my terminally ill father, tried (as an only child) to be supportive of my mother during his illness, and attempted to cope with a job that was not working out. Eventually, my father died and I left the large financial institution that had been my employer to open a business of my own. I moved three times during this period and sold property that was jointly held in my previous relationship. There was a fair amount of stress, but that is not why I needed to talk to someone.

I needed to talk to someone who could give me an objective assessment of my reactions to the rather intense experiences happening to me and around me. I think Dr. X helped me to see things in perspective and ensured that I didn't do anything rash. I certainly avoided drinking, drugs, and hurting other people and the other destructive things people do when they are overwhelmed by their lives.

Of course, I could have just lied when I filled out the insurance application and said I had never consulted a psychologist or a psychiatrist. I don't think anyone would have found out. It simply didn't occur to me that admitting this on the application would cause me any harm.

The letter I received from the insurance company declining my application was a kind of form letter and it definitely had a rubber-stamp signature. It said in total:

"We have today written to Dr. X advising the reasons for the action taken in connection with your above-mentioned application. We trust you will better understand our action after discussing this with Dr. X."

Dr. X was completely mystified why her two-sentence description of our therapy session (not very different from my description in this article) was a reason for a company not to insure me.

I am still strying to get insurance, now from another company. But this time I wear a scarlet letter. "Have you ever had an application for insurance rejected . . . ?" I check the YES box and it sets off alarms for the prospective insurer. They call and ask if I can tell them why I was rejected. "Because I visited a psychologist" doesn't satisfy them. They're sure there must be something really wrong that I'm not telling them about.

Talk shows are filled with entertainers promoting their careers through revealing all. However, if you're not a star, letting an insurance company, or your employer, know you've seen a shrink might be a mistake. (Browne, 1994)

When I finished reading Mr. Browne's piece, I could understand his anger at not getting disability insurance. After all, he seemed like a deserving, competent, aspiring, high-PA individual. As Kelvin said, his reasons for seeing a psychologist were not all that remarkable. His "problems" began when he ran into a streak of taxing life events, even by populationwide "objective" measures. His father was dying, his relationship of fifteen years had ended, he quit his old job, he sold personal property, and he opened a business.

But, despite these "problems," high-need-for-control Kelvin did not wilt and die. Instead, he called on his stress energy reserves and flew from one end of the country (Toronto) to the other (Vancouver)—repeatedly—to be with his dying father. He ended one relationship and got emotionally involved with another person. He was emotionally supportive to his mother during his father's illness and after his death. He left one job in search of a more aspiring one—one that he could be "in total control of." And he sold personal property from his past relationship.

I asked myself after reading his passage, if Kelvin could do all of this in a peak distress period, how much more did I think Kelvin could do in a peak eustress period? I simply could not answer my own question.

I respected the "personal control" that Kelvin seemed to possess and was able to retain. His story smacked of "high need for control." How could I tell? Well, I noticed that he NEVER EVER told me what his physical symptoms of distress were. He led me on, hoping I'd beg him for the answer. But HE maintained control. He never did succumb to my need "to know" the details of his pain and suffering.

Why didn't Kelvin tell me his symptoms? Probably because he didn't think that I, the insurance company, or his employer needed to know that sort of personal information. And he's right. It is, in the larger picture, immaterial what his stress symptoms were.

What is important to the insurance companies, his employers, and me is that Kelvin Browne recognized his symptoms of distress, he accepted that he had a "stress problem," he went to get professional help for it, he "gave it all that he had" in an effort to rehabilitate himself, and he regained his "mind-behavior balance." His story should have ended there.

But it didn't end. Like Warren Potts's story, Kelvin Browne's story got worse before it got better. Instead of being rewarded for seeking professional help when he needed it—which is the heroic "thing" to do—Kelvin Browne was punished by the insurance companies who refused him disability coverage. That is why he is angry. And he, I concluded, deserves to be angry.

In closing, let us reward Kelvin Browne for his heroic stress-reduction efforts. As we leave this session, let us commit ourselves to be more understanding in the workplace when one of our organizational members tells us, in confidence, that he or she has a stress problem. Let us encourage that organizational member to consider getting some professional assistance, if he or she cannot resolve his or her dilemma alone. Let us not—like the insurance companies that Kelvin described—further lower the self-esteem of a valued organizational member by presenting more blows to the apparently bruised "roots" of control.

I have to confess that I was curious to know what happened to Kelvin Browne. So I did something that I would normally not do. I telephoned him and talked with him for about twenty minutes.

I felt relieved to discover that Kelvin Browne is very much as I had appraised him to be. Today, he is alive, well, and kicking—just as a high-need-for-control, competent, aspiring, high-PA should be. And the good news is that he got a good return on his newspaper piece. An insurance company offered him disability insurance.

At the end of our conversation, Kelvin told me that his anger had dissipated somewhat, and that he was now getting on with bigger and better things in his life. I thought to myself, "Oh, how PA-ish."

STRESS-COPING SUMMARY POINTS

1. To ward off performance-inhibiting reactions, organizational members should regularly complete self-report inventories to determine if they are, effectively, "in control."

2. In order to complete this task, four inventories that work well for this purpose include:

    a. Warr's "Mind-Behavior Well-being" Inventory,
    b. The Social Readjustment Rating Scale (SRRS),
    c. The Perceived Stress Scale (PSS), and
    d. The PANAS Scale.

3. To reduce the amount of distress experienced during taxing life events, organizational members should attempt three Cognitive Reappraisal Strategies:

    a. Comparative Frame of Reference Cognitive Reappraisals;
    b. Devaluation of a Particular Success Outcome (or Reward); and
    c. Characterological (Self-Blame) Attribution Reformulation.

4. To reduce the amount of distress experienced during such events, organizational members might also attempt such behavioral strategies as counting to ten before responding and cue-induced muscle relaxation therapy.

5. If self-help cognitive reappraisal and behavioral modification strategies like those just listed do not bring adequate distress (and/or NA predisposition) relief, organizational members should consider getting help from a mental-health or stress-management professional.

Appendix 3.1
A Measurement of Your Well-Being

Questions About Your Job

In the past few weeks, HOW MUCH OF THE TIME has your job made you feel each of the following?

Please fill in the blank with one of the following numbers:

1 never; 2 occasionally; 3 some of the time; 4 much of the time; 5 most of the time; 6 all of the time

A.

_____ Tense	_____ Depressed	_____ Calm	_____ Cheerful
_____ Uneasy	_____ Enthusiastic	_____ Contented	_____ Relaxed
_____ Worried	_____ Gloomy	_____ Miserable	_____ Optimistic

In the past few weeks, HOW has your job made you feel? Please disagree or agree with each item presented, using the following scale:

1 strongly disagree; 2 disagree; 3 neither disagree nor agree; 4 agree; 5 strongly agree

B.
1. I can do my job well. _____
2. I sometimes think I am not very competent at my job. _____
3. In my job, I like to set myself challenging targets. _____
4. I am not very interested in my job. _____
5. After I leave work, I keep worrying about job problems. _____
6. I can deal with just about any problem in my job. _____
7. I find my job quite difficult. _____
8. I find it difficult to unwind at the end of a work-day. _____
9. I enjoy doing new things in my job. _____
10. I prefer to avoid difficult activities in my job. _____
11. I feel used up at the end of the work-day. _____
12. I feel I am better than most people at tackling job difficulties. _____
13. In my job, I make a special effort to keep trying when things seem difficult. _____
14. I am not very concerned how things turn out in my job. _____
15. My job makes me feel quite exhausted by the end of a work-day. _____
16. In my job, I often have trouble coping. _____

Appendix 3.1 (continued)

Questions About Your Life Outside of Your Job

In the past few weeks, HOW MUCH OF THE TIME has your personal life made you feel each of the following?

Please fill in the blank with one of the following numbers:

1 never; 2 occasionally; 3 some of the time; 4 much of the time;
5 most of the time; 6 all of the time

C.

_____ Tense	_____ Depressed	_____ Calm	_____ Cheerful
_____ Uneasy	_____ Enthusiastic	_____ Contented	_____ Relaxed
_____ Worried	_____ Gloomy	_____ Miserable	_____ Optimistic

In the past few weeks, HOW has your personal life made you feel?
Please disagree or agree with each item presented, using the following scale:

1 strongly disagree; 2 disagree; 3 neither disagree nor agree;
4 agree; 5 strongly agree

D.
17. I can deal with just about any problem in my personal life. _____
18. I enjoy doing new things in my personal life. _____
19. I am not very interested in the world around me. _____
20. I sometimes think I am not very competent in my personal life. _____
21. I like to set myself challenging targets in my personal life. _____
22. Most things I do, I do well. _____
23. I find my personal life quite difficult. _____
24. I prefer to avoid difficult activities in my personal life. _____
25. I feel I am better than most people at tackling difficulties. _____
26. I often have trouble coping in my personal life. _____
27. I make a special effort to keep trying when things seem difficult. _____
28. I am not very concerned how things turn out in my personal life. _____

Source: Warr, P. (1990). The measurement of well-being and other aspects of mental health. *Journal of Occupational Psychology, 63,* 193–210.

Appendix 3.2
A Measurement of Recent Life Events

Mark with an X each life-event that you had in the past year:

ITEM	Life Event	"X"
1	Death of spouse	
2	Divorce	
3	Marital separation	
4	Jail term	
5	Death of family member	
6	Personal injury/illness	
7	Marriage	
8	Fired at work	
9	Marital reconciliation	
10	Retirement	
11	Change in family member's health	
12	Pregnancy	
13	Sex difficulties	
14	Gain of new family member	
15	Business readjustment	
16	Change in financial state	
17	Death of close friend	
18	Change to different line of work	
19	Change in number of arguments with spouse	
20	Mortgage over $10,000	
21	Foreclosure of mortgage/loan	
22	Change in responsibilities at work	
23	Son or daughter leaving home	
24	Trouble with in-laws	
25	Outstanding personal achievement	
26	Wife begins or stops work	
27	Begin or end school	
28	Change in living conditions	
29	Revision of personal habits	
30	Trouble with boss	
31	Change in work hours or conditions	
32	Change in residence	
33	Change in schools	
34	Change in recreation	
35	Change in church activities	
36	Change in social activities	
37	Mortgage or loan less than $10,000	
38	Change in sleeping habits	
39	Change in number of family get-togethers	
40	Change in eating habits	
41	Vacation	
42	Christmas	
43	Minor violations of the law	

Source: Holmes, T. H., & Rahe, R. H. (1967). The social readjustment rating scale. *Journal of Psychosomatic Research, 11,* 214.

Appendix 3.3
A Measurement of Perceived Stress

INSTRUCTIONS:
The questions in this scale ask you about your feelings and thoughts during the last month. In each case, you will be asked to indicate **how often** you felt or thought a certain way. Although some of the questions are similar, there are differences between them and you should treat each one as a separate question. The best approach is to answer each question fairly quickly. That is, don't try to count up the number of times you felt a particular way, but rather indicate the alternative that seems like a reasonable estimate.

For each question below, choose from the following response alternatives:
  0 never; 1 almost never; 2 sometimes; 3 fairly often; 4 very often

ITEMS:

1. In the last month, how often have you been upset because of something that happened unexpectedly?
2. In the last month, how often have you felt that you were unable to control the important things in your life?
3. In the last month, how often have you felt nervous and "stressed"?
4. In the last month, how often have you dealt successfully with irritating life hassles?
5. In the last month, how often have you felt that you were effectively coping with important changes that were occurring in your life?
6. In the last month, how often have you felt confident about your ability to handle personal problems?
7. In the last month, how often have you felt that things were going your way?
8. In the last month, how often have you found that you could not cope with all the things that you had to do?
9. In the last month, how often have you been able to control irritations in your life?
10. In the last month, how often have you felt that you were on top of things?
11. In the last month, how often have you been angered because of things that happened that were outside of your control?
12. In the last month, how often have you found yourself thinking about things that you have to accomplish?
13. In the last month, how often have you been able to control the way you spend your time?
14. In the last month, how often have you felt difficulties were piling up so high that you could not overcome them?

Source: Cohen, S., Kamarck, T., & Mermelstein, R. (1983). A global measure of perceived stress. *Journal of Health and Social Behavior*, 24, 385–396.

Appendix 3.4
The PANAS

This scale consists of a number of words that describe different feelings and emotions. Read each item and then mark the appropriate answer in the space next to that word. Indicate to what extent you have felt this way during the PAST FEW WEEKS. Use the following scale to record your answers:
1 very slightly or not at all
2 a little
3 moderately
4 quite a bit
5 extremely

Items:
_____ interested
_____ distressed
_____ excited
_____ upset
_____ strong
_____ guilty
_____ scared
_____ hostile
_____ enthusiastic
_____ proud

This scale consists of a number of words that describe different feelings and emotions. Read each item and then mark the appropriate answer in the space next to that word. Indicate to what extent you have felt this way during the PAST FEW WEEKS. Use the following scale to record your answers:
1 very slightly or not at all
2 a little
3 moderately
4 quite a bit
5 extremely

Items:
_____ irritable
_____ alert
_____ ashamed
_____ inspired
_____ nervous
_____ determined
_____ attentive
_____ jittery
_____ active
_____ afraid

This scale consists of a number of words that describe different feelings and emotions. Read each item and then mark the appropriate answer in the space next to that word. Indicate to what extent you have felt this way during the PAST YEAR. Use the following scale to record your answers:
1 very slightly or not at all
2 a little
3 moderately
4 quite a bit
5 extremely

Items:
_____ interested
_____ distressed
_____ excited
_____ upset
_____ strong
_____ guilty
_____ scared
_____ hostile
_____ enthusiastic
_____ proud

This scale consists of a number of words that describe different feelings and emotions. Read each item and then mark the appropriate answer in the space next to that word. Indicate to what extent you have felt this way during the PAST YEAR. Use the following scale to record your answers:
1 very slightly or not at all
2 a little
3 moderately
4 quite a bit
5 extremely

Items:
_____ irritable
_____ alert
_____ ashamed
_____ inspired
_____ nervous
_____ determined
_____ attentive
_____ jittery
_____ active
_____ afraid

Source: Watson, D., Clark, L. A., & Tellegen, A. (1988). Development and validation of brief measures of positive and negative affect: The PANAS scales. Journal of Personality and Social Psychology, 54, 1063–1070.

Scoring Appendix 3.1

Appendix 3.1.A.1 Score

Are you job-anxious or job-contented?

(a) "Reverse-score" your answers to "tense," "uneasy," and "worried" in Part A. Use the following conversion: 1=6; 2=5; 3=4; 4=3; 5=2; 6=1.

(b) Total your converted scores for "tense," "uneasy," and "worried."

(c) Total your original scores for "calm," "contented," and "relaxed."

(d) Total b + c. This is your final score. Mark it here:_____ (Range 6-36)

The lower your score, the more job-anxious you are.

The higher your score, the more job-contented you are.

(e) To obtain a "mean" score, divide your final score by 6. Mark it here: _____

Appendix 3.1.A.2 Score

Are you job-depressed or job-enthusiastic?

(a) "Reverse-score" your answers to "depressed," "gloomy," and "miserable" in Part A. Use the following conversion: 1=6; 2=5; 3=4; 4=3; 5=2; 6=1.

(b) Total your converted scores for "depressed," "gloomy," and "miserable."

(c) Total your original scores for "cheerful," "enthusiastic," and "optimistic."

(d) Total b + c. This is your final score. Mark it here:_____ (Range 6-36)

The lower your score, the more job-depressed you are.

The higher your score, the more job-enthusiastic you are.

(e) To obtain a "mean" score, divide your final score by 6. Mark it here: _____

Appendix 3.1.C.3 Score

Are you personally-anxious or personally-contented?

(a) "Reverse-score" your answers to "tense," "uneasy," and "worried" in Part C. Use the following conversion: 1=6; 2=5; 3=4; 4=3; 5=2; 6=1.

(b) Total your converted scores for "tense," "uneasy," and "worried."

(c) Total your original scores for "calm," "contented," and "relaxed."

(d) Total b + c. This is your final score. Mark it here:_____ (Range 6-36)

The lower your score, the more personally-anxious you are.

The higher your score, the more personally-contented you are.

(e) To obtain a "mean" score, divide your final score by 6. Mark it here: _____

Appendix 3.1.C.4 Score

Are you personally-depressed or personally-enthusiastic?

(a) "Reverse-score" your answers to "depressed," "gloomy," and "miserable" in Part C. Use the following conversion: 1=6; 2=5; 3=4; 4=3; 5=2; 6=1.

(b) Total your converted scores for "depressed," "gloomy," and "miserable."

(c) Total your original scores for "cheerful," "enthusiastic," and "optimistic."

(d) Total b + c. This is your final score. Mark it here:_____ (Range 6-36)

The lower your score, the more personally-depressed you are.

The higher your score, the more personally-enthusiastic you are.

(e) To obtain a "mean" score, divide your final score by 6. Mark it here: _____

Scoring Appendix 3.1 (continued)

Appendix 3.1.B.5 Score

Do you see yourself as being job-competent?
- (a) "Reverse-score" your answers to items 2, 7, and 16 in Part B. Use the following conversion: 1=5; 2=4; 3=3; 4=2; 5=1.
- (b) Now total your scores for items 1, 2, 6, 7, 12, and 16. This is your final score. Mark it here:_____ (Range 6-30)
  The higher the score, the more job-competent you perceive yourself to be.
- (c) To obtain a "mean" score, divide your final score by 6. Mark it here: _____

Appendix 3.1.B.6 Score

Do you see yourself as being job-aspiring?
- (a) "Reverse-score" your answers to items 4, 10, and 14 in Part B. Use the following conversion: 1=5; 2=4; 3=3; 4=2; 5=1.
- (b) Now total your scores for items 3, 4, 9, 10, 13, and 14. This is your final score. Mark it here:_____ (Range 6-30)
  The higher the score, the more job-aspiring you perceive yourself to be.
- (c) To obtain a "mean" score, divide your final score by 6. Mark it here: _____

Appendix 3.1.B.7 Score

Is there a negative carry-over from your job to your personal life?
- (a) Total your scores for items 5, 8, 11, and 15 in Part B. This is your final score. Mark it here: _____ (Range 4-20)
  The higher the score, the more negative carry-over there is.
- (b) To obtain a "mean" score, divide your final score by 4. Mark it here: _____

Appendix 3.1.D.8 Score

Do you see yourself as being personally-competent?
- (a) "Reverse-score" your answers to items 20, 23, and 26 in Part D. Use the following conversion: 1=5; 2=4; 3=3; 4=2; 5=1.
- (b) Now total your scores for items 17, 20, 22, 23, 25, and 26. This is your final score. Mark it here:_____ (Range 6-30)
  The higher the score, the more personally-competent you perceive yourself to be.
- (c) To obtain a "mean" score, divide your final score by 6. Mark it here: _____

Appendix 3.1.D.9 Score

Do you see yourself as being personally-aspiring?
- (a) "Reverse-score" your answers to items 19, 24, and 28 in Part D. Use the following conversion: 1=5; 2=4; 3=3; 4=2; 5=1.
- (b) Now total your scores for items 18, 19, 21, 24, 27, and 28. This is your final score. Mark it here:_____ (Range 6-30)
  The higher the score, the more personally-aspiring you perceive yourself to be.
- (c) To obtain a "mean" score, divide your final score by 6. Mark it here: _____

Source: Warr, P. (1990). The measurement of well-being and other aspects of mental health. *Journal of Occupational Psychology*, 63, 193–210.

Scoring Appendix 3.2

Social Readjustment Rating Scale (SRRS) Score

Are you at risk for moving out-of-control and for developing stress-related
disorders as a result of recent life-events?
  (a) Turn to Table 3.2 and mark in your Appendix 3.2 "X" column the mean
      values associated with your life-events.
  (b) Total the values in the "X" column. Mark your total score here: _____.
  (c) Research with the SRRS scale has shown that 80% of individuals with total
      scores over 300 and 53% of individuals with scores between 150 and 300
      suffer significant health-disabilities (i.e., heart attacks, acute
      respiratory illnesses, and death) during the period following
      stressful life-events. Individuals with scores below 150 have a low
      incidence of major health disorders. Where does your "risk factor" fall?

Mark an X by the statement that best describes your health-disability risk:

Low Risk: Score Less Than 150 _____   Moderate Risk: Score 150-300 _____

                    High Risk: Score Over 300 _____

Source: Holmes, T. H., & Rahe, R. H. (1967). The social readjustment rating scale. Journal
    of Psychosomatic Research, 11, 213–218.

Scoring Appendix 3.3

Perceived Stress Scale (PSS)

Have you appraised your life events as being "stressful" in the past month?
  (a) Turn to your responses for Appendix 3.3. Now "reverse-score" your
      responses to items 4, 5, 6, 7, 9, 10, and 13 using the following
      conversion: 0=4; 1=3; 2=2; 3=1; 4=0.
  (b) Now total your responses for all 14 items. This is your final score.
      Mark it here:_____ (Range 0-56).
      The higher your score, the greater you appraised your life-events as being
      "stressful" in the past month.
  (c) For community adult "norms" already collected, females generally score
      slightly higher than males on the PSS. In community samples, the mean
      "global measure" score for females is 25.6 (standard deviation 8.24), while the
      mean "global measure" score for males is 24.0 (standard deviation 7.80).
  (d) How does your global measure score compare with the mean scores for community
      adults of your gender? Does your total PSS score fall below or above the
      stated means? By how much? What does your score tell you about your past month
      and your reaction to life-events during that month? Would you have gotten the
      same or different results if you had completed the PSS two months ago? What about
      six months ago? What about a year ago?
  (e) Would your PSS score indicate that you coped well with stress and remained in
      control over the past month?
      Mark one: Yes _____ No _____

Source: Cohen, S., Kamarck, T., Mermelstein, R. (1983). A global measure of perceived stress. *Journal of Health and Social Behavior*, 24, 385–396.

Scoring Appendix 3.4

The PANAS: The Past Few Weeks
Have you been PA- or NA-predominant over the past few weeks?
(a) Turn to Appendix 3.4. Record and total your scores for the following:
_____interested
_____excited
_____strong
_____enthusiastic
_____proud
_____alert
_____inspired
_____determined
_____attentive
_____active
This is your PA score for the past few weeks. Mark your PA score here:
_____ (Range 10-50)
The higher the score, the higher your positive-affect for the past weeks.
(b) Now turn to Appendix 3.4. Record and total your scores for the following adjectives:
_____distressed
_____upset
_____guilty
_____scared
_____hostile
_____irritable
_____ashamed
_____nervous
_____jittery
_____afraid
This is your NA score for the past few weeks. Mark your NA score here:_____ (Range 10-50)
The higher the score, the higher your negative-affect for the past weeks.

The PANAS: The Past year
Have you been PA- or NA-predominant over the past year?
(a) Turn to Appendix 3.4. Record and total your scores for the following:
_____interested
_____excited
_____strong
_____enthusiastic
_____proud
_____alert
_____inspired
_____determined
_____attentive
_____active
This is your PA score for the past year. Mark your PA score here:
_____ (Range 10-50)
The higher the score, the higher your positive-affect for the year.
(b) Now turn to Appendix 3.4. Record and total your scores for the following adjectives:
_____distressed
_____upset
_____guilty
_____scared
_____hostile
_____irritable
_____ashamed
_____nervous
_____jittery
_____afraid
This is your NA score for the past year. Mark your NA score here:_____ (Range 10-50)
The higher the score, the higher your negative-affect for the year.

Source: Watson, D., Clark, L. A., & Tellegen, A. (1988). Development and validation of brief measures of positive and negative affect: The PANAS scales. Journal of Personality and Social Psychology, 54, 1063–1070.

REFERENCES

Abramson, L. Y., Seligman, M. E. P., & Teasdale, J. D. (1978). Learned helplessness in humans: Critique and reformulation. *Journal of Abnormal Psychology*, 87, 49–74.

Bandura, A. (1977). Self-efficacy: Toward a unifying theory of behavioral change. *Psychological Review*, 84, 191–215.

Bradburn, N. M. (1969). *The Structure of Psychological Well-Being*. Chicago: Aldine.

Browne, K. (1994). The scarlet letter: Why I am not insurable. *The Globe and Mail*, April 14, A26.

Burger, J. M. (1984). Desire for control, locus of control, and proneness to depression. *Journal of Personality*, 52, 71–89.

Burger, J. M. (1985). Desire for control and achievement-related behaviours. *Journal of Personality and Social Psychology*, 48, 1520–1533.

Burger, J. M., & Arkin, R. M. (1980). Prediction, control and learned helplessness. *Journal of Personality and Social Psychology*, 38, 482–491.

Burger, J. M., & Cooper, H. M. (1979). The desirability of control. *Motivation and Emotion*, 3, 381–393.

Burke, M. J., Brief, A. P., & George, J. M. (1993). The role of negative affectivity in understanding relations between self-reports of stress and strain: A comment on the applied psychology literature. *Journal of Applied Psychology*, 78, 402–412.

Chen, P. Y., & Spector, P. E. (1991). Negative affectivity as the underlying cause of correlations between stressors and strain. *Journal of Applied Psychology*, 76, 398–407.

Cohen, S., & Hoberman, H. M. (1983). Positive life events and social supports as buffers of life change stress. *Journal of Applied Social Psychology*, 13, 99–125.

Cohen, S., Kamarck, T., & Mermelstein, R. (1983). A global measure of perceived stress. *Journal of Health and Social Behavior*, 24, 385–396.

Evans, P., & Bartolome, F. (1980). *Must Success Cost So Much?* London: Grant McIntyre.

Herzberg, F. (1966). *Work and the Nature of Man*. Chicago: World Publishing Company.

Holmes, T. H., & Rahe, R. H. (1967). The social readjustment rating scale. *Journal of Psychosomatic Research*, 11, 213–218.

Jahoda, M. (1958). *Current Concepts of Positive Mental Health*. New York: Basic Books.

Lazarus, R. S. (1966). *Psychological Stress and the Coping Process*. New York: McGraw-Hill.

Maslow, A. H. (1973). *The Farther Reaches of Human Nature*. London: Penguin.

Near, J., Rice, R., & Hunt, R. (1980). The relationship between work and non-work domains: A review of empirical research. *Academy of Management Review*, 5, 415–429.

Pearlin, L. I., Menaghan, E. G., Lieberman, M. A., & Mullan, J. T. (1981). The stress process. *Journal of Health and Social Behavior*, 22, 337–356.

Piotrkowski, C. S. (1978). *Work and the Family System*. New York: Free Press.

Rahe, R. H. (1972). Subjects' recent life changes and their near-future illness susceptibility. *Advances in Psychosomatic Medicine*, 8, 2–19.

Warr, P. (1990). The measurement of well-being and other aspects of mental health. *Journal of Occupational Psychology*, 63, 193–210.

Watson, D., & Clark, L. A. (1984). Negative affectivity: The disposition to experience aversive emotional states. *Psychological Bulletin*, 96, 465–490.

Watson, D., Clark, L. A., & Tellegen, A. (1988). Development and validation of brief measures of positive and negative affect: The PANAS scales. *Journal of Personality and Social Psychology*, 54, 1063–1070.

Weidner, G., & Andrews, J. (1983). Attributions for undesirable life events, type A behavior, and depression. *Psychological Reports*, 53, 167–170.

Chapter 4

Assessing the Organization's Ability to Maintain Control

A CASE IN POINT

William Bartell, Human Resource Manager for Wyler Industries Limited, was about to begin his second session on "Control," the first element in the stress C-O-P-E-ing model. Whereas the first session focused on control from a personal, or microsystem, perspective, this second session focuses on control from an organizational, or macrosystem, perspective. Of particular interest to participants in this session would be how the organization can best help its organizational members to maintain control in the workplace, along with sound productivity.

The first control session, William reflected, was not all that difficult to explain to his audience because over the last 30 years there has been a fair amount of consistency among experts about what constitutes personal control, or lack of it. After the release of Lazarus's work in 1966, for example, stress experts have generally accepted that personal control and stress appraisal are dynamic, subjective, and integrally related processes.

This second session on organizational control, he reflected, was somewhat more difficult to explain because of the varied opinion among researchers about ways of optimizing organizational control across work groups and across cultures. William decided to begin his second control session by leveling with the participants about the varied nature of organizational control investigations that have occurred over the past 30 years.

THE OPENING ADDRESS: THE DIFFICULTIES OF DEFINING AND MEASURING "ORGANIZATIONAL CONTROL"

William began his session on organizational control:

When we had our first session on personal control, we talked about the relative consistency in thought among researchers about what it means to be "in control" as an individual. We suggested that individuals are in control when they appraise themselves as moving toward their goals for on-the-job and off-the-job competence and aspiration. We further reflected on the words and anger of Kelvin Browne, who was rejected for disability insurance because he tried to maintain his sense of control by seeking help from a psychologist during a particularly stressful life period. Based on our reflections around his case, we concluded that as managers we need to daily promote the mind-behavior well-being of all of our organizational members. We recognized that the only way to do this is to continually respect—through our words and through our actions—our members' needs for respect, human dignity, and safety in the workplace.

Most of you here today are probably wondering what it is that organizations can do to help their organizational members, on a widespread basis, to maintain control. Today's session on organizational control attempts to fill this void. We'll continue the push for empowerment as we did in our first session on control, for research over the past 30 years has consistently shown that the best way for organizations to help their members maintain personal control on a widespread basis is to provide them with a safe and healthy work environment and with the day-to-day possibilities to manage both their work and their stress levels. Beyond this basic requirement, the research findings in the recent past have been less consistent about the particular organizational factors that ensure personal control across job families, work groups, and cultures.

Despite the very important need to empower organizational members at all times, in difficult economic times, many managers in industry allegedly "preach" but do not "walk" stress management and work-empowerment. Instead, they develop a closed-system, "crisis style of operating," which includes downsizing "to the bone" and expecting more and more output from organizational members with fewer and fewer resources, particularly human resources. Most organizational members can tolerate such short-term taxing energy demands and are willing to commit themselves to such an organizational survival plan when an economic crisis does exist. The problem comes, however, when management's "crisis style of operating" outlives the crisis—and organizational members recognize this fact. Eventually, organizational members begin to complain in large numbers about the lack of trust that they have in management, the low morale that pervades the organization, and the low job satisfaction that hangs like a black cloud over their workstations. In such chronically taxing times, it is not uncommon for these organizational members to openly conjecture about the number of stress-disability cases and work disruptions that will surface if management does not "get their act together" and intervene in the stress-excess problem. And in the final stages of energy exhaustion, there are rampant reports of organizational members who have "burned out" because of management's willingness to take from their employees but not to provide for them.

This session focuses on how organizations can proact to prevent the aforementioned macrosystem problems from occurring. Proacting against excessive stress in the workplace is what organizational control is about. Thus, this organizational control session has as its objective the maintenance of organizational members' personal control and the prevention of organizationally disabling conditions like widespread low morale and job dissatisfaction, poor organizational member psychological, behavioral, and physical well-being, and a workforce that is too "burned-out" to function.

So as not to bias your responses to the inventories you are about to complete, *I would ask that you please turn to the appendix for this session* (i.e., Chapter 4 Appendixes) *and complete as honestly as you can the inventory items that appear before you. Please do not score these inventory items until asked to do so. After you have finished responding, please join us for further discussions of this material.*

WHAT IT MEANS FOR ORGANIZATIONS TO BE "IN CONTROL"

Within the last 30 years, experts investigating organizational control have warned managers that if organizational control is what they desire, they should, at a minimum, provide their organizational members with a work environment that is informationally open rather than informationally closed and that is trust enhancing rather than mind and body endangering. The reason that an informationally open, climatically eustressful, and safe work environment is critical to maintaining organizational control is that organizational members throughout the organization must genuinely and unquestionably feel that they are their own Personal Control Boards. Genuinely and unquestionably feeling that one is one's own Personal Control Board means not being punished for suggesting better ways of getting work tasks accomplished or not being laid-off for remarking that the work environment is perceived to be unsafe.

Researchers have consistently argued that organizational control cannot exist without widespread appraisals by organizational members of personal-control maintenance. Accepting this point, management's primary organizational-control function becomes one of ensuring an open, empowering work environment and the resources needed by organizational members to accomplish the work that needs to be accomplished by them in order to keep the organization alive and functioning—in the good economic times and in the bad.

The premise underlying this approach to organizational control is that organizational members know best the resources needed by them to not only get their required tasks done efficiently and effectively but also mind-and-body safely. Lazarus's transactional model of stress and strain, as discussed in the previous session on personal control, suggests that organizational members' unique abilities to appraise changing environmental demands enable the organization to remain adaptive, productive, energy-efficient, and competitive. Thus, if managers can commit themselves and adhere to a well-founded organizational-control strategy, they would likely find it unnecessary to "cut to the bone" and to overstress their employees in difficult economic periods.

In the organizational and job-stress literature, organizations are said to be "in control" when their organizational members, in large number, report and are found to be psychologically, physiologically, and behaviorally "healthy" and "in control." Conversely, organizations are said to be "out of control" when their organizational members, in large number, report and are found to be psychologically and/or physiologically and/or behaviorally "unhealthy" and "out of control." The indicators commonly used to provide an assessment of an organization's "control health" include subjective and objective measurements of organizational members' mental, physical, and behavioral well-being as well as their degrees of job satisfaction.

The knowledge that we have about how to design a well-founded organizational-control strategy has been accumulated from hundreds of research studies over the last three decades. Each of these decades has had special organizational-control themes ascribed to them (Ganster & Schaubroeck, 1991). In the 1960s, for example, organizational researchers studied how role stressors influence organizational control; thus, the 1960s has been become known as the "Role-Stress Era." In the 1970s, researchers discovered that a basic ingredient for organizational control is the empowerment of organizational members; thus, the 1970s has become known as the "Empowerment Era." In the 1980s, researchers investigated the causes and effects of organizational members' extreme mental and physical exhaustion caused by chronically taxing work demands—a condition labeled as "burnout"; thus, the 1980s has become known as the "Burnout Identification Era." Each of these decades and the contributions made by researchers within them will now be described.

THE 1960s: THE ROLE-STRESS ERA

The 1960s was really the start of the organizational control era. As a result of studies completed at the University of Michigan's Institute for

Social Research in the 1960s and with the publication of a study in 1964 by researchers Kahn, Wolfe, Quinn, Snoek, and Rosenthal, researchers around the world became interested in how role-conflict, role-ambiguity, and role-workload detracted from or enhanced organizational members' mental, physical, and behavioral well-being. Studies of this nature continued well into the 1980s.

Most of the role-stressor studies conducted during the 1960s defined the three major elements contributing to organizational members' role-induced distress and a loss of control in terms resembling the following:

- *Role-conflict* exists when organizational members in a particular work role are torn by conflicting job demands or by having to do things that they do not want to do or do not think are part of the job specification. This condition often occurs when organizational members are caught between two groups of people who either demand different kinds of job behaviors or who have conflicting expectations about a particular job's functions.

- *Role-ambiguity* exists when organizational members or their colleagues have inadequate information about a particular work role—particularly, the scope and responsibilities pertaining to that role.

- *Role-overload/role-underload* exists when organizational members have been assigned quantitatively too much/too little to do, or when they have been given qualitatively too difficult/too easy a task to do. (Kahn et al., 1964)

Although the measurement of role-distress outcomes varied from study to study during this twenty-year period, some of the more common assessments made included:

- Subjective appraisals by organizational members of the physiological disorders suffered by them, such as frequent headaches, sleep disorders, and stomach upsets;

- Subjective appraisals by organizational members of their psychological well-being, or lack of it, as manifested by anxiety onsets, depression onsets, low job satisfaction, and feelings of a loss of personal control;

- Objective readings by researchers on the physiological symptoms of distress presenting in organizational members, such as elevated blood pressure, elevated adrenaline and serum uric acid, and elevated cortisol; and

- Objective macrosystem readings by researchers on the behavioral symptoms of distress presenting in the organization, such as widespread low morale, reduced organizational productivity, increased absenteeism and turnover rates, and increased rates of on-the-job accidents (Kahn et al., 1964).

Starting in the mid-1960s, and particularly as a result of the release of Lazarus's work emphasizing the importance of organizational members' appraisals of job stress and loss of personal control, the research designs investigating the relationships between role-stressors and control maintenance became, increasingly, subjective in nature and mental well-being fixated. In fact, by the mid-1980s, over 200 studies assessing the relationship between subjectively appraised role-stress factors and organizational members' psychological well-being had been reported (Ganster & Schaubroeck, 1991).

Despite the wealth of information provided by researchers during this twenty-year period on the impact of role stressors on personal and organizational control, the "trend" findings relating role-stressors to across-the-board mental, physical, and behavioral well-being of organizational members remained ill defined, and often inconsistent. For example, it was not uncommon for a role-stress study to find that role ambiguity was statistically related to organizational members' subjective reports of mental health but not statistically related to researchers' objective assessments of their physical health.

Then, in 1985, Jackson and Schuler's meta-analytic (i.e., large-scale statistical) review of the organizational-control and job-stress literature found that the most consistently reported "trend" findings on role stress and control were related to organizational members' subjective measurements of their psychological well-being, particularly their appraisals of the occurrence of job-induced anxiety. These researchers said that studies consistently reported that role-ambiguity correlates about .47 and role-conflict correlates about .43 with organizational members' job-induced anxiety levels (Jackson & Schuler, 1985).

Since 1987, other researchers have reported that role-overload correlates about .40 with job-induced anxiety, and that this relationship seems to hold across-the-board for blue-collar, professional, and managerial organizational members (Matthews et al., 1987).

The "bottom-line" 1960s advice for managers wanting to optimize personal and organizational control is that organizational members need to feel "appropriately" informed about their roles in the organization and they need to feel "appropriately" taxed by their workloads.

THE 1970s: THE ORGANIZATIONAL MEMBER EMPOWERMENT ERA

Beginning in the 1970s and continuing into the present, researchers have investigated other macrosystem stressors besides role-related ones that seem to be related to personal and organizational control. Such stressors investigated have included organizational members' abilities to problem solve at work, to have control over their work pace, to utilize their job skills, to have job security, to have eustressful boss and coworker relationships, and to perceive trust, faith, and confidence in their organization's management team.

As with the literature in the 1960s on role-stress and personal/organizational control, there had been considerable debate in the 1970s about which macrosystem factors—if any—would ensure that organizational members across work groups and across cultures would feel, in large numbers, "in control." Then, in 1987, researchers Matthews, Cottington, Talbott, Kuller, and Siegel, after investigating job distress and lack of organizational control in blue-collar organizational members, suggested that part of the problem with the inconsistent findings from the 1960s and 1970s was likely not that a significant relationship failed to exist between macrosystem stressors and personal control on a widespread basis, but that researchers needed to improve their assessment procedures and research designs. They argued that if measured appropriately, "empowering" kinds of organizational factors like those just listed should be shown to statistically affect organizational members' multifaceted dimensions of well-being (Matthews et al., 1987).

Perhaps one of the most important research contributions made during the 1970s was the Swedish sawmill study of Johansson, Aronsson, and Lindstrom (1978). The latter set the stage for the development of a conceptual basis for job stress and organizational control above and beyond just a trial-and-error searching for critical control factors. The "activation theory of job stress" was generated by this group of researchers. Briefly, their theory suggested that organizational members' psychological, behavioral, and physiological well-being should be maximized at intermediate, or moderated, levels of intrinsic (i.e., "built-in") job arousal or stimulation.

Researcher Peter Warr from the United Kingdom later drew a parallel between "the activation theory of job stress" and "a vitamin model of job characteristics" in trying to explain how jobs allowing for moderated levels of arousal, or stimulation, should theoretically produce maximum microsystem, and therefore macrosystem, well-being (Warr, 1990a). A certain level of vitamins, Warr affirmed, is required for physical health up to but not beyond a certain level; after that level, increased vitamin intake can actually be useless or harmful, rather than beneficial. A similar nonlinear, or plateauing relationship between organizational stressors and microsystem health should be found empirically, Warr argued, particularly when the stressors are likely to be appraised by organizational members as being "threatening" or "endangering." For example, observed associations between organizational members' workloads and their mental and physical well-being should be a nonlinear one, noted Warr, with a midrange plateau of workload being perceived by the majority of organizational members as beneficial or eustressing, and with extremely low or high values of workload being perceived by the majority as less beneficial or even endangering (Warr, 1990a).

Research empirically investigating the activation theory or vitamin theory of organizational stress led to such positive international developments on the stress-reduction and organizational-control front as the development of the person-environment (P-E) fit theory and the job demands/job control theory for helping managers to design organizational control strategies, and to the passing of public policy in Sweden legislating organizations to "empower" organizational members to be daily able to "moderate" their stressors on the job.

The P-E fit approach to moderating job stress advocated the implementation of "enriched" work for organizational members at all levels of the hierarchy so that their jobs would be appraised by them as being psychologically rewarding, and therefore, "appropriately fitting" and "eustressing." This theory was popularized in the United States by researchers Hackman and Oldham (1980) in the late 1970s and reached its heyday in the early 1980s. The basic tenet of the P-E fit theory was that the degree of "fit" existing between organizational members' needs and their jobs largely determined the degree of personal control, psychological well-being, and job satisfaction experienced by them. The reason that this theory was accepted widely in industry in its time is that the developers also provided managers with a survey instrument, known as the Job Diagnostic Survey, and normative data across job families for assessing their organizational work groups' "control" health and readiness for job-enrichment interventions.

Then, in the late 1970's, the job demands/job control theory came on the industrial scene and continues to dominate the organizational control literature today. It was popularized by Karasek in the United States and by Warr, Cook, and Wall in the United Kingdom (Karasek, 1979; Warr, Cook, & Wall, 1979). Organizational experts promoting this theory advocate open, empowering work environments so that organizational members can daily appraise their varying job demands and, when necessary, moderate them in order to remain "in control." This theory assumes that intrinsic job demands and job latitude largely determine whether organizational members will become "eustressed" with their jobs and remain healthy, or become "distressed" with their jobs and eventually present with stress-disabling conditions. Two major points have emerged from this theory which help managers plan organizational control strategies:

- Positive psychological, physiological, and behavioral outcomes seem to derive when organizational members perceive that they occupy "appropriately" arousing and intrinsically-rewarding (or refueling) jobs. That is, they feel that their jobs allow for "appropriate" amounts of both job demands and job control; but

- Excessive distress and strain occur when jobs leave organizational members appraising themselves as being "high" in job demands but "low" in job control.

According to the job demands/job control model, when a job situation is appraised by organizational members as being "appropriately arousing," they become eustressed rather than distressed by their work. Chronically "eustressed" organizational members seem to consistently report feeling job-contented, job-enthusiastic, job-satisfied, and energy-refueled by their jobs. At peace within themselves and in harmony with their work environments, these organizational members tend to be psychologically, physiologically, and behaviorally "healthy."

Conversely, when a high-demand/low-control work combination exists, a kind of physiological and psychological war erupts within organizational members. They become chronically physiologically "aroused" by their required and taxing job demands—to the point that energy is continually released from their body stores to meet these demands—but they become chronically psychologically and behaviorally "constrained" by the low degree of control that they perceive they have over their work. At war within themselves and with their organizations, these chronically stressed organizational members are left feeling hopeless and helpless because their energy cannot be channeled into "appropriate" mind-behavior responses and because they see management as not caring. Thus, these members become chronically frustrated, angry, job-dissatisfied, and pathologically stressed. They often present with anxiety attacks, cardiovascular disease, and burnout.

Empirical validation studies based on both the P-E fit and the job demands/job control theories have consistently found, like role-stress studies, that organizational members' psychological well-being, in particular, is optimized under work-empowering and "good fit" conditions, although the particular organizational factors essential to such eustressful work conditions seem to vary between work groups within companies and between cultures (Ganster & Schaubroeck, 1991).

THE 1980s: THE BURNOUT-IDENTIFICATION ERA

Research tactics on organizational control took on a whole new "crisis" orientation with the release of Freudenberger's landmark 1974 study describing the prevalence of "burned out" organizational members working in the free-clinic movement in the United States (Freudenberger, 1974). Beginning in the late 1970s and certainly by the early 1980s, organizational members around the world became, increasingly, paranoid about becoming "burned out" by their work.

Organizational and stress researchers around the world attempted to ameliorate the situation by conducting detailed investigations into the signs and work causes of the condition described by Freudenberger. As a result of the multitudes of studies published on the topic, "burnout" became quickly known to those in the mental health field and in organizations as THE syndrome characterized by overstressed and multidimensionally exhausted organizational members. Thus, the 1980s decade became known in the organizational-control literature as the Burnout-Identification Era.

More than 300 burnout study results were published in the 1980–1985 period alone (Shirom, 1989).

What became clear even in the early writings on the subject is that no organizational group—blue-collar, white-collar, or professional—is exempted from this multifaceted stress disorder if job-distressing conditions chronically prevail (Shirom, 1989).

Most stress and organizational experts say that burnout feels as bad as it sounds. Freudenberger defined "burnout" as becoming failed, worn-out, and energy-exhausted by unrelenting, taxing work demands and organizational environments that do not allow for energy-refueling (Freudenberger, 1974). Thus, organizational members eventually "burnout" in a number of ways and with varying degrees of intensity.

So that participants can understand what is meant by this condition and why it is desirable for organizations to prevent it if they wish to keep their organizations and their members "in control," let us look briefly at the case of an organizational member who is burning out, supposedly because of management's ten-year "overuse" of a crisis style of managing—a style which they have packaged as "continuous reorganization necessary for survival." This company's continuous reorganizing has been accompanied by continuous organizational member "pruning." This case is an excerpt from a classic piece written by Harry Levinson in the *Harvard Business Review* in May–June 1981, and entitled, "When executives burn out" (p. 75):

I've been with this company for nearly 15 years and have changed jobs every 2 to 3 years. Most of our managers are company men, like me. We have always been a high-technology company, but we have been doing less well in marketing than some of our competitors. Over the past 10 years we have been going through a continuous reorganization process. The organization charts keep changing, but the underlying philosophy, management techniques, and administrative trappings don't. The consequence is continuous frustration, disruption, resentment, and the undermining of "change." You don't take a company that has been operating with a certain perspective and turn it around overnight.

With these changes we are also being told what we must do and when. Before, we were much more flexible and free to follow our noses. These shifts create enormous pressures on an organization that is used to different ways of operating. On top of that, a continuous corporate pruning goes on. I am a survivor, so I should feel good about it and believe what top management tells me, namely, that the unfit go and the worthy remain. But the old virtues—talent, initiative, and risk taking—are not being rewarded. Instead, acquiescence to corporate values and social skills that obliterate differences among individuals are the virtues that get attention. Also the reward process is more political than meritocratic.

I don't know if we're going to make it. And there are a lot of others around here who have the same feeling. We're all demoralized.

This excerpt suggests that burnout results in large part from a chronic loss of personal control. As is evident from this case, there exists within the minds of burned-out organizational members a sense of despair over the reality that management seems not to want to moderate workplace stress or empower its members to control their own work pace and energy demands. It would rather "prune." Thus, over extended periods of this type of "control deprivation," these organizational members begin to present with signs of low job satisfaction, low morale, and reduced productivity. In due course, their presentations become much more intense. When they reach the burnout stage, they are markedly demotivated with work, wrought with anxiety and/or depression, and hopeless that there will be improvements in the workplace environment. Reductions in self-esteem commonly ensue.

Despite the rather high degree of paranoia that has existed and continues to exist around the topic of burnout, the organizational-control literature has consistently reported that jobs allowing for the following work opportunities, or "eustressors," go a long way to diminishing the occurrence of burnout for the bulk of organizational members:

- The opportunity for members to use their job skills and to have "appropriate" levels of problem solving and decision making on the job;
- The opportunity for members to determine and maintain a workload that is organizationally "appropriate" as well as organizational member-safe;
- The opportunity for members to feel "appropriately aroused" by their jobs, as assessed by their reports of psychological well-being and job satisfaction.
- The opportunity for members to work in a socially supportive and informationally open organizational climate, whereby they can resolve personal and workplace "poor fits" and "endangerments"—and thus stay physiologically, psychologically, and behaviorally "healthy" and in control. (Matthews et al., 1987)

Although there have been numerous excellent burnout studies emerging from the 1980s, one study in particular showed the importance of refueling opportunities in the work environment as an effective burnout-prevention remedy for organizational members. This study is interesting because it involves an occupation that is known to be excessively stressful because of work overloads: air-traffic controllers. When individuals are asked to "free-associate" to the occupation *air-traffic controller*, they often blurt out the word "burnout"—because most individuals believe that air-traffic controllers are excessively drained of energy on the job and are not allowed to refuel "appropriately."

To empirically investigate whether this perception about air-traffic controllers is valid and "a given," in the early 1980s, a team of researchers headed by Rose (Rose et al., 1982a, 1982b, 1982c) completed a comprehensive, five-year stress and personal control study on 200 male air-traffic controllers. Multiple objective and subjective measures of job stressors and organizational members' stress responses were taken. Much detailed data were generated for assessment. For example, participants' blood was drawn for blood cortisol readings (a physiological indicator of stress elevation) every twenty minutes for five hours on three or more days over a three-year period.

At the end of their data analysis period, and contrary to popular belief, this team of researchers found that there was only a slight increase in neuroendocrine physiological response (as shown with the cortisol readings) with corresponding increases in both objectively- and subjectively-measured workloads. Even more surprising, the air-traffic controllers who were high-cortisol responders were subsequently *less ill, more satisfied with their jobs*, and were described by their peers as being *more competent* than the low-cortisol responders.

Rose and colleagues explained these somewhat surprising findings by concluding that the high-cortisol responders were "engaged in" and "appropriately stressed" by their job demands. That is, as a group, these organizational members seemed to be stressfully "in control" rather than stressfully "out of control." Rather than reflect a physiological, psychological, and behavioral state of intense "distress" leading to burnout, their study results more accurately reflected a healthy state of job-induced "arousal" and resultant "channeling" for these members. In short, these organizational members seemed to have been provided by their organizations with opportunities to not only channel their arousal energy on their jobs "appropriately" but to refuel in ways that they, individually and as a group, appraised as being personally rewarding.

In terms of its usefulness in "control" strategy building, the critical point to the air-traffic controller study (and to other burnout studies reported during the 1980s) is that subjective appraisals made by organizational members of the energy expenditures required by their jobs as well as the energy-refueling allowed by their organizations make a critical difference between organizational members' experiencing widespread "distress" and "burnout" or widespread "eustress" and "personal control."

KEY EMPIRICAL STUDIES ON ORGANIZATIONAL CONTROL FROM THE LAST 30 YEARS

Intrinsic Job Stressors, Psychological Well-Being, and Job Satisfaction: An Individual or Micro-System Perspective

Recall from the session on personal control (Chapter 3) that Peter Warr conducted a large-scale organizational study on 1,686 working adults in the United Kingdom to determine how psychological well-being is related to personal control. Warr's research on this study sample has also produced some useful findings and insights into organizational factors that likely enhance or reduce organizational members' personal control and psychological well-being on a large-scale basis.

For example, Warr hypothesized that organizational members' psychological well-being would be significantly enhanced by their appraised opportunities to:

• Use valued skills on the job;

• Maintain personal control by having the latitude to make decisions and to have discretion over their tasks and conduct during the workday; and

• Regulate their workloads so that these loads would be organizationally appropriate but organizational member-safe. (Warr, 1990a)

Consistent with the job demands/job control model discussed earlier, Warr conjectured that moderate, rather than low, levels of these three job-intrinsic factors would "appropriately" stress organizational members, such that they would appraise themselves as being psychologically "well." His 1990b study findings on this group of 1,686 working adults supported this conjecture. The correlation coefficients indicating the linear associations between these three job stressors, measured only from low to medium values, and the participants' nine psychological well-being measures are given in Table 4.1 (Warr, 1990b, p. 203).

Some observations from Table 4.1 are worthy of note from an organizational control perspective:

1. Consistent with the job demands/job control model of job stress and with the International Labour Office's (ILO's) position on the need for empowerment in th e workplace to catalyze widespread organizational control, "medium" rather than "low" levels of personal control were associated with psychological well-being in these organizational members—as reflected by high scores on job-contentment, job-enthusiasm, job-competence, and job-aspiration, and by low scores on negative carryover.

2. Consistent with the role-stress findings on workload and well-being from the 1960s and contrary to the suppositions of the job demands/job control model, even at the "medium" levels workload was associated with arousal and inappropriate channeling, as reflected in job-anxiety ($r = -.10$) and negative carryover ($r = .23$) scores. Thus, job-induced anxiety likely results when organizational members feel concomitantly aroused but endangered by taxing job demands.

3. Consistent with the clinical psychology literature, "depressed" feelings in these participants seemed to be associated with appraised "job deprivations"—such as having to contend with low levels of skill usage or personal control on the job. Also consistent with the clinical psychology literature, "anxious" feelings in these participants seemed to be associated

Table 4.1
Correlations between Perceived Job Characteristics (from low-to-medium levels)
and Nine Indices of Mental Health (N = 1,686)

	Skill Use	Personal Control	Work-load
Affective well-being			
1. Job anxiety-contentment	.01	.25	-.10
2. Job depression-enthusiasm	.26	.37	.17
3. Non-job anxiety-contentment	.04	.17	-.01
4. Non-job depression-enthusiasm	.14	.22	.11
Other aspects of mental health			
5. Reported job competence	.02	.13	.00
6. Reported job aspiration	.45	.40	.39
7. Negative carry-over	.10	-.14	.23
8. Reported non-job competence	.09	.17	.13
9. Reported non-job aspiration	.13	.20	.18

Note: Values greater than .07 are significant at the $p < .001$ level.
Source: Warr, P. (1990b). The measurement of well-being and other aspects of mental health.
   Journal of Occupational Psychology, 63, 203.

with appraised "endangerments" to their well-being (and possibly their safety)—such as having to contend with heavy workloads on the job.

4. Of all three job-intrinsic stressors assessed, workload had the greatest negative carryover from work to home for these participants, a finding discussed earlier in terms of the personal control literature (see Chapter 3).

5. Of all three job-intrinsic stressors assessed, personal control on the job appeared to allow for large degrees of psychological returns and energy-refueling for this study's participants. A positive rather than a negative carryover from work to home was present in the data. Participants who felt "in control" at work had high scores on job contentment, job enthusiasm, job competence, job aspiration, personal contentment, personal enthusiasm, personal competence, and personal aspiration.

To clarify whether there existed a linear or a nonlinear, plateaulike association between workload and psychological well-being and to assess the relationships between job demand and job control and job satisfaction (i.e., the overall affective feeling—positive or negative—that one has about his or her job), Warr investigated the presence of linear and nonlinear relationships between participants' appraised:

- Job demands (including workload) and their job satisfaction;
- Job demands and their job contentment;

Table 4.2
Relationships between Job Demands and Job Latitude on Organizational
Members' Affective Well-Being and Job Satisfaction: Linear and Nonlinear
Contributions

Job Demands and	Linear r	Non-linear Significance
Job Satisfaction	.10	.001
Anxiety-Contentment	-.26	.001
Depression-Enthusiasm	.05	.001
Job Latitude and		
Job Satisfaction	.40	.01
Anxiety-Contentment	.06	
Depression-Enthusiasm	.32	

Source: Warr, P. (1990a). Decision latitude, job demands, and employee well-being. Work
    and Stress, 4, 285–294.

• Job demands and their job enthusiasm;
• Job latitude (i.e., personal control on the job) and their job satisfaction;
• Job latitude and their job contentment; and
• Job latitude and their job enthusiasm. (Warr, 1990a)

The correlation coefficients for the linear relationships are shown in the
first column of Table 4.2 (Warr, 1990a, p. 289). The statistical significance
levels for the nonlinear relationships are shown in the second column of
Table 4.2. A blank in the second column indicates a nonsignificant finding.
For the first column, the larger the coefficient, the stronger the linear relationship (positive or negative). For the second column, the smaller the
coefficient, the greater the level of statistical significance.

Some observations from Table 4.2 are worthy of note from an organizational control perspective:

1. Consistent with the low-to-medium workload findings in Table 4.1,
the linear results in Table 4.2 show that for these 1,686 working adults,
"job demand" distress was associated more with job anxiety than with job
depression.

2. Consistent with the low-to-medium personal-control findings in Table
4.1, the linear results in Table 4.2 show that for these working adults, "job
latitude" distress was associated more with job depression than with job
anxiety.

3. Consistent with the psychological well-being outcomes in Table 4.1,
job satisfaction for these participants was more closely associated with job
latitude ($r = .40$) than with job demands ($r = .10$). This finding makes

Table 4.3

The Relationship between Job Demands and Job Latitude on Organizational
Members' Affective Well-Being and Job Satisfaction: Scores from Low to High
Values on Each Job Feature

	1	2	3	4	5	6	7
Job Demands and							
Satisfaction	2.98	3.31	3.38	3.49	3.42	3.39	3.35
Anxiety-Contentment	4.29	4.47	4.37	4.23	4.07	3.96	3.78
Depression-Enthusiasm	4.33	4.60	4.65	4.59	4.52	4.55	4.54
Job Latitude and							
Satisfaction	2.60	3.06	3.22	3.47	3.55	3.61	3.69
Anxiety-Contentment	4.07	4.18	4.14	4.19	4.19	4.14	4.26
Depression-Enthusiasm	4.09	4.38	4.48	4.57	4.69	4.73	4.94

Source: Warr, P. (1990a). Decision latitude, job demands, and employee well-being. *Work
and Stress*, 4, 285–294.

sense, given that job satisfaction is an affective outcome that (like job latitude) more likely reflects appraised concomitant "arousal" and "nondeprivation" (i.e., refueling) rather than appraised concomitant "arousal" and
"endangerment" (like work overloads).

4. In support of the job demands/job control theory of job stress, the
results in the second column of Table 4.2 indicate that for these participants, there appears to be a significant nonlinear and plateaulike relationship between:

• Job demands and psychological well-being;
• Job demands and job satisfaction; and
• Job control and job satisfaction.

5. The results in the second column of Table 4.2 indicate that there
appears to be a strong linear but no significant nonlinear relationship between job latitude and psychological well-being (as assessed by the job
contentment and job enthusiasm scores).

To illustrate more clearly the linear and nonlinear relationships depicted
in Table 4.2, Warr ranked the mean values on each job feature from low
to high for seven approximately equal subgroups. These results are shown
in Table 4.3 (Warr, 1990a, p. 290).

Some observations from Table 4.3 are worthy of note from an organizational control perspective:

6. Rather consistent with the job demands/job control model of job

stress, organizational members' job satisfaction began to increase after the low levels of job demand were appraised by group 1, leveled off at moderated job-demand levels, and then decreased at high job-demand levels (see, for example, group 7).

7. Consistent with a linear model of "unbridled empowerment" rather than with the nonlinear model of job demands/job control, organizational members' job satisfaction increased with increasing job latitude.

8. Rather consistent with the nonlinear job demands/job control model of job stress and with the clinical psychology literature on endangerment, organizational members' job anxiety was low at low and moderated levels of job demand (see, for example, groups 1 through 4) but increased at high job-demand levels (see, for example, groups 5 through 7).

9. Consistent with a linear model of "unbridled empowerment" and with the clinical psychological literature on nondeprivation, organizational members' job enthusiasm increased noticeably with increasing levels of job latitude.

Intrinsic Job Stressors, Psychological Well-Being, and Job Satisfaction: A Group Perspective

Having noted some interesting distinctions in individual members' affective well-being and job satisfaction when "nondepriving" and "endangering" job stressors were investigated, Peter Warr and other organizational researchers became interested in knowing whether similar relationships held for a broader range of "nondepriving" and "endangering" job stressors and across blue-collar, professional, and managerial groups.

Two empirical validation studies reported in the organizational control literature were of particular interest to Warr. One study was reported by Wall, Clegg, Davies, Kemp, and Mueller (1987) and involved 246 shop-floor assembly organizational members of both genders in a large micro-electronics factory. The other study was reported by Shapiro, Barkham, Hardy, and Morrison (1990) and involved 120 professional and managerial organizational members of both genders who were engaged in psychotherapy to reduce high job-stress levels.

Both teams of researchers used earlier versions of Warr's (1990b) inventory to assess psychological well-being (see Chapter 3) of group members, as well as other context-free clinical inventories to assess poor mental health. For the shop-floor assembly study, Goldberg's General Health Questionnaire, a screening test for detecting minor psychiatric disorders, was used. For the managerial and professional organizational member study, the Beck Depression Inventory, a screening test for detecting depression (or inwardly vented anger), was used. Thus, low scores on the two context-free inventories indicate psychological well-being.

For both studies, the relationships between group members' psycho-

Table 4.4

Correlations between Perceived Job Characteristics and Organizational Members'
Mental Well-Being: Shop-Floor and Professional/Managerial Participants

	Shop-Floor Participants (N =248)		Professionals and Managers (N = 96)	
	Job Anxiety-Contentment	Job Depression-Enthusiasm	Job Anxiety-Contentment	Job Depression-Enthusiasm
Intrinsic Job Satisfaction	.21[a]	.40[a]	.34[c]	.52[c]
Extrinsic Job Satisfaction	.31[a]	.33	.40	.45
Reported Control Opportunity	.12[a]	.31[a]	.29	.34
Reported Task Complexity and Task Variety	.18[a]	.47[a]	.02	.19
Reported Work Overload	-.40[a]	-.09[a]	-.39[b]	-.10[b]
Reported Skill Use	.15[a]	.46[a]	.30[c]	.51[c]
Context-free Well-Being	-.46	-.39	-.09	-.24

Legend:
[a]Significance level < .001 between a pair of correlations.
[b]Significance level < .01 between a pair of correlations.
[c]Significance level < .05 between a pair of correlations.
Source: Warr, P. (1990b). The measurement of well-being and other aspects of mental health.
    Journal of Occupational Psychology, 63, 205–206.

logical well-being and the following job satisfaction outcomes and job stressors were investigated:

- Intrinsic job satisfaction outcome (i.e., that resulting from "built-in" job features,
  such as amount of responsibility involved);
- Extrinsic job satisfaction outcome (i.e., that resulting from the rewards allocated
  by management, including salaries paid);
- Control opportunity allowed (i.e., the amount of conscious control and planning
  allowed above and beyond just doing the job tasks);
- Task complexity and task variety designed in the job;
- Work overloads assigned; and
- Skill-usage allowed.

The correlation coefficients showing the linear associations between
group members' mental well-being and the cited job satisfaction outcomes
and job stressors are shown in Table 4.4 (Warr, 1990b, pp. 205–206).
    Several points from Table 4.4 are worthy of note from an organizational
control perspective:

1. For both the shop-floor and the professional/managerial groups, intrinsic job satisfaction, self-directed control, and skill usage were more highly associated with "nondeprivation" job enthusiasm than with "endangerment" job anxiety. Similar findings were also reported by Warr for individual systems.

2. For both the shop-floor and the professional/managerial groups, extrinsic job satisfaction was more highly associated with "nondeprivation" job enthusiasm than with "endangerment" job anxiety. This finding was not earlier reported by Warr for individual systems, but indicates the importance of management's commitment to fair reward allocations for work groups throughout the organization.

3. For both the shop-floor and the professional/managerial groups, task complexity and task variety were more highly associated with "nondeprivation" job enthusiasm than with "endangerment" job anxiety. This finding was not earlier reported by Warr for individual systems, but indicates the importance of "appropriately" arousing and "enriching" jobs on group members' well-being for all groups throughout the organization.

4. For both the shop-floor and the professional/managerial groups, work overload was associated with "endangerment" job anxiety (as illustrated by the negative correlation coefficients between overload and well-being in all four table cells). As expected, there was not as strong an association between work overload and job depression. These findings are consistent with those reported by Warr for microsystems.

5. As expected, for both the shop-floor and the professional/managerial groups, high well-being scores using versions of Warr's 1990a instrument were associated with low scores on the two context-free well-being inventories that measured minor psychiatric disorders and depression.

Combining the findings of these two studies on shop-floor and professional/managerial organizational members with those on the 1,686 working adults, the appraised presence of intrinsic job factors of a "personal control," or "empowering," or "nondeprivation," or "refueling" nature tended to result in levels of psychological well-being for individual and group members, regardless of the type of work group within the organization. Conversely, the appraised presence of "endangering" job-intrinsic factors like work overloads tended to result in levels of anxiety for group members.

Organizational Climate, Psychological Well-Being, and Job Satisfaction: A Macrosystem Perspective

In recent years, researchers have investigated the relationships between organizational climate stressors and individuals' and group members' mental well-being, job satisfaction, and behavioral well-being. Two of these study results will now be discussed.

In 1980, Cook and Wall investigated the linear relationships between blue-collar groups' anxiety levels, their behavioral well-being (i.e., work productivity), their job satisfaction, and their appraisals of the following organizational climate stressors:

• Trust in fellow workers and in management;
• Faith in peers' intentions;
• Confidence in peers' actions;
• Faith in management's intentions;
• Confidence in management's actions;
• Organizational commitment (i.e., wanting to stay with the organization until retirement);
• Organizational identification (i.e., personally relating to the organization);
• Organizational involvement (in tasks and planning); and
• Organizational loyalty (i.e., standing behind the organization's values). (Cook & Wall, 1980)

The obtained correlation coefficients are presented in Table 4.5 (Cook & Wall, 1980). Coefficients greater than or equal to .13 were statistically significant at the .01 level.

Several points from Table 4.5 are worthy of note from an organizational control perspective:

1. Consistent with earlier findings on "refueling" job-intrinsic stressors and job satisfaction, this study's results indicated positive linear relationships between all of the preceding "refueling" organizational climate factors and blue-collar members' work productivity and job satisfaction. Thus, "nondeprivation" and "refueling" kinds of organizational climate factors seem to create a sense of organizational group members' feeling behaviorally "in control" and affectively "job-satisfied."

2. Consistent with earlier findings on "refueling" job-intrinsic stressors and low anxiety in organizational members, this study's results indicated negative linear relationships between all of the above "refueling" organizational climate factors and blue-collar members' anxiety levels—except for confidence in management. The more confidence blue-collar organizational members perceived they had in management, the higher their anxiety. Perhaps the latter association results from a fear by group members of becoming too accepting of management in case the trustworthy managers "are replaced" or "decide to change their ways."

In 1981, Wall collaborated with Clegg to investigate the appraised levels of many of the aforementioned organizational climate stressors by managerial, supervisory, white-collar, and blue-collar members employed in a large engineering factory in the United Kingdom (Clegg & Wall, 1981). Another variable thought to be important from a P-E "fit" perspective-

Table 4.5

Correlations between Perceived Organizational Environment Characteristics and
Three Indices of Mind-Behavior Well-Being for 650 Blue-Collar Participants

Item	(a)	(b)	(c)	(d)	(e)	(f)	(g)	(h)	(i)
(a) Trust									
(b) Faith-peers	.64								
(c) Confidence-peers	.61	.57							
(d) Faith-Management	.75	.22	.12						
(e) Confidence-management	.76	.21	.14	.63					
(f) Organizational commitment	.56	.30	.23	.61	.42				
(g) Organizational identification	.56	.32	.23	.59	.43	.86			
(h) Organizational involvement	.41	.25	.20	.42	.30	.76	.54		
(i) Organizational loyalty	.42	.17	.11	.50	.31	.84	.57	.43	
(j) Job Satisfaction	.58	.32	.28	.57	.43	.62	.59	.41	.52
(k) Anxiety	-.30	-.20	-.15	-.25	.25	-.23	-.22	-.15	-.22
(l) Work Productivity	.28	.19	.21	.25	.18	.39	.31	.33	.38

Source: Cook, J., & Wall, T. (1980). New work attitude measures of trust, organizational
    commitment, and personal need non-fulfillment. *Journal of Occupational Psychology*, 53,
    48.

was also assessed: Higher-order need strength—the importance organizational members attach to higher-order, personal-control needs like job
competence and job aspiration.

Normative data on these 659 organizational members of both genders
and across work groups are presented in Table 4.6 (Clegg & Wall, 1981).
An * beside the stressors in column one indicates that significant differences
in mean scores were found among the organizational groups tested.

Several points from Table 4.6 are worthy of note from an organizational
control perspective:

1. The appraisals made by group members on nine of the ten organizational climate factors increased significantly as one moved from the "blue-
collar" column through the "white-collar" through the "supervisors" column through the "managers" column.

Table 4.6

Normative Data on Occupational-Control Variables, Higher-Order Need Strength, and Job Satisfaction for Managerial, Supervisory, White-Collar, and Blue-Collar Members

Variable	Sample Size	Sample Mean and (Standard Deviation)	Subgroup Mean and (Standard Deviations):			
			Managers	Supervisors	White-collar	Blue-collar
Intrinsic Job Characteristics*	608	31.19 (7.67)	40.67 (4.92)	36.84 (5.31)	32.97 (6.32)	28.61 (7.33)
Need Strength	636	36.45 (4.46)	36.83 (4.66)	37.16 (3.39)	36.38 (3.85)	36.30 (4.82)
Job Satisfaction*	574	71.90 (13.58)	79.15 (10.79)	77.57 (8.50)	74.00 (10.29)	69.38 (14.96)
Trust in Management*	632	28.38 (7.94)	33.00 (4.36)	30.68 (5.82)	29.19 (7.03)	27.25 (8.57)
Faith in Management's Intentions*	644	14.04 (4.33)	16.83 (2.34)	15.83 (3.11)	14.29 (3.94)	13.38 (4.59)
Confidence in Management's Actions*	640	14.30 (4.23)	16.17 (2.61)	14.94 (3.53)	14.85 (3.70)	13.84 (4.55)
Organizational Commitment*	633	32.74 (6.49)	36.50 (4.64)	35.26 (4.35)	32.94 (5.72)	31.84 (7.00)
Organizational Identification*	649	11.09 (2.70)	12.13 (2.26)	12.05 2.11)	11.23 (2.42)	10.76 (2.87)
Organizational Involvement*	648	11.80 (2.24)	13.23 (1.01)	12.83 (1.12)	11.89 (1.95)	11.44 (2.45)
Organizational Loyalty*	637	9.86 (2.99)	11.13 (2.49)	10.38 (2.73)	9.84 (2.88)	9.65 (3.09)

Source: Clegg, C. W., & Wall, T. D. (1981). A note on some new scales for measuring aspects of psychological well-being at work. Journal of Occupational Psychology, 54, 233.

2. The one important exception to this increasing appraisal trend across groups was higher-order need strength. No significant difference between mean scores was found among the four groups assessed. That is, the blue-collar organizational members felt as strongly about the need for job competence and job aspiration (i.e., personal control) in the work environment as did the white-collar, supervisory, and managerial group members. But although all group members had the same need to be "in control" at work, the findings from this 1981 study indicate that—at least for the organizational members employed in this large factory—the chances for fulfillment of organizational members' "control needs" increases as one moves up the organizational ladder.

Taken as a composite, these study results highlight, once again, the importance of organizational members appraising themselves as being "in control" and "empowered" at work. When the appraisal for organizational control and self-control is affirmative, there are microsystem and macrosystem "returns" in terms of organizational members' reporting greater job competence and job aspiration, reduced anxiety, greater work productivity, and higher job satisfaction. The problem with organizational control seems to present at the lower group levels, with organizational members further from "the top" reporting a lack of fulfillment in higher-order needs and a lack of job empowerment.

ORGANIZATIONAL FEEDBACK: HOW "IN CONTROL" AND HOW JOB-SATISFIED ARE YOU WITH YOUR APPRAISED JOB LATITUDE AND JOB DEMANDS?

Participants can now receive feedback on how "in-control" they feel as a function of their current intrinsic job characteristics. *Please now score your responses to the job latitude inventory* (in Appendix 4.1).

Participants should now have five mean scores in their possession:

1. a job anxious–contentment score (ranging from 1 to 6);
2. a job depression–enthusiasm score (ranging from 1 to 6);
3. a job satisfaction score (ranging from 1 to 5);
4. a job decision–latitude score (ranging from 1 to 7); and
5. a job workload score (ranging from 1 to 7).

Considering their five obtained scores, participants should now decide in which of the group cells from (1 to 7) in Table 4.3 that they see their "P-E fit" scores placing. Are your scores near the low end of "poor fit," near the high end of "poor fit," or in the moderated range of "appropriate fit"—according to the job demands/job control theory?

Given their responses to these questions, participants should now be able to conclude:

- If they have appraised "appropriate," "empowering," and "refueling" levels of job-demands and personal-control in the jobs that they currently possess.

ORGANIZATIONAL FEEDBACK: HOW "IN CONTROL" AND JOB-SATISFIED ARE YOU, GIVEN YOUR ORGANIZATIONAL CLIMATE? ARE YOU AN IN-CONTROL "10"?

Participants can now receive feedback on how "in control" they feel in their job environments. *Please now score your responses to the job satisfaction inventory* (in Appendix 4.2).

Participants should now have ten scores to review:

1. Intrinsic job characteristics (i.e., the organizational member's appraisal of the presence of built-in job features which might give rise to job satisfaction);

2. Higher-order need strength (i.e., the organizational member's appraisal of the importance of higher-order, personal-control needs such as job competence and job aspiration);

3. Total job satisfaction (i.e., the organizational member's appraisal of the degree to which he or she reports emotional pleasure with intrinsically imparted and managerially imparted features of the job);

4. Trust in management (i.e., the organizational member's degree of faith in the trustworthy intentions of management and the confidence that he or she has in management's ability to follow through on their intentions);

5. Faith in management's intentions (i.e., the organizational member's belief that management's intentions are honorable and respectful of organizational members' human dignity);

6. Confidence in management's actions (i.e., the organizational member's degree of believing that management's actions will parallel their words, that they will "walk the empowerment and stress management talk");

7. Organizational commitment (i.e., the organizational member's affective reaction to the characteristics of his or her employing organization, especially attachment to its goals and values);

8. Organizational identification (i.e., the organizational member's pride in and internalization of the goals and values of his or her employing organization);

9. Organizational involvement (i.e., the organizational member's "psychological absorption" in and "positive arousal" by the activities of his or her work role); and

10. Organizational loyalty (i.e., the organizational member's affection for and attachment to the employing organization, particularly a "wish to stay").

Participants should now compare their ten organizational climate/job satisfaction scores with those of the normative sample of 659 organizational members, discussed earlier. Using the "Sample Mean" column in Table 4.6 as the standard, go down the column with your scores, noting if your scores "meet" or "exceed" those listed. Give yourself 1 mark on each of the factors if your score meets or exceeds the sample mean standard.

So how "in control" do you feel, given your organization's factors? Of a maximum "in control" score of 10, where was your score? Are you nearer the out-of-control "1" end or nearer the in-control "10" end?

If you were to give this inventory to work groups throughout your organization, do you think that their mean scores would reflect an organization that allows organizational members, in large numbers, to be "in control"? Do you think that certain "pockets" of "in-control" organizational members would be found? If so, where in the organizational hierarchy would they likely be found?

Given participants' responses to these questions, they should now be able to conclude:

- If there are "appropriate" levels of "nondepriving" and "refueling" organizational stressors for the bulk of organizational members within the organization, such that there exists a "healthy" degree of organizational control.

EXECUTIVES' PSYCHOLOGICAL WELL-BEING AND JOB SATISFACTION ACROSS CULTURES

With the globalization of business, in recent years researchers have become interested in understanding cultural differences, if any, in organizational members' appraisals of personal and organizational control. A study completed by Cary Cooper (1984) on 1,065 senior and executive officers in organizations in ten countries around the world is particularly interesting. Briefly, the study's objective was the measurement of executives' appraised levels of job satisfaction, psychological well-being, and organizational stressors.

The following organizational stressors were conjectured by Cooper to negatively affect executives' and senior officers' job satisfaction and psychological well-being:

- Lack of autonomy and personal control;
- Work "excesses" such as work overloads, unrealistic time pressures/deadlines, long working hours, and having to take work home;
- Work "shortcomings" such as work underloads and doing jobs below one's level of competence;
- Interpersonal conflicts such as hiring and firing organizational members, dealing with shareholders, and dealing with unions; and

Table 4.7

Percentage of Executives at Risk for Mental Disability and Percentage Who Report Being Job-Dissatisfied (by rank)

% at Risk for Mental Disability		% Job-Dissatisfied	
Egypt	41.6	Egypt	34.7
Brazil	40.9	Brazil	34.0
Singapore	32.7	Japan	34.0
Nigeria	32.4	Singapore	30.8
Japan	31.8	Nigeria	25.7
South Africa	28.0	Britain	25.0
Britain	25.2	United States	22.1
United States	18.5	South Africa	20.4
Sweden	14.5	Sweden	18.0
Germany	10.8	Germany	17.9

Source: Cooper, C. L. (1984). Executive stress: A ten-country comparison. *Human Resource Management*, 23, 400.

• Negative carryover such as experiencing a negative attitude by the spouse about one's job, having family member relationships interrupted, and seeing the demands of work adversely affect one's private and social life.

Using a criterion of mental ill health scores at least 25% higher than the norm (i.e., falling close to psychiatric outpatient group mean scores), Cooper ranked the 1,065 executives in the ten countries on the percentage who seemed to be at risk for mental-stress disability, given their mental health scores. He also ranked them, by percentage, on their self-reported job dissatisfaction.

The ranking results are presented in Table 4.7 (Cooper, 1984, p. 400). The stressors cited by these senior officers as causing job dissatisfaction are summarized, by country, in Table 4.8 (Cooper, 1984, pp. 401–404).

Several points from Tables 4.7 and 4.8 are worthy of note from an organizational control perspective:

1. Examining the data for executives with mental ill health scores at least 25% higher than the norm, one can see from Table 4.7 that in the developing countries and those with rapid economic change (i.e., Egypt, Brazil, Singapore, Nigeria, and Japan), where "control" at the macrolevel is threatened, over 30% of the executives appear to be "at risk" for stress-induced mental disability. In contrast, in the developed countries (i.e., the United States, Sweden, and Germany), where "control" at the societal macrolevel is relatively unthreatened, the proportion of executives "at risk" for stress-induced mental disability is under 20%. Britain and South Africa fall be-

Table 4.8
Job and Organizational Stressors Cited by Executives in Ten Countries

Sweden	Lack of autonomy; negative job carryover; dealing with strong unions
Germany	Lack of autonomy; time pressures/deadlines; inadequately trained organizational members
United States	Lack of autonomy; incompetent boss; beliefs conflicting with the organization; negative job carryover
Japan	Work overload; time pressures/deadlines; keeping up with new technology
Britain	Keeping up with new technology; work-related travel
South Africa	Long working hours; negative coworker relations; inadequately trained organizational members; negative job carryover
Singapore	Inability to transmit ambitious aspirations and skills to other organizational members
Nigeria	Inadequately trained organizational members; long working hours; job below level of competence; negative job carryover
Brazil	Time pressures/deadlines; keeping up with new technology; job below level of competence; inadequately trained organizational members; interpersonal conflicts with organizational members
Egypt	Work overload; inadequately trained organizational members; negative job carryover

Source: Cooper, C. L. (1984). Executive stress: A ten-country comparison. *Human Resource Management*, 23, 401–404.

tween the two mental-disability "risk" extremes, which likely reflects their comparative economic positions and degree of "control" threat.

2. Examining the data in Table 4.7 for executives with high percentages of job dissatisfaction, one can readily see that those in the developing or rapidly changing cultures also reported the highest percentages of job dissatisfaction.

3. Examining trends in the organizational stressors cited in Table 4.8, one can readily note that even in the relatively "job-empowered" and "economically in control" cultures of Sweden, Germany, and the United States, lack of autonomy or personal control was the common distressor cited by

senior officers. Consistent with earlier study findings on organizational members "lower" in the organization, these senior officers seem to have an unsated need for personal control within their organizations. Other "endangering" stressors like unrealistic time pressures and negative work-to-home carryover were also cited.

4. Examining trends in organizational stressors in Table 4.8, one can readily note that in the countries undergoing economic and social change, the distressors were varied but consistently "endangering" by work overloads, time pressures/deadlines, long working hours, inadequately trained organizational members, and negative work carryover).

These findings at the societal macrosystem levels seem to portray a picture of organizational control similar to those at the microsystem and group levels; namely, that "refueling" and "nondepriving" job and organizational stressors seem to linearly and positively contribute to organizational members' psychological and behavioral well-being, as well as to their job satisfactions. "Arousing" but "endangering" job and organizational stressors seem to be tolerated by organizational members at low to moderate levels but are anxiety producing at high levels. Finally, organizational members at all levels of the organizational ladder seem to want but do not get enough job control or empowerment.

SUGGESTIONS FOR ASSESSING AND "REPAIRING" ORGANIZATIONAL-CONTROL PROBLEM AREAS

Like stress and personal control, organizational control is dynamic rather than static. Therefore, managers wanting accurate readings of their organizational members' appraisals of personal control need to assess such readings of presence at least once a year.

As noted by Lazarus (1966), because the existence of organizational control lies largely in the minds of the organizational "beholders," the best way to measure large-scale perceptions of control is through a survey design, as was common practice in most of the empirical validation studies described here. Because, as noted in some of the studies described here, there can be a variation in appraised control for groups within organizations, it is essential that managers wanting a comprehensive picture of organizational control survey members across organizational groups.

Once organizational distressors adversely affecting organizational members' psychological well-being, productivity, and job satisfaction are identified, managers might want to do some macrosystem rehabilitation. A listing of procedures known to be useful for dealing with organizational-control problem areas has been developed by Connor and Worley (1991) and is provided in Table 4.9. Most of these procedures can be implemented cost effectively with the help of organizational consultants experienced in the key areas listed.

Table 4.9
Managerial Strategies for Dealing with Organizational-Control Problem Areas

Role Clarification	Help organizational members define their work roles, thus reducing role ambiguity and role conflict within organizations
Reasonable Performance Standards	Have managers set reasonable performance standards with organizational members and have them clearly communicate these standards over time in order to reduce role organizational members' uncertainty, role ambiguity, and work over/underload
Individual Goal Setting	Use individual goal-setting to help organizational members to clarify their understanding of their jobs as well as to reduce role uncertainty, role ambiguity, role conflict, and stress caused by unreasonable time pressures and deadlines
Organizational Goal Setting	Use organizational goal-setting, together with open communication, to clarify for managers and organizational members, alike, personal-organizational "fits" and problems of role ambiguity
Time-out	Allow organizational members to take "time-out" from tasks to use stress-coping techniques like meditation or deep-breathing exercises to reduce debilitating mind-body stress symptoms and work over/under-load pressures
Fair and Reasonable Feedback and Performance Evaluations	Evaluate organizational members against clearly-specified behaviors and goals, and provide feedback that is specific and immediate in order to reduce role ambiguity
Training Programs	Give training programs, of both a knowledge and skills nature, to organizational members on stress management so that they can reduce or prevent stress-induced mind-body disabilities

Table 4.9 (continued)

"Empowering" Job Restructuring	Restructure jobs to include such changes as job enrichment for organizational members wanting greater autonomy and skill variety in order to reduce work over/underloads, unrealistic time pressures/deadlines, role ambiguity and role conflict
Improved Selection and Placement Policies	Update selection and placement policies to improve individual-job "fit" and to reduce stress-related problems like organizational minority culture insensitivity, work over/underloads, and unrealistic time pressures/deadlines
Time Management	Give time-management training to organizational members to improve their goal-setting, delegating, and managing skills and to reduce work over/underloads, unrealistic time pressures/deadlines, and low participation in decision-making and problem-solving
Management Stress Education Programs	Update managers' training to help them to monitor excessive stress levels in their work areas and to give them additional knowledge and skill training in open systems and organizational-member "empowerment"
Open Communication Channels	Communicate openly with organizational members to allow them to predict and understand organizational events occurring around them so that they can effectively adapt to their changing environments and manage their own stress levels
Decentralization in Decision-Making	Involve organizational members at all levels in decisions affecting them in order to reduce several causes of high stress, including low decision-making participation, member alienation, role conflict, role ambiguity, and role over/underloads
Development of Cohesive Work Groups	Team-build to help reduce organizational members' stress levels caused by a lack of perceived trust in management and in coworkers
Group Leadership Training	Train group leaders in areas like effective leadership and communication to reduce stress resulting from game playing, inconsiderate or inequitable leadership, organizational-member conflict, and low participation by organizational members in decision-making and problem-solving

Source: Connor, P. E., & Worley, C. H. (1991). Managing organizational stress. *Business Quarterly* (Summer), 1–7.

CONCLUSION

This session on organizational control opened on a somewhat pessimisic note but closes on an optimistic one. Thirty years of research on organizational control issues has shown that job-related anxiety, job-related depression, low organizational morale, and job burnout are, to a large degree, preventable. Managers wanting to prevent these stress-disabling conditions from presenting within their organizations need to be committed to organizational member empowerment. Empowerment means that managers are not only committed to ensuring that "refueling," "nondepriving," and "nonendangering" work conditions prevail but that managers are prepared to intervene and to correct the situation when "job-distressing" or "job-endangering" work conditions present. Unlike the "burning out" organizational member at the start of this session who worked daily in a work environment that drained but did not refuel organizational members, today's concerned managers need to develop organizational control strategies that energize rather than deplete their organizational members. A good place to start building trust and a sense of control throughout the organization is to daily "walk" the empowerment and stress-management "talk."

STRESS-COPING SUMMARY POINTS

1. To assess organizational control, managers should annually ask their organizational members throughout the organization to complete "control" inventories.

2. To accomplish this objective, two "control" inventories that work well are those presented in the appendixes of this chapter.

3. To reduce the probability of stress-related mental disability, low productivity, low job satisfaction, and burnout, companies need to ensure that organizational members, in large number, feel "in control" and "safe" in the workplace. Organizational-control studies from the 1960s through the present have emphasized the need for providing organizational members at all levels of the hierarchy with "appropriate" amounts of "nondepriving" and "nonendangering" job and organizational stressors. Research has shown that the latter objective is considerably more difficult to accomplish in developing countries than in developed ones because of a continuously changing economic environment.

Appendix 4.1
A Measurement of Your Job Characteristics

Questions About Your Job

A. In the past few weeks, HOW MUCH OF THE TIME has your job made you feel each of the following?
   Please fill in the blank with one of the following numbers:
   1 never; 2 occasionally; 3 some of the time; 4 much of the time;
   5 most of the time; 6 all of the time

_____Tense	_____Depressed	_____Calm	_____Cheerful
_____Uneasy	_____Enthusiastic	_____Contented	_____Relaxed
_____Worried	_____Gloomy	_____Miserable	_____Optimistic

B. In the past few weeks, HOW JOB SATISFIED have you been?
   Please CIRCLE one response for each item. Please be honest.
   1. Taking all things together, how do you feel about your job?
      a. I really enjoy my job and couldn't enjoy it more
      b. I enjoy it very much
      c. I enjoy it quite a lot
      d. I just about enjoy it
      e. I don't enjoy it
   2. Taking all things together, how do you feel about your job?
      a. I am extremely satisfied with my job
      b. I am very satisfied
      c. I am quite satisfied
      d. I am just about satisfied
      e. I am not at all satisfied
   3. Taking all things together, how do you feel about your job?
      a. I am extremely happy about my job and couldn't be more happy
      b. I am very happy
      c. I am quite happy
      d. I am just about happy
      e. I am not happy

C. Overall, HOW WOULD YOU RATE EACH of these characteristics for your job? Place an X on the blank that reflects how you feel:
   1. I have total influence over the way my work is planned.

   _____ _____ _____ _____ _____ _____
   totally disagree   totally agree
   2. I have full opportunity to use my abilities in my job.

   _____ _____ _____ _____ _____ _____
   totally disagree   totally agree
   3. My workload is extremely heavy.

   _____ _____ _____ _____ _____ _____
   totally disagree   totally agree

Appendix 4.2
A Measurement of Your Organizational Characteristics

Questions About Your Organization

A. Intrinsic Job Characteristics. How much of each feature is present in your job?

Please use this 1-5 scale:

1 There's none in my job
2 There's just a little of that in my job
3 There's a moderate amount of that in my job
4 There's quite a lot of that in my job
5 There's a great deal of that in my job

ITEMS:

A1 The freedom to choose your own method of working
A2 The amount of responsibility you are given
A3 The recognition you get for good work
A4 Being able to judge your work performance, right away, when actually doing the job
A5 Your opportunity to use your abilities
A6 The amount of variety in your job
A7 Your chance of promotion
A8 The attention paid to suggestions you make .
A9 The feeling of doing something which is not trivial, but really worthwhile

B. Job Needs. How important are the following "Job Needs" for you?

Please use this 1-7 scale:

1 Not at all important
2 Not particularly important
3 I'm not sure about its importance
4 Moderately important
5 Fairly important
6 Very important
7 Extremely important

B1 Using your skills to the maximum
B2 Achieving something that you personally value
B3 The opportunity to make your own decisions
B4 The opportunity to learn new things
B5 Challenging work
B6 Extending your range of abilities

C. Job Satisfaction. How satisfied are you with each of the following job features?

Please use this 1-7 scale:

1 I'm extremely dissatisfied
2 I'm very dissatisfied
3 I'm moderately dissatisfied
4 I'm not sure
5 I'm moderately satisfied
6 I'm very satisfied
7 I'm extremely satisfied

ITEMS:

C1 The physical work conditions
C2 The freedom to choose your own method of working
C3 Your fellow workers
C4 The recognition you get for good work
C5 Your immediate boss
C6 The amount of responsibility you are given
C7 Your rate of pay
C8 Your opportunity to use your abilities
C9 Industrial relations between management and workers in your firm
C10 Your chance of promotion
C11 The way your firm is managed
C12 The attention paid to suggestions you make
C13 Your hours of work
C14 The amount of variety in your job
C15 Your job security
D. Trust and Commitment in Management. How much do agree with the following?
   Please use this 1-7 scale:
   1 No, I strongly disagree   5 Yes, I agree just a little
   2 No, I disagree quite a lot   6 Yes, I agree quite a lot
   3 No, I disagree just a little 7 Yes, I strongly agree
   4 I'm not sure
D1 Management at my firm is sincere in its attempts to meet the organizational members'
   point of view.
D2 Our firm has a poor future unless it can attract better managers
D3 Management can be trusted to make sensible decisions for the firm's future
D4 Management at work seems to do an efficient job
D5 I feel quite confident that the firm will always try to treat me fairly
D6 Our management would be quite prepared to gain advantage by deceiving the workers
D7 I am quite proud to be able to tell people who it is I work for
D8 I sometimes feel like leaving this employment for good
D9 Even if the firm were not doing too well financially, I would be reluctant to change
   to another employer.
D10 I feel myself to be part of the organization
D11 In my work, I like to feel I am making some effort, not just for myself but for the
   organization as well.
D12 To know that my own work had made a contribution to the good of the organization
   would please me.

Source: Warr, P., Cook, J., & Wall, T. (1979). Scales for the measurement of some work attitudes and aspects of psychological well-being. *Journal of Occupational Psychology,* 52, 129–148; Cook, J., & Wall, T. (1980). New work attitude measures of trust, organizational commitment and personal need non-fulfillment. *Journal of Occupational Psychology,* 53, 39–52.

Scoring Appendix 4.1

Appendix 4.1.A.1 Score

Are you job-anxious or job-contented?

(a) "Reverse-score" your answers to "tense," "uneasy," and "worried" in Part A. Use the following conversion: 1=6; 2=5; 3=4; 4=3; 5=2; 6=1.

(b) Total your new scores for "tense," "uneasy," and "worried."

(c) Total your original scores for "calm," "contented," and "relaxed."

(d) Total b+c. This is your final score. Mark it here:_____ (Range 6-36) The higher your score, the more job-contented you are.

(e) To calculate your "mean" score, divide your total (d) by 6. _____

Appendix 4.1.A.2 Score

Are you job-depressed or job-enthusiastic?

(a) "Reverse-score" your answers to "depressed," "gloomy," and "miserable" in Part A. Use the following conversion: 1=6; 2=5; 3=4; 4=3; 5=2; 6=1.

(b) Total your new scores for "depressed," "gloomy," and "miserable."

(c) Total your original scores for "cheerful," "enthusiastic," and "optimistic."

(d) Total b+c. This is your final score. Mark it here:_____ (Range 6-36) The higher your score, the more job-enthusiastic you are.

(e) To calculate your "mean" score, divide your total (d) by 6. _____

Appendix 4.1.B Score

Are you job-satisfied?

(a) For items 1-3 in Part B, convert letters to numbers, such that: a=5; b=4; c=3; d=2; e=1

(b) Total your scores for the three items.

(c) Divide the total by 3. This is your average job-satisfaction score. Mark it here:_____ (Range 1-5)

The lower your score, the less job-satisfied you are.

The higher your score, the more job-satisfied you are.

Appendix 4.1.C.1 Score

Do you have much decision-latitude on your job?

(a) For items 1-2, convert your blank to a number. Starting with the blank closest to the "totally disagree," begin with number 1 and continue until number 7.

(b) Total your answers for questions 1 and 2.

(c) Divide your total in (b) by 2. This is your average decision-latitude score. Mark it here: _____ (Range 1-7)

The higher your score, the more decision-latitude you have.

Appendix 4.1.C.2 Score

Do you have a heavy work-load on your job?

(a) For item 3, convert your blank to a number. Starting with the blank closest to the "totally disagree," begin with number 1 and continue until number 7.

(b) This is your workload score. Mark it here: _____ (Range 1-7)

The higher your score, the heavier the work-load you have.

Scoring Appendix 4.2

Intrinsic Job Characteristics Score:
Total your response to Items A1 through A10 (range 10-50)
Mark it here: _____

Higher-Order Need Strength Score:
Total your response to Items B1 through B6 (range 6-42)
Mark it here: _____

Job Satisfaction:
Total your response to Items C1 through C15 (range 15-105)
Mark it here: _____

Trust in Management Score:
(a) "Reverse-score" your response to Items D2 and D6 (7=1;
   6=2; 5=3; 4=4; 3=5; 2=6; 1=7)
(b) Total your response now to Items D1 through D6 (range 6-42)
Mark it here: _____

Faith in Management's Intentions Score:
(a) "Reverse-score" your response to Item D6 (7=1; 6=2; 5=3; 4=4; 3=5;
   2=6; 1=7)
(b) Total your response now to Items D1, D5, and D6 (range 3-21)
Mark it here: _____

Confidence in Management's Actions Score:
(a) "Reverse-score" your response to Item D2 (7=1; 6=2; 5=3; 4=4. . .)
(b) Total your response now to Items D2, D3, and D4 (range 3-21)
Mark it here: _____

Organizational Commitment Score:
(a) "Reverse-score" your response to Item D8 (7=1; 6=2; 5=3; 4=4. . .)
(b) Total your response now to Items D7 through D12 (range 6-42)
Mark it here: _____

Organizational Identification Score:
Total your response to Items D7 and D10 (range 2-14)
Mark it here: _____

Organizational Involvement Score:
Total your response to Items D11 and D12 (range 2-14)
Mark it here: _____

Organizational Loyalty Score:
(a) "Reverse score" your response to Item D8 (7=1; 6=2; 5=3; 4=4. . .)
(b) Total your response now to Items D8 and D9 (range 2-14)
Mark it here: _____

REFERENCES

Clegg, C. W., & Wall, T. D. (1981). A note on some new scales for measuring psychological well-being at work. *Journal of Occupational Psychology*, 54, 221–225.

Connor, P. E., & Worley, C. H. (1991). Managing organizational stress. *Business Quarterly* (Summer), 1–7.

Cook, J., & Wall, T. (1980). New work attitude measures of trust, organizational commitment, and personal need non-fulfillment. *Journal of Occupational Psychology*, 53, 39–52.

Cooper, C. L. (1984). Executive stress: A ten-country comparison. *Human Resource Management*, 4, 395–407.

Freudenberger, H. J. (1974). Staff burn-out. *Journal of Social Issues*, 30, 159–165.

Ganster, D. C., & Schaubroeck, J. (1991). Work stress and employee health. *Journal of Management*, 17, 235–271.

Hackman, J. R., & Oldham, G. R. (1980). *Work Redesign*. Reading, MA: Addison-Wesley.

Jackson, S. E., & Schuler, R. (1985). A meta-analysis and conceptual critique of research on role ambiguity and role conflict in work settings. *Organizational Behavior and Human Decision Processes*, 36, 16–78.

Johansson, G., Aronsson, G., & Lindstrom, B. O. (1978). Social psychological and neuroendocrine reactions in highly mechanized work. *Ergonomics*, 21, 583–589.

Kahn, R., Wolfe, D., Quinn, R., Snoek, J., & Rosenthal, R. (1964). *Organizational Stress: Studies in Role Conflict and Ambiguity*. New York: Wiley.

Karasek, R. (1979). Job demands, job decision latitude, and mental strain: Implications for job redesign. *Administrative Science Quarterly*, 24, 285–306.

Lazarus, R. S. (1966). *Psychological Stress and the Coping Process*. New York: McGraw-Hill.

Levinson, H. (1981). When executives burn out. *Harvard Business Review* (May-June), 73–81.

Matthews, K., Cottington, E., Talbott, E., Kuller, L., & Siegel, J. (1987). Stressful work conditions and diastolic blood pressure among blue collar factory workers. *American Journal of Epidemiology*, 126, 280–291.

Rose, R. M., Jenkins, C. D., Hurst, M., & Hall, R. P. (1982a). Endocrine activity in air traffic controllers at work. II. Biological, psychological, and work correlates. *Psychoneuroendocrinology*, 7, 113–123.

Rose, R. M., Jenkins, C. D., Hurst, M., Kreger, B. E., Barrett, J., & Hall, R. P. (1982b). Endocrine activity in air traffic controllers at work. III. Relationship to physical and psychiatric activity. *Psychoneuroendocrinology*, 7, 125–134.

Rose, R. M., Jenkins, C. D., Hurst, M., Livingston, L., & Hall, R. P. (1982c). Endocrine activity in air traffic controllers at work. I. Characterization of cortisol and growth hormone levels during the day. *Psychoneuroendocrinology*, 7, 101–111.

Shapiro, D. A., Barkham, M., Hardy, G. E., & Morrison, L. A. (1990). The Second Sheffield Psychotherapy Project: Rationale, design and preliminary outcome data. *British Journal of Medical Psychology*, 63, 97–108.

Shirom, A. (1989). Burnout in work organizations. In C. L. Cooper & I. Robertson (Eds.), *International Review of Industrial and Organizational Psychology 1989*. Chichester, England: Wiley.

Wall, T. D., Clegg, C. W., Davies, R. T., Kemp, N. J., & Mueller, W. S. (1987).
    Advanced manufacturing technology and work simplification: An empirical
    study. *Journal of Occupational Behavior*, 8, 233–250.
Warr, P. B. (1990a). Decision latitude, job demands, and employee well-being.
    Work and Stress, 4, 285–294.
Warr, P. (1990b). The measurement of well-being and other aspects of mental
    health. *Journal of Occupational Psychology*, 63, 193–210.
Warr, P., Cook, J., & Wall, T. (1979). Scales for the measurement of some work
    attitudes and aspects of psychological well-being. *Journal of Occupational
    Psychology*, 52, 129–148.

Part III

The Outward Sign Issue

Chapter 5

Assessing One's Own Outward Signs of Distress

A CASE IN POINT

William Bartell, Human Resource Manager for Wyler Industries Limited, was pleased with the way that the Stress-Empowerment sessions were being received. Participants remarked at the end of the sessions on Control that they had a clearer picture of whether they were recently able to remain "in control" and if their organizations were recently able to maintain a "talking-walking" semblance of Control. Now participants seemed eager to complete the first of the outward signs of distress sessions, the second element in the stress C-O-P-E-ing model.

Given that some degree of stress and strain in life is normal, how above or below "normal" their recently experienced symptoms of distress appear to be and how effectively participants appear to be coping with their taxing energy demands would be of particular interest to participants in this session. After the personal control session, a number of participants felt that more feedback was needed before they could answer with confidence, "Should I consider seeking professional assistance to reduce my presenting stress symptoms—or do I seem to be 'coping' okay?" This session, William affirmed, was designed to help fill this information void.

THE OPENING ADDRESS: THE HIGH COST OF DISTRESS TO SOCIETY

William began his first session on outward signs of distress:
In talking through the case of Warren Potts earlier on, we managers at Wyler Industries Ltd. began to empathize with employers in the United

States who feel burdened by the high costs of stress disability cases in the workplace. We were able to understand more fully why it is that stress experts have estimated that excessive job stress costs the U.S. economy approximately $150 billion a year for stress-related presentations, including absenteeism, accidents, disability claims, and replacement costs for stress-disabled organizational members. Then, we reflected, if the United States, a highly developed nation economically, technologically, and controlwise, faces these sorts of incredible stress-related costs, what sorts of stress-related costs do less developed nations face? We stopped reflecting at the macrosystem level and decided to plan appropriate actions at our work site to help alleviate pathological distress symptoms for our organizational members. That planning has resulted in these stress-empowerment sessions.

Throughout our sessions on control, we measured the degrees of anxiety, depression, and job satisfaction that were appraised by us as being generated by our jobs. Today, we will look more closely at our personal outward signs of distress. The objective of this session is to give participants an opportunity to assess the degree to which their physiological, psychological, and behavioral distress symptoms are presenting and to determine if these outward signs fall within the "normal range" or the "pathological range."

Up to now we have often talked in global figures about the costs of pathological levels of distress to industry. It is interesting to note that on a broader societal plane, in 1980 a team of experts headed by B. P. Dohrenwend completed a comprehensive review of epidemiological estimates of mental illness in the United States and found that approximately 25% of the general population report significant levels of anxiety and distress symptoms. These experts called this condition "demoralization." Canadian mental-health expert Carl D'Arcy (1982) estimates the Canadian figure of mental demoralization to be closer to 20% of the general population. Moreover, mental-health experts report that about half of those self-reporting as "demoralized" are clinically impaired, which means that their quality of life is significantly hampered by their psychological disabilities.

Certain segments of the population seem to consistently report higher levels of mental ill health. Women report more "demoralizing" symptoms than men, and lower socioeconomic groups report more "demoralizing" symptoms than those in higher socioeconomic groups. Around the world, epidemiological studies reflect that anxiety and depression have a greater prevalence and incidence than are generally expected.

Because depression may often masquerade as another illness, its diagnosis is often missed. However, anxiety is relatively simple to detect and, thus, is more likely to be reported. Clark (1989) suggests that the one-year prevalence rate for anxiety "panic attacks" may be in the below 3% range, while the one-year prevalence rate for generalized anxiety disorders is in the 3–6% range. Klerman (as quoted in Brand, 1972) estimates that one North American out of every eight will suffer a depression sometime during his or her life. Lehmann estimates the prevalence of depression at 3–4% of the general population, and of these, only 1 in 5 will likely be treated, 1 in 50 will likely be hospitalized, and 1 in 200 will likely commit suicide (see Beck & Beamesderfer, 1974).

Besides psychological disabilities, certain physiological conditions, often lifestyle and stress induced, have been known to disable individuals to the point where they are dysfunctional or near death. Heart disease, digestive system disease, respiratory disease, cancer, and injury have been among the top disabling contenders receiving experts' attention in recent years.

Cardiovascular disease develops in almost all human populations exposed to stress-induced atherogenic environments. In North America, cardiovascular diseases (including heart disease, hypertension, and cerebrovascular disease) have been the leading cause of death for men and women since the 1940s. In North America, declines of about 27% have been noted within the last decade, largely due to improved information on the causes, warning signs, prevention, and rehabilitation of cardiovascular disease. Today, cardiovascular disease is responsible for about 40% of all adult deaths annually in Canada and in the United States. Decreasing trends in cardiovascular disease mortality have also been noted in other developed countries around the world (i.e., Austria, Finland, Norway, Italy, and France). However, increases have been reported in the developed nations of Scotland, England, Wales, and Ireland and in the economically and politically volatile countries of Hungary, Poland, Romania, Bulgaria, and Yugoslavia (U.S. National Center for Health Statistics, 1987; Statistics Canada, Canadian Centre for Health Information; Cooper, 1986).

In North America, cancer is the second-leading cause of death for men and women. Accidental and violent deaths are generally the third-ranking cause of death in men—with more than half of these deaths being attributed to motor vehicle accidents and suicides. Respiratory diseases (headed by pneumonia and influenza and followed by chronic bronchitis, emphysema, asthma, and other chronic airway obstruction) are generally the third-ranking cause of death in women (U.S. National Center for Health Statistics, 1987; Statistics Canada, Canadian Centre for Health Information, 1987; Cooper, 1986).

Within the last five years, the five most frequent conditions requiring hospitalization in Canada for men (in descending order) were heart diseases, diseases of the digestive system, diseases of the respiratory system, injury/poisoning, and cancer. The five most frequent conditions requiring hospitalization in Canada for women (in descending order) were complications of pregnancy and childbirth, diseases of the digestive system, heart diseases, diseases of the respiratory system, and diseases of the genitourinary system (Statistics Canada, Canadian Centre for Health Information, 1993). As is typical in most countries around the world besides Canada, causes of illness and hospitalization often mirror the causes of death.

Although international trends associated with mental and physical ill health and with extreme violence (such as suicide and homicide) have been documented to some degree, the behavioral incidences of other behaviors caused by anger—such as interpersonal aggression, system sabotage, theft, and substance use—have been sparsely reported in the health and organizational-stress literature. Of those cited, alcoholism/substance abuse is the most well publicized.

In a 1985 National Household Survey conducted in the United States, 19% of employed Americans, aged 20–40 years, reported using illegal substances at least once in the preceding month. In a more recent 1987 report, 95% of 60 U.S. employers surveyed reported having direct experience with a substance abuse problem. The majority (98%) believed it is as bad or worse than it was five years ago, with 58% of the respondents citing cocaine abuse as a special problem in the present-day workplace (Spector, 1975, 1978; Chen & Spector, 1992; Friedman et al., 1992).

What is critical from a stress management perspective is that with proper education, self-awareness, lifestyle changes, and professional/medical intervention, experts around the globe believe that the major known causes of adult death and morbidity can be decreased significantly. In short, "health-empowering" individuals to recognize their own early signs of poor stress-coping—psychologically, physiologically, and behaviorally is—without question, the best disability-prevention strategy that societies around the world can promote.

This session has as its objective the recognition of common outward signs of distress and an initial assessment of individuals' stress-coping strategies.

So as not to bias your responses to the inventories you are about to complete, *I would ask that you please turn to the appendix for this session* (i.e., Chapter 5 Appendixes) *and complete as honestly as you can the inventory items that appear before you. Please do not score these inventory items until asked to do so. After you have finished responding, please join us for further discussions of this material.*

THE PSYCHOPHYSIOLOGY OF HUMAN STRESS

The relationship between stress and physiological, psychological, and behavioral presentations is a complex one, and even in the present this process is not fully understood.

We begin this session on a positive note, recognizing as we have in other sessions, that stress is not necessarily a bad thing. Some degree of stress and energy consumption is a normal and necessary part of living. Moreover, energy consumption can be very desirable, particularly when there is some perceived return on the energy investment.

Hans Selye (1974), the founder of stress physiology, wrote decades ago that contrary to widespread belief, stress is not simply nervous tension nor the result of damage. Above all, it is not something to be avoided. Stress, or arousal, is associated with the expression of all humans' innate drives. Without some degree of stress, humans would be unable to gain mastery or to self-actualize. Stress ensues as long as any demand is made on any part of the body. And the only time that individuals are truly stress free and demand free is when they are dead.

What is destructive to human beings is too much distress—which is by its very nature, a "condition" that derives uniquely within each individual. We have spoken at length in earlier sessions about how an individual's unique appraisal of a stressor (be it real or imagined) is what determines whether eustress or distress will result. Numerous studies in recent years have revealed that too many distressors or one "really disastrous" distressor (such as that which causes post-traumatic stress disorder, or PTSD) can create major physiological, psychological, and behavioral havoc within individuals. The question since the beginning of the twentieth century has been, How is it that distressors destroy?

To begin to answer this question, a basic understanding of the stress-strain relationship is needed. In physical terms, stress exists when force is applied to distort "a body." The effect of the force on the body presents as "elastic" distortion (i.e., the impact is reversible and the body is able to "bounce back") or "nonelastic" distortion (i.e., the impact is nonreversible and the body is unable to "bounce back"). Distortion is measurable as the degree of "strain" experienced by the body.

The relationship between stress and strain can be plotted; what results is a curve that illustrates that with the initial application of stress or force, some unmeasurable change likely occurs in the body. As the stressor, or force, continues, the curve indicates a measurable strain or distortion being experienced, which is directly proportional to the amount of force being exerted. This area in the curve is known technically as the "elastic distortion region," which means that if the stressor is removed, then the strain on the body will disappear. In lay language, the strain (or "harm" or "discomfort") experienced by the body is reversible to this point.

There is a point on the curve, however, when the force or stress is such that there is no longer a direct proportional relationship between the amount of stress applied and the amount of strain experienced. At this point, the body changes its character in some way, and the resulting strain is not reversible but becomes part of an "injured" or "permanently distorted" body. This area in the curve is known technically as the "nonelastic distortion region." In lay language, the strain (or "harm" or "disease state") experienced by the body is nonreversible. A common analogy used to demonstrate nonelastic distortion is an elastic band that has been forced to stretch beyond its capability; at the point of "nonelastic distortion," it either remains overstretched and dysfunctional, or it breaks.

There is a psychophysiological analogue to this stress and strain relationship in humans. The initial portion of the curve of stressor application would be nonmeasurable, and would likely be experienced by the individual as some cellular or biochemical response of the mildest form. As the stress level increases, various physiological, psychological, and behavioral changes, or strains, would be observed in the human, such that the strain experienced would be proportional to the level of stress being applied. (Common "changes" or "strains" cited by stressed individuals are outlined in Table 1.1.) At this point, the strain experienced would be reversible if the stressor (were) removed. Thus, the area in the chart would constitute the "elastic distortion region."

With further increases in stress, the area of "nonelastic distortion," or pathology, would eventually present. In lay language, the individual would have been stressed and strained beyond the level of "adaptation." Thus, his or her adaptive life resources would have been drained to excess, and his or her mind-body behavior changes, or strains, would not be fully reversible (at least not without professional intervention). Distressful "trauma"—mental, physical, and/or behavioral—would result. Common traumas presenting at this nonelsastic distortion stage include those cited earlier: cardiovascular disease, cancer, and mental ill health.

As noted in earlier sessions on control, humans have been programmed to not only want to be "in control" but to maintain a healthy degree of control—with some elasticity—in order to be able to deal with stressors that arise. To further understand the complexities of human psychophysiological responses to distressors, one needs to understand that humans' cells are all programmed to physiologically contribute to the body's state of coordinated control. The purpose of the human physiological function, then, is to help humans maintain a controlled internal bodily environment, or homeostasis, so that individuals can deal effectively with externally demanding eustressors and distressors. Even in relatively unstrained times, the body consumes considerable amounts of finite life energy just to keep the mind and body in a healthy state of "dynamic" equilibrium.

In high-stress periods, when demands on the human body become taxing, some degree of "control" inherent in individual body cells becomes "changed" or "distorted" by special biochemicals called "hormones." Hormones are secreted by the glands of the body's endocrine system.

The overall coordination and control of the endocrine system are accomplished via the human central nervous system, through "networking" with the human autonomic nervous system. The principles of "control" that are in force are based on a set of preset bodily standards. Whether these bodily standards are being maintained or not is monitored by a sensory mechanism in the brain, which transmits or feeds back information to coordinating centers in the brain.

In the brain coordinating centers, incoming information is continually being compared with that of these preset standards. If "significant" variation or distortion is appraised as occurring, instructions are transmitted by the nervous system and the endocrine system to the body's cells to make appropriate "changes" in function for "coping" with the distortion. Thus, stressors can provide the stimulus for marked changes in the cells' preset limits. But how does this marked change occur, and how does the body restore its equilibrium once the distortion has been relieved? Early work in physiological laboratories sought to identify general patterns of response of living systems to externally imposed stressors.

Walter Cannon (1929) demonstrated the important role of the sympathetic nervous system (i.e., that part of the autonomic nervous system which serves the viscera, glands, heart, blood vessels, and smooth muscles) and the adrenal medullary system for aiding animals (including humans) to rapidly respond to "threatening" or "endangering" environmental stimuli. For Cannon, these "threatening" stimuli were those producing pain, anger, hunger, fear, and rage. A fast approach of an appraised "enemy" would illustrate this kind of "threatening" stimulus. The coordination of the sympathetic nervous system and the adrenal medullary system would allow the animal to "choose" the appropriate response to the threatening stimulus: either fight it, or flight from it.

Cannon called this aggressive-withdrawal "coping" response set the "fight-or-flight" stress reaction. He said that it is associated with activation of the adrenal medullary system, which releases the catecholamines adrenaline and noradrenaline and which results in increased cardiac output, elevated blood pressure, and an increased heart rate. Simply stated, the body survives the "threatening crisis" by informing the bodily systems that certain marked changes "from the norm" are needed. Namely, that oxygen in the blood needs to be drawn away from the situationally nonessential organs (like the digestive system) and redistributed to areas where it is more critically needed for fighting or fleeing: the limbs. In short, Cannon's work highlighted the importance of one aspect of the adrenergic system to help living systems cope with "threatening" or "endangering" stressors and to regain immediate control over "the enemy."

In the 1930s, Hans Selye questioned what would happen to living systems if they could not flee or fight the stressor as a means of regaining control. Certainly this possibility happens at work and in the home on a daily basis. In an attempt to discover the answer, Selye exposed animals in the laboratory to noxious stimuli such as cold, toxins, and traumatic injury. His reports twenty years later demonstrated the importance of the adrenal cortex in helping human systems respond to externally imposed "distressors" (Selye, 1950). In his initial research, Selye injected rats with various impure and toxic gland "distressors" and reported physiological responses to these stressors such as enlargement and hyperactivity of the adrenal cortex, deduction in the thymus gland and lymph nodes, and excessive gastric acid and ulcer production. In his later research, Selye reported these same physiological responses to other distressing or noxious stimuli that could not be relieved. He thus concluded that living creatures, including humans, have a pattern of "stereotyped" physiological responses to uncontrollable distressors. He termed this stereotypic pattern of response the "general adaptation syndrome," or GAS.

The GAS, said Selye (1983), consists of the following three stages:

Alarm Stage. Triggered when the human system is suddenly exposed to stimuli to which it is not adapted, the alarm phase represents a "call to arms" of the body's defenses, and has two subphases for coping with "the crisis": the shock phase and the countershock phase.

The shock phase is immediate and presents such immediate crisis-reactive outward signs of distress as loss of muscle tone, decreased body temperature, and decreased blood pressure.

The countershock phase immediately follows and is a rebound reaction to the shock. Somehow, the presence of a "distressor" signals the hypothalamus, a complex bundle of nerve cells in the brain, to act as a crisis-surviving "bridge" between the brain, the endocrine system (which releases life-saving hormones into the bloodstream to help body organs adapt to the "crisis"), and the autonomic nervous system (which regulates the cardiovascular, respiratory, temperature, and water regulatory subsystems at all times). To aid the body in coping with the "crisis," a complex series of biochemical and body changes are thus stirred into action. For example, the resulting nervous signals reach certain neuroendocrine cells in the hypothalamus, where they are transformed into a chemical messenger for releasing corticotrophic hormones. A message is relayed to the pituitary (a small, rounded gland at the base of the brain), causing a discharge of adrenocorticotrophic hormone (ACTH) into the bloodstream. Upon reaching the adrenal cortex, ACTH triggers the secretion of corticoids, particularly cortisol. Many anti-inflammatory corticoid hormones supply a readily available source of energy for meeting the demands made by the stressor, facilitate other adaptive enzyme responses, and suppress immune reactions and inflammation, thereby helping the body to temporarily "coexist" with the presenting distressor. Usually secreted in lesser amounts, the proinflammatory corticoid hormones stimulate the reactivity of the body's connective tissue, protecting the body against possible physical invasion by "the stressor."

This crisis-surviving chain of events seems to be cybernetically controlled by several short-loop and long-loop biofeedback mechanisms existing within the human body that continually monitor the existing levels of hormones and compare these levels with those required for adaptation. For example, if there is an abundance of ACTH appraised as existing, a short-loop feedback returns some of it to the hypothalamus-pituitary axis, which then terminates further ACTH production.

Simultaneously with these processes, the catecholamines are liberated as another means of adaptation. Noradrenaline and adrenaline are secreted to make energy available from the body stores, to accelerate the pulse rate, to elevate the blood pressure and the rate of blood circulating to the muscles, and to stimulate the central nervous system. They also enhance the blood coagulation mechanism as protection against excessive bleeding in case injuries are sustained "in the battle" with the stressor.

Numerous other hormonal and biochemical changes "check and balance" the body's functioning and stability. The coordination of all these mind-body systems constitute an arsenal of survival weapons by which the human system can defend itself "against the stressor." In other words, the body becomes prepared psychologically, physiologically, and behaviorally to cope with the stressor that presents. After the "crisis" subsides, resistance begins.

Resistance Stage. Resisting the stressor and all of the changes in the body that have been provoked thus far, this phase is triggered by a decrease in adrenocortical secretions. Unlike in the alarm stage, where the adrenal cortex discharges its secretory granules into the bloodstream, in the resistance stage, the adrenal cortex becomes particularly rich in secretory granules. Throughout the body, cells are desperately engaged in processes that will return the body to homeostasis. Opposite biochemical and hormonal reactions to those described for the alarm stage are called into play. At the end of this stage, most of the earlier outward signs of distress disappear, as the body develops an adaptation to the formerly "stressful condition."

It is often argued by stress experts—and this argument is opposed by some—that this resistance stage is associated with the development of such mind-body (or psychosomatic) disorders as gastric ulcers, high blood pressure, colitis, asthma, migraine headaches, and arthritis in certain biologically predisposed individuals. What is less controversial is the recognition by experts that the human's capacity to resist stressors in this phase is limited, and should the factors creating distress be sufficiently severe or endure sufficiently long, the body moves on to the third GAS stage.

Exhaustion Stage. Presenting outwardly as psychological, physiological, and behavioral "trauma" (i.e., heart attacks, cancer, chronic depression), this third phase of "nonelastic distortion" may lead to exhaustion or death if the outward signs of distress are not "reversed" or if the stressor is sufficiently severe and prolonged. Exhaustion occurs because of an ongoing biochemical and hormonal "war" within the human body, caused by the body's attempts to adapt to the stressor and then resist it. This "war" causes premature aging of the human system. Premature aging then leads to a greater predisposition for disease conditions, or mind-body "trauma."

In his more recent work, Selye (1974) emphasizes that some degree of stress is essential to life, and that alarm reactions are not only unavoidable but serve as good sources of "feedback" that the human system is capable of being stressed and strained to some degree in order to adapt. When these outward signs of distress become too frequent or too uncomfortable, however, a "warning light" should go on within the human's mind, telling him or her that certain life changes may be in order if the individual wants to stay healthy and productive. Therefore, Selye characterized the first two stages of the GAS as a "good thing" from a survival perspective, and said that they should be differentiated from the third stage—which is irreversible damage. Of course, whether the third stage is reached is a function, in large part, of whether the first two stages of the GAS are overused and abused.

Besides defining the GAS, Selye's research made a number of significant contributions to our understanding of the psychophysiology of stress. First, Selye emphasized that the body's ability to adapt to environmental changes is elastic but limited. Given that homeostasis, stress-coping, and homeostasis-regaining all require life energy from a limited "pool," under unrelenting stress conditions, multidimensional system drainage and damage can occur. It can be extensive and life-threatening, leading to exhaustion (or "burnout"). Therefore, human beings must constantly manage their adaptive resources and finite life energy in order to survive to their biologically preprogrammed age. Moreover, if inordinate amounts of energy are consumed just "to physiologically survive," there is little life energy left for sustaining competence or for self-actualization.

Selye admitted that although stress experts still do not know precisely *what* is lost in living and in stress-coping—except that it is not merely caloric energy—humans' best defense is a good energy offense: moderate negative returns and accentuate positive returns on energy investments. Moreover, humans need to keep their physiological systems in good working order by regularly getting enough sleep, food, physical exercise, and mental "relaxation" (Selye, 1983).

Second, Selye emphasized that long-term adaptation entails learning from one's past stress experiences. He compared the relative "maturity" of humans' adaptation capabilities to biological life stages. Selye suggested that childhood, with its characteristic low resistance and excessive response to any kind of stimulus, represents low adaptation capability. Adulthood, during which the body has adapted to most commonly encountered stimuli and has increased resistance, represents moderate adaptation capability. Old age (particularly over age 70), characterized by loss of adaptability and eventual exhaustion, represents a life stage of low adaptation capability (Selye, 1983). Given this scenario, it is little wonder, he suggests, that individuals between the ages of 30 and 65 generally have adequate adaptive reserves to get through most taxing life situations, including raising children, advising teenaged children, and caring for aging parents—not to mention being productive at work.

Third, Selye recognized that stressors affect individuals differently. Individuals' responses are based on many endogenous factors, including genetic and hereditary predispositions, gender, age, and early childhood conditioning and patterning. Furthermore, their responses are based on exogenous factors, including "healthful" substance intake, physical environment health and safety, and dietary balance. In the human body, suggested Selye, there exist systems (respiratory, cardiovascular, mental, and so on) that, based on some combination of heredity and environmental exchanges, are weak. These weak systems are likely to be affected early on by pathological stress levels.

Following Cannon's and Selye's important stress process contributions, Henry and Stephens (1977) helped to clarify *what* it is that causes human systems to move into a more "passive" (and potentially destructive) phase of resistance to stressors via the extensive GAS response, as compared to a shorter, more "active" phase of resistance via the fight-or-flight response. Their answer: the perceived inability of the human system to control the stressor(s). Their animal research studies indicated that when living systems are "challenged" and given the opportunity to exert control over their environment and the stressors in it, they show increased activity, responding to the challenge with aggression and with activation of the adrenergic system (as detailed by Cannon). However, when living systems are "challenged" but not given the opportunity to exert control (i.e., they are immobilized or defeated), they show a withdrawal response, with activation of the adrenocortical hormones (as described by Selye).

Similar findings were reported for humans by Frankenhauser (1980). Moreover, animal studies conducted by Corley, Mauck, and Shiel (1975) investigating (1) the combination of chronic distress along with some opportunity to exert effort to control the distress and (2) the combination of chronic distress without an opportunity to exert effort to control the distress led to excessive sympathetic arousal results in animals, with hypertension occuring for combination 1 and with death ensuing for combination 2.

Lazarus's (1976) work, as detailed in earlier sessions on control (see Chapters 3 and 4), further emphasized the importance of humans' appraisals of control over stressors and the coping resources accumulated by them over time for dealing with stressful demands. Rather than concluding that humans need to fight, flee, or self-destruct in order to cope with life's many distressors, Lazarus noted that the relationship of stress to disease in humans has much more flexibility and is determined by such critical aspects as the amount of control a stressful situation permits and the unique cognitive characteristics of the individual. Thus, an individual's unique way of thinking and feeling about the situation as well as the individual's conditioning to past stressors determines to a large degree whether he or she will be consumed by anger and disease or remain self-healing—even under highly stressful life conditions.

Research within the last decade has shown that, over time, an individual's access to social support during high-stress periods, his or her number of appraised positive life events, and his or her ability to maintain a "moderated" physical exercise program can all effectively moderate the relationship between chronic negative life stress and stress-disabling symptomology (Cohen & Hoberman, 1983; Kirkcaldy & Shephard, 1990).

MEASURING OUTWARD SIGNS OF PSYCHOPHYSIOLOGICAL DISTRESS

As suggested by Selye, nature seems to have given humans warning signs for detecting if they are becoming chronically overstressed. Most individuals can describe their "outward signs of distress" by talking about their feelings of anxiety and depression. But at what stage do these stress symptoms become serious—and, perhaps, in need of expert attention?

Whereas the good news is that there are warning signs of distress, the bad news is that stress-related disease can be so generalized that it is often overlooked as "a problem," even by health experts who are trained to do the recognizing. Physicians who have been trained to recognize and treat disease often report having difficulty recognizing highly stressed patients, even though, *on face*, the patients' outward signs of distress are presenting "loud and clear." To assist physicians in assessing the degree of stress-related symptomology reported by their clients, stress experts have spent considerable time and talent developing inventories for this purpose. Today, various versions of the General Health Questionnaire (or GHQ) (Goldberg, 1972; Goldberg et al., 1970) and the Symptom Checklist (SCL) (Derogatis et al., 1974) are used by clinicians throughout the world as effective stress-symptom screening tools.

The approaches of the GHQ and the SCL are somewhat different for assessing "normals" (i.e., meaning exhibiting within-normal-range stress symptomology) and "stress cases" (meaning exhibiting clinical stress symptomology). The GHQ assumes that individuals' outward signs of distress are potentially pathological if established routines are being upset by excessive stress levels. The SCL assumes that individuals' outward signs of distress are potentially pathological if the individuals' quantity and intensity of stress symptomology are excessive and debilitating.

Because both the GHQ and the SCL are self-reports, which means that an individual answers the items in the inventory without assistance from a professional, these instruments can provide useful feedback to individuals as to whether their stress-induced symptomology is "normal," "below average," or "excessive." In this manner, individuals can then decide whether they should seek the advice of a physician or a stress counselor.

In its original British form, the GHQ is a self-administered questionnaire consisting of 30 or 60 items. All items are concerned with psychological distress or altered behavior. For each item, respondents are asked to compare their "recent states" with their "usual states." In the scoring of degree of routine upset, an item is counted as presenting concern only if the disruption is being experienced "more than usual." Thus, the 30-item GHQ generates an outward-sign-of-distress score between 0 and 30. Outward sign scores of concern are considered to be above 4, although some stress counselors like D'Arcy use 6 as the critical cut-off (Goldberg et al., 1976).

The Lipman-Rickels Scale, better known as the symptom checklist (or SCL), varies in number of items presented. The 35–item version of the Hopkins symptom checklist (SCL) is one commonly used around the world. It includes many of the symptoms of distress outlined in Table 1.1 and consists of a listing of physical and psychological symptoms likely experienced in recent stressful times by respondents. Each symptom is scored by the respondent on a frequency scale from "not at all" to "extremely." The 35-item SCL generates a frequency-intensity outward sign score between 0 and 105. Outward sign scores of concern are considered to be above 16 (Goldberg et al., 1976).

To compare the effectiveness of the screening of the two self-report questionnaires and to investigate the effects of demographic variables on the screening characteristics of these inventories, Goldberg, Rickels, Downing, and Hesbacher (1976) completed a study using 244 patients in five general practitioners' offices. Patients who did not necessarily self-diagnose themselves as being "stressed" completed both the GHQ and the SCL while waiting in their physicians' offices. Fifty patients were then "randomly" asked if they were willing to be interviewed by another physician, who was actually a psychiatrist. At the study's conclusion, the researchers reported that both the GHQ and the SCL self-report scores correlated equally well with the psychiatrist's interview assessments of clients' "overall stress symptom severity." That is, correlation coefficients exceeded .70 for both the SCL and GHQ with the psychiatrist's assessed distress ratings. Moreover, both the SCL and the GHQ scores were positively and significantly correlated with the psychiatrist's interview assessments of clients' "anxiety" and "depression" signs. The correlation coefficients for the SCL and the GHQ with "anxiety at interview" were both .53. The correlation coefficients for the SCL and the GHQ with "depression at interview" were .62 and .67, respectively.

From a point of view of screening, Goldberg's research team then divided the clients by their GHQ and SCL inventory scores into: correctly identified stress cases and normals (i.e., true positives and true negatives), normals with high scores (i.e., false positives), and stress cases with low scores (false negatives). Using this method, these researchers found that the sensitivities (i.e., true positives × 100/cases) for the SCL and GHQ were a high 84% and 86%, respectively. They therefore concluded that:

1. The GHQ was slightly preferred as a screening test for psychological distress cases because it has fewer false positives (i.e., assesses an individual as a "stress case" when he or she is "normal") for females than the SCL has, and it includes items of outwardly observable behavior (which is an asset for physicians and laypersons). The GHQ's observed shortcoming is that it can miss assessing individuals with long-standing stress disorders.

2. The SCL also works well as a screening test for psychological distress cases because it tends not to miss long-standing stress disorders, the symptoms are readily identifiable by the self-reporters, and the SCL furnishes diagnostic subscales on a number of disorders that are not readily available with the GHQ, including depression ("feeling blue"), anxiety ("feeling nervousness or shakiness inside"), and anger ("having impulses to beat, injure, hurt someone"). The shortcoming of the SCL is that it tends to misclassify middle-users of the response scale, who play it safe by endorsing "a little" to many of the items and thus manage to accumulate a score in the morbid range (i.e., being in a diseased or abnormal state).

3. Both tests function better as psychological distress detection screens for men than for women and for white clients than for black clients in terms of misclassifications, but neither seems to be adversely affected by the social class or the age of the respondent.

Carl D'Arcy (1982) investigated the responses to the GHQ by 2,000+ adult Canadians to ascertain if Canadians respond in similar ways to Europeans and Americans on the GHQ inventory. His study conclusions were as follows:

1. Consistent with previous study findings on other adult populations, D'Arcy found that women had significantly higher GHQ scores than men.

2. For Canadian women as for other study populations, there were significant age variations; the scores were markedly higher for women in the 18–19 age group and fell drastically after age 29.

3. For Canadian men as for other study populations, there was a U-shaped distribution; the mean GHQ score was slightly elevated in the 18–19 age group, was in the "normal" range for ages 20–60, and became elevated in the 70+ age category.

4. Respondents in good general health, having fulfilling relationships with spouse/others and having an ability to remain "in control" were found to report low stress symptomology.

The respondent characteristics associated with low scores on the GHQ for D'Arcy's (1982) Canadian study group are summarized in Table 5.1.

D'Arcy's study found that depression and anxiety were the major patterns of distress most frequently cited by stressed Canadian adults. Thus, he concluded, stress-symptom screening inventories like the GHQ seem to work well across cultures for detecting individuals in the general population who are becoming "demoralized" by excessive stress levels.

Table 5.1
Respondent Characteristics Associated with Low Scores on the GHQ

Relationship With Spouse Can turn to spouse with problems; share interests; emotionally supportive; sexually compatible; intellectually compatible; similar views on family matters; similar social values; overall happiness with family life
Relationship With Others Seldom or never feel lonely; good relationships with neighbors; positive perception of the community of residence; good reputation of work place in the community; good relationships with co-workers; satisfactory interactions with people
Problem Solving and Personal Control Maintenance Able to maintain an internal locus of control; do not keep problems to oneself; do not go off by oneself to solve problems; do not drink alcohol to solve a problem
General Health State Good general health state; no long-term health problems; have not recently taken more than 3 days off from work; have not visited the hospital emergency room frequently in the past year; have not been hospitalized in the last 12 months
Use of Medicines Do not use pain relievers more than once a month; do not use skin ointment more than once a month; do not use sleeping pills; do not take tranquilizers; do not take other medicine more than once a month
Sociodemographics Over age 29 and under 70; male; married (not single, separated, or divorced); employed

Source: Adapted from D'Arcy, C. (1982). Prevalence and correlates of nonpsychotic psychiatric symptoms in the general population. *Canadian Journal of Psychiatry, 27,* 320–321.

PERSONAL FEEDBACK: HOW SEVERE ARE YOUR OUTWARD SIGNS OF DISTRESS?

Participants can now receive feedback on the severity of their outward signs of distress. *Please now score your responses to the symptom checklist (SCL) and the general health questionnaire (GHQ) inventories* (in Appendixes 5.1 and 5.2, respectively).

Considering your total score for Appendix 5.1, and given a "concern" score of 16, did your total SCL score fall below or above this point of concern? That is, in the past two weeks, have the frequency and intensity of your distress symptoms been in the "above-normal range"? Would your total score also apply to the last month, or over the past six months? Are there particular stressors that could be the likely cause of your presenting distress?

When you get stressed, do your outward signs of distress cluster on anxiety, depression, anger, or perfectionism, or on some combination of these four? High scores on the subscales indicate that professional assistance may be in order to help participants cope more effectively with particular stress cluster discomforts. High-concern marks for anxiety, depression, anger, and perfectionism would be 5, 5, 2, and 3, respectively. How many of your subscale clusters (i.e., anxiety, depression, anger, and perfectionism) approach or exceed a score of high concern?

Considering your total score for Appendix 5.2, and given a conservative concern score of 4, did your GHQ score fall below or above this point of concern? That is, in the past two weeks, has your routine deviated markedly from your own "norm" (be it healthy or not)? Would your total GHQ score also apply to the last month, or over the past six months? Are there particular stressors that could be the likely cause of your routine-disruption distress?

Participants should now be able to conclude:

• If their outward signs of distress and deviations from routine exceed the "healthy" and within-normal-range standards previously observed; and
• If their subscale patterns of distress on anxiety, depression, anger, or perfectionism exceed the "healthy" or within-normal-range standards.

Besides post-traumatic stress disorder—which is a relatively rare phenomenon (see Chapter 1)—anxiety, depression, and anger are the three outward-sign discomforts for which highly stressed individuals most often seek professional assistance from physicians and mental health experts. How experts define and treat each of these outward sign clusters will now be described.

HOW EXPERTS DEFINE AND TREAT ANXIETY

Anxiety Defined

Anxious individuals perceive considerable endangerment in their current life circumstances; thus, their anxiety is a response to these perceptions or misperceptions of reality. Anxiety may be defined as an unpleasant emotional experience varying in degree from mild unease to intense dread that is associated with the anticipation of impending or future disaster.

Recent research (Clark, 1989) suggests two different types of anxiety: recurrent "panic attacks" and "generalized anxiety disorder" (i.e., unrealistic or excessive worry). In recurrent panic attacks, which can occur unexpectedly and in almost any situation, individuals experience an intense feeling of apprehension or impending doom which is sudden and which is associated with a wide range of outward signs of distress: breathlessness, palpitations, chest pain, choking, dizziness, tingling in the hands and feet, hot and cold flashes, sweating, faintness, trembling, and feelings of unreality. The unexpected and highly distressing nature of these outward signs lead the sufferers to think that they are in danger of some physical or mental disaster such as fainting, a heart attack, losing control, or going insane. Whereas some sufferers experience calmness between the storms of panic, most sufferers remain chronically stressed between attacks because they ruminate about when the next attack will occur and where.

In generalized anxiety disorder, arising out of basic life circumstances, individuals suffer such wide-ranging outward signs of distress as muscle tension, twitching and shaking, restlessness, easy fatiguability, breathlessness, palpitations, sweating, dry mouth, dizziness, nausea, diarrhea, flushes or chills, frequent urination, difficulty swallowing, feeling "on edge," difficulty concentrating, insomnia (i.e., sleep disturbances), and irritability. Although thoughts associated with excessive worry and anxiety are varied, they generally involve an appraisal of not being able to cope, receiving negative evaluations from others at work or at home, performance fears at work or at home, and diffuse health state concerns.

Panic disorder often starts suddenly, with onsets commonly occurring in the mid- to late twenties. Generalized anxiety states generally begin in early teenhood, or later. For both anxiety disorders, stressful life events involving a threat of future "crisis" or "danger" are common around the time of anxiety onset. In mixed anxiety and depressive states, these stressful life events usually also involve some perceived element of loss (Clark, 1989).

The central notion in Lazarus's work and in cognitive models of emotional disorders is that it is not "objective" life events but "subjective" appraisals of these events—or cognitions—which produce negative emotions such as anxiety, depression, and anger. In anxiety, the important cognitions, as noted, center on perceived physical or psychosocial danger. Beck, Emery, and Greenberg (1985) maintain that in chronic anxiety states, individuals systematically overestimate the danger inherent in any given life situation. Such "overestimates" automatically activate the "anxiety program," which is a type of flight-or-fight response:

- There are changes in autonomic arousal as preparation for in which fleeing, fighting, or fainting (a form of escape from the threatening stimulus);
- There is inhibition of ongoing and aspiring behaviors; and
- There is selective scanning of the environment for possible sources of danger.

The kinds of stress-inducing cognitions that typically trigger generalized anxiety revolve around issues of acceptance (Beck, Emery, & Greenberg, 1985) (e.g., "I am nothing unless I am loved"), competence (e.g., "If I make a mistake, I will fail"), responsibility (e.g., "I am mainly responsible for the way my children turn out"), control (e.g., "I have to be in control all the time"), and the symptoms of anxiety themselves (e.g., "It is dangerous to show signs of anxiety at work"). Once an individual is in a state of anxiety, his or her attentional and behavioral changes further contribute to the maintenance of the anxiety problem. For example, an individual who is anxious about public speaking tends to "clue in" to audience members who yawn during his or her speech—which reinforces and adds further credibility to the individual's belief that he or she is a poor public speaker.

The kinds of stress-inducing cognitions that typically trigger panic anxiety revolve around issues of bodily sensations that are appraised as catastrophic (Clark, 1989). The sufferers generally misinterpret normal anxiety responses—breathlessness and dizziness—as indicative of an immediately impending physical or mental threat (e.g., "My feeling of breathlessness is evidence of my impending cessation of breathing and, of course, my consequent death!") This misinterpretation then triggers a state of intense apprehension, which triggers a scanning for similar "threatening" bodily sensations, which triggers interpretations of sensations of catastrophe, and so on, in an anxiety-escalating fashion.

Besides the SCL, which detects anxiety predispositions, the State-Trait Anxiety Inventory and the Self-Rating Anxiety Scale (SAS) are two widely used anxiety-detection measures (Spielberger, Gorusch, & Lushene, 1970; Zung, 1974).

Anxiety Treatments

Cognitive-Behavioral Therapy. Because anxiety is a cognition disorder coupled with "inappropriate" behavior, effective treatments for this disorder usually always include some form of cognitive-behavioral therapy (CBT). Briefly, cognitive behavior therapy aims to reduce anxiety by teaching individuals how to identify, evaluate, control, and modify their negative danger-related thoughts and associated behaviors. A variety of CBT techniques exist for treating generalized anxiety and panic attacks, with most CBT sessions requiring five to twenty weekly sessions (Clark, 1989).

The cognitive procedures used for generalized anxiety and panic attacks include identifying and challenging sufferers' evidence for their misperceptions of danger or catastrophe, substituting more realistic interpretations, and restructuring images. An illustration of the cognitive procedures used for "breaking" chronic panic attacks is presented below. In this example, the therapist (Th) is helping the client (Cl) challenge his erroneous belief that he will faint and collapse in a panic attack. This script was written by one of the world's leading experts on cognitive behavior therapy for panic attacks, Dr. David M. Clark from the University of Oxford.

Cl: In the middle of a panic attack, I usually think I am going to faint or collapse.

Th: How much do you believe that sitting here right now and how much would you believe it if you had the sensations you get in an attack?

Cl: 50% now and 90% in an attack.

Th: OK, let's look at the evidence you have for this thought. Have you ever fainted in an attack?

Cl: No.

Th: What is it then that makes you think you might faint?

Cl: I feel faint and the feeling can be very strong.

Th: So, to summarize, your evidence that you are going to faint is the fact that you feel faint?

Cl: Yes.

Th: How can you then account for the fact that you have felt faint many hundreds of times and have not yet fainted?

Cl: So far, the attacks have always stopped just in time or I have managed to hold onto something to stop myself from collapsing.

Th: Right, so one explanation of the fact that you have frequently felt faint, had the thought that you will faint, but have not actually fainted, is that you have always done something to save yourself in time. However, an alternative explanation is that the feeling of faintness that you get in a panic attack will never lead to you collapsing, even if you don't control it.

Cl: Yes, I suppose so.

Th: In order to decide which of these two possibilities is correct, we need to know what has to happen to your body for you to actually faint. Do you know?

Cl: No.

Th: Your blood pressure needs to drop. Do you know what happens to your blood pressure during a panic attack?

Cl: Well, my pulse is racing. I guess my blood pressure must be up.

Th: That's right. In anxiety, heart rate and blood pressure tend to go together. So, you are actually *less* likely to faint when you are anxious than when you are not.

Cl: That's very interesting and helpful to know. However, if it's true, why do I feel so faint?

Th: Your feeling of faintness is a sign that your body is reacting in a normal way to the perception of danger. Most of the bodily reactions you are experiencing when anxious were probably designed to deal with the threats experienced by primitive man, such as being approached by a hungry tiger. What would be the best thing to do in that situation?

Cl: Run away as fast as you can.

Th: That's right. Now, on the basis of what we've discussed so far, how much do you believe you might faint in a panic attack?

Cl: Less, say 10%.

Th: And if you were experiencing the sensations?

Cl: Maybe 25%. (Clark, 1989, pp. 76–77)

Typically, this sort of "cognitive" discussion is followed by behavioral assignments that are specifically designed to test the client's negative predictions. In this instance, the patient was encouraged to intentionally provoke feelings of dizziness by hyperventilating and by going into phobic situations; then he was not to do anything to control these anxious feelings—such as holding onto something or sitting down. In this way, he discovered that the dizziness that is characteristic of a panic attack does not lead to a collapse (Clark, 1989).

The usual behavioral procedures prescribed for overcoming panic attacks include inducing feared sensations by hyperventilation, reading pairs of words representing feared sensations/catastrophes, and focusing attention on the body to demonstrate to the client the "true" cause of panic symptoms. Other behavioral procedures for panic attacks include having the clients practice exposure to feared situations in order to allow them to disconfirm their negative predictions about the dire consequences of anxiety symptoms.

In trials conducted in five different centers and in four countries (England, Germany, Sweden, and the United States), on the average, 85% of the clients became panic-free after three months of CBT, and these gains were maintained at follow-ups lasting up to one year (Clark & Ehlers, 1993).

With generalized anxiety, similar cognitive reappraisal techniques are used. The particular behavioral experiment devised for the client depends on the specific beliefs that it is designed to test. These assignments can be one of the most effective ways of changing beliefs. The following behavioral experiment, again offered by Dr. Clark, was devised for a businessman who reportedly felt anxious when speaking in public:

He believed that his colleagues would see that he was anxious (belief = 65%) and, as a consequence, cease to respect him (belief = 40%). When asked what evidence he had for the idea that others could see he was anxious, it transpired that he believed that because he *felt* anxious, others must be able to see that he was anxious. As a test for this prediction, the therapist asked him to give a short speech while being videotaped. During the taping he felt very anxious. However, to his surprise, he was unable to detect any external signs of anxiety when subsequently viewing the video. This then reduced his belief that others could see he was anxious (30%). (1989, p. 82)

Relaxation Techniques. Relaxation can be an effective way for clients who are anxious to demonstrate to themselves that they can have control over their distress symptoms. Researchers have found that relaxation increases the accessibility of positive information in memory and, thus, makes it easier for clients to find alternatives to endangering thoughts. One of the simplest ways of achieving relaxation is by planning eustressful activities regularly and by planning breaks in busy routines. However, for severe anxiety, applied relaxation training, facilitated by a professional trainer, is typically advised. It is further advisable to demonstrate each of the stages in applied relaxation during a treatment session rather than just giving clients tapes of each set of relaxation exercises, for studies consistently indicate that audiotapes alone are rarely effective (Clark, 1989; Beck & Beamesderfer, 1974).

Before clients engage in applied relaxation training, they should understand the rationale behind it (Ost, 1987). When an individual becomes anxious, three different components to the stress reaction occur: a physiological component (i.e., increased heart rate, sweating, muscle tension), a cognitive component (i.e., negative thoughts), and a behavioral component (i.e., trying to escape). The relative strength of these components varies from person to person, but generally, individuals experience the physiological change, followed by the negative thought, which increases the physiological reaction. As anxiety builds very quickly, a technique is needed that can stop the cycle anywhere and quickly (say, in 20–30 seconds). This is the objective of applied relaxation training.

As it is easiest to control anxiety if the client starts to relax before anxiety reaches its peak, training starts with teaching the client the early stages of anxiety. The most often cited early signs of anxiety are increased heart rate and butterflies in the stomach. The six stages of Ost's applied relaxation training are briefly outlined in Table 5.2, with the expected time it should take a client to relax at each stage in the training program given in parentheses. In most of the controlled trials investigating its effectiveness, the applied relaxation training program has extended from eight to twelve sessions.

Alternative Treatments. Benzodiazepines, beta blockers, and tricyclic antidepressants are the most frequently used alternatives to CBT for treating anxiety. While the short-term use of benzodiazepines may be helpful for managing acute emotional crises, these drugs appear to be of little value in more persistent anxiety—and may even lead to dependency (Clark, 1989). Within recent years, imipramine had been administered as an effective antipanic agent, but controlled studies have shown that clients treated with imipramine are significantly more likely to relapse and require further treatment than those treated with CBT or CBT and relaxation training (Clark & Ehlers, 1993).

Besides drug therapy, sessions on time management are often found to be particularly useful for clients who are highly time-anxious. The princi-

Table 5.2
Ost's Stages of Applied Relaxation Training

STAGE ONE: PROGRESSIVE RELAXATION (15-20 MIN). Involves the progressive relaxation technique in which the body is divided into a series of large muscle groups, and each group is tensed and then relaxed. By alternating tension and relaxation, clients are taught to discriminate between these two stages and to become more aware of the parts of the body in which they are particularly tense. Clients sit in a comforable chair. The facilitator shows how the different groups of muscles should be tensed and relaxed. The client does the exercises; the facilitator checks to see that these are done correctly. Then the client closes his/her eyes and the facilitator takes him/her through tensing and releasing the different muscle groups in the right order and at the right tempo. Tension is normally maintained for about five seconds, with the subsequent relaxation of a muscle group lasting 10-15 seconds. Normally, each muscle group is tensed and relaxed only once. In the first session, relaxation of the hands, arms, face, neck, and shoulders is practiced. In the second session, the rest of the body is also included. Following each session, clients are asked to practice the progressive relaxation for approximately 15-20 minutes, twice a day. Clients should choose a place and time where they will be comfortable and unlikely to be interrupted.

STAGE TWO: RELEASE-ONLY (5-7 MIN). Involves a reduction in the time it takes to relax by omitting tension. A session starts with the client being asked to breathe calmly and to relax as much as possible while doing so. The facilitator then instructs him/her to relax each muscle group, starting at the top of the head and moving through the body to the tip of the toes. Homework involves practicing release-only relaxation twice a day, keeping a record of the time taken to relax and the amount of relaxation achieved. After 1-2 weeks of practice, most clients are ready to move onto the third stage.

STAGE THREE: CUE-CONTROLLED RELAXATION (2-3 MIN). Involves a further reduction in time to relax by focusing on breathing and establishing a form of conditioning between the self-instruction "relax" and increases in feelings of relaxation. The session starts with the client relaxing using release-only (i.e., without detailed instruction from the facilitator) and signalling when a satisfactory state of relaxation has been achieved. The facilitator then gives the following instructions, cued to the client's breathing pattern. Just before an inhalation, the facilitator says, "inhale," and just before an exhalation, the facilitator says, "relax." This sequence is repeated five times, and then the client is instructed to continue the sequence silently. Normally, cue-controlled relaxation is practiced twice in a session. As in the preceding stages, homework involves practicing this type of relaxation twice a day, recording the time taken to relax and the amount of relaxation achieved on each occasion. Normally, 1-2 weeks of practice is needed before proceeding onto the fourth stage.

STAGE FOUR: DIFFERENTIAL RELAXATION (60-90 SEC). Involves learning how to relax while engaged in everyday activities, not just sitting in an armchair. The first session starts with the client using cue-controlled relaxation to relax while sitting in an armchair. Then he/she is instructed to move body parts while at the same time concentrating on keeping the rest of the body relaxed by frequently scanning for signs of unnecessary tension, and relaxing as appropriate. Once the client has practiced these sessions while sitting in an armchair, the same movements are practiced while sitting at a desk (where practice in staying relaxed while writing or talking on the phone is included). In the second session, these exercises are extended to relaxing while standing and while walking. By the end, the time it takes clients to relax has usually reduced to 60-90 seconds. Homework involves practicing differential relaxation twice a day, with 1-2 weeks' practice being necessary before progressing to the next stage.

Table 5.2 (continued)

STAGE FIVE: RAPID RELAXATION (20-30 SEC). Involves further reduction in time to relaxation and to give clients extensive practice in relaxing in natural, non-stressful situations. The facilitator and client identify a series of cues which can be used to remind the client to relax in his or her "natural" environment. The client aims to relax 15-20 times a day in natural, non-stressful situations. When relaxing, he/she is instructed to:
(1) take 1-3 deep breaths, slowing exhaling after each breath;
(2) think "relax" before each exhalation;
(3) scan the body for tension and try to relax as much as possible in the situation.
Once clients have practiced rapid relaxation for 1-2 weeks and are able to relax in 20-30 seconds, the final stage of applied relaxation is introduced.

STAGE SIX: APPLICATION TRAINING AND MAINTENANCE. Involves practicing applying the relaxation skills in anxiety-provoking situations. Practice usually involves frequent but relatively brief (10-15 minutes) exposure to a wide range of anxiety-arousing situations. The aim of this exposure is to show clients that they can cope with any anxiety experienced, and eventually learn to control it. To promote control, the client is reminded that it is important to start relaxation as soon as the first sign of anxiety is perceived. Techniques such as hyperventilation, physical exercise, and imaging anxiety-arousing events can be used to produce anxiety both in treatment sessions and during homework practice. Clients are encouraged to develop the habit of scanning their body for tension at least once a day and to use rapid relaxation to remove it. Clients are encouraged to practice rapid relaxation once or twice a week in order to maintain relaxation skills over the longer term.

Source: Ost, L. G. (1987). Applied relaxation: Description of a coping technique and review of controlled studies. *Behaviour Research and Therapy, 25,* 397-410.

Table 5.3
Principles of Time Management

---

1. Review your GOALS. Decide what you want to get out of the day at work, the weekend, etc.

2. Make a LIST of the things you think you have to do and things you would like to do, with time estimates.

3. If tasks and activities exceed the time available, decide on PRIORITIES. What **must** be done today, what can wait, and until when? What do I **want** done today? Can I **delegate** anything? If I can, to whom? What will happen if I don't do X? If nothing, consider omitting X.

4. Select an ORDER or SEQUENCE for tasks to be done. Find the sort of sequence that suits you best. For example, some people find that the day is more pleasurable if they start with a task they must do and then follow it with a task they enjoy. In that way, they have something to look forward to and the unpleasant task doesn't play on their mind all day.

5. Try to do ONE TASK AT A TIME and try to FINISH what you start. Don't jump from one task to another leaving behind a stack of partially completed activities. In general, each task takes longer this way as you waste time getting repeatedly started on the same task, and uncompleted tasks remain on your mind, interfering with the present task.

6. Don't rush immediately from task to another. Instead, PAUSE. Plan brief BREAKS and times to relax; tea breaks, lunch breaks, times for yourself.

7. REVIEW priorities and progress midway through the day.

8. Look out for PROCRASTINATION. Are you putting it off because you're setting yourself too high a standard? Are you being realistic about what you could do? Could you do it now and get it out of the way?

9. At the end of the day, REMEMBER what you have achieved and GIVE YOURSELF CREDIT.

Source: Clark, D. M. (1989). Anxiety states: Panic and generalized anxiety. In K. Hawton, P. Salkovskis, J. Kirk, & D. M. Clark (Eds.), *Cognitive Behaviour Therapy for Psychiatric Problems: A Practical Guide.* Oxford: Oxford University Press, 73.

ples of time management advocated by Dr. David Clark (1989, p. 73) in his anxiety treatment sessions are outlined in Table 5.3.

PERSONAL FEEDBACK: ARE YOU AN "ANXIOUS" PERSON?

Participants have already received feedback from the SCL about whether they are predisposed to anxiety. Having heard more details on the topic of generalized anxiety and on panic attacks, participants are in a better position to reflect on their own conditioned patterns of thinking and behaving when they become highly stressed. Do you think that you become anxious "inappropriately" or "too frequently"? Following this reflection, participants should now be able to conclude:

• If they should seek further advice from a professional about anxiety management.

HOW EXPERTS DEFINE AND TREAT DEPRESSION

Depression Defined

As noted earlier, the central notion in cognitive models of emotional disorders is that it is not events, per se, but individuals' appraisals of events that are responsible for the production of anxiety, depression, and anger. In depression, the interpretations that are considered important relate to perceived loss of a relationship, status, or competence.

Depression is used in a number of ways, with three of them being the most prevalent. Depression can be used to describe an individual's mood, to describe a syndrome, or to describe an illness. As a mood, depression is part of the normal range of human experience, usually developing in response to some frustration or disappointment in life. The syndrome of depression consists of a depressive mood together with other outward signs of distress, like weight loss, inability to concentrate, and so on. The clinical depression illness involves the presence of the syndrome of depression and also implies that the state is not transitory and that it is associated with significant functional impairment. Individuals who are clinically depressed are often unable to work or are able to do so with significantly reduced efficiency.

It has often been claimed by experts that there are two distinct types of depression, one known as psychotic or endogenous depression (which includes the depressive phase of manic-depressive illness), and the other known as neurotic or reactive depression. Endogenous depressions are further subdivided by many into unipolar (recurrent depression) and bipolar (manic-depressive) types, each having distinctive genetic and gender differences. The evidence for this dichotomy is tenuous, but experts around the world often classify "cases" by it. Probably the best way to look at depression is via a continuum, with the typical psychotic stereotype at one pole, the typical neurotic stereotype at the other pole, and the majority of depression sufferers somewhere between the two.

Although reactive depression is often triggered by negative life events (by society's standards), it can also be triggered by positive life events (by society's standards), such as being told that one is getting a promotion or that one is pregnant. What is critical is not that a positive or a negative life event triggers illness but that the individual who owns the life event is feeling depressed. A major outward sign of depression is anhedonia, a markedly diminished interest in pleasurable life experiences, such as food, sex, hobbies, and leisure-time activities. Thus, while grief and other negative life events often complicate a diagnosis of depression because they trigger anhedonia, one big difference between the former and depression is that depression does not respond to common sense. A depressed person takes a vacation but does not feel better. A friend tries to cheer the depressed person, but he or she feels worse (O'Reilly, 1994).

Depressive illness is common around the world and ranks close behind coronary disease as one of the major causes of morbidity. Studies have shown that approximately twice as many women report being depressed as men, but this female preponderance is likely due to the high frequency of relatively mild reactive depressions occurring in women between the ages of 25 and 45. After the age of 60, there is little difference in depression rates cited for men and women.

Moreover, argue some researchers, the incidence of depression has been rising. Because of heightened stress levels, say some, people born since the 1940s are more likely to report a depression than those born earlier. Whether this is indeed the case or whether people are less inhibited about seeking assistance for mental illness nowadays remains debatable. At any rate, the figures speak for themselves: Depressive psychoses are said to currently account for 40% of all mental hospital admissions in the United Kingdom.

Contrary to popular belief, a tendency to depression is not a self-indulgence. Many researchers believe that it is a condition caused, in part, by an imbalance of chemicals in the brain. Clinical depression (i.e., that requiring medical intervention) is one of the diseases that Selye suggested is genetically dependent. That is, clinical depression seems to run in families; the parents, siblings, and children of a clinically depressed individual are at higher risk for chronic bouts of depression than are those having no relatives with the disease (O'Reilly, 1994).

Consequently, the biochemistry of depression has attracted increasing attention in recent years, although much of the research on the disorder has focused on the more severe forms. The clinical observation that endocrine disturbances of various kinds are often associated with chronic depression has led to a search for hormonal abnormalities. Thus, much research has found that severe depressions are accompanied by elevated blood cortisol levels, which seem to revert to normal levels once the depression is lifted. What continues to be a mystery in research circles is whether this increased cortisol production is etiologically important or whether it is simply a nonspecific stress response to affective arousal. Most researchers tend to favor the latter hypothesis over the former.

What should be clear by now is that, regardless of how they are labeled, depression bouts vary widely in their symptomology, in their course, and in their response to treatment. Common outward signs of depression include (Beck & Beamesderfer, 1974) depressed mood, pessimism, a sense of failure, a lack of satisfaction—life and job, feeling guilty, a sense of punishment, self-dislike, self-accusations, suicidal wishes, crying spells, irritability, social withdrawal, indecisiveness, inability to concentrate or make decisions, distortion of body image, work inhibition, sleep disturbance, fatigue, loss of appetite, weight loss, bodily symptom preoccupation, and a loss of sex drive.

Although a number of scales (besides the generalized SCL) exist for detecting depression, the Short Form of the Beck Depression Inventory, developed by Beck and Beamesderfer, has been specifically designed to determine individuals' depth of depression (Beck & Beamesderfer, 1974). A "moderate" or "severe score" classification on this Beck Inventory should prompt individuals to seek medical assistance immediately. Severe bouts of depression can last for six months.

Depression Treatments

Most of the major antidepressants on the drug market today have shown to be effective in alleviating depression, although sometimes individuals find greater relief from one drug than from another. Drugs commonly prescribed include such trade names as Prozac (by Eli Lilly), Paxil (by SmithKline Beecham), and Zoloft (by Pfizer). Comprehensive depression treatment programs generally combine drug therapy with psychotherapy. The U.S. Department of Health and Human Services reports that a typical trial on medication for mild to moderate cases of depression lasts four to six weeks; psychotherapy usually lasts from six to eight weeks (O'Reilly, 1994).

For the client who thinks he or she may be depressed, the sooner he or she gets professional assistance, the better. As Winston Churchill, a well-known sufferer of depression, once remarked, "If the black dog [of depression] starts biting you, don't ignore it." Like any disease, depression is harder to treat the more severe it gets. Severe cases generally require much more intensive psychotherapy and drug treatment than mild to moderate cases. Sometimes the modern version of electroconvulsive therapy—which is safe for most severely depressed patients and usually effective—is prescribed.

PERSONAL FEEDBACK: HOW SEVERE ARE YOUR "DOWN" MOODS?

Participants can now receive feedback on the severity of their outward signs of depression. *Please now score your responses to the short form of the Beck Depression ("down moods") Inventory* (in Appendix 5.3).

Considering your total score for Appendix 5.3, and given "high concern" for scores 8 and above (i.e., in the moderate and high depression range), does your depression score indicate that you may have a need for professional assistance?

Participants should now be able to conclude:

• If they should seek professional advice for possible depression.

HOW EXPERTS DEFINE AND TREAT ANGER

Anger Defined

Anger is the third emotional disorder that is cognitively based. Like depression, which entails a perceptual loss over one's personal domain, anger entails a perceptual loss of control over one's "personal rules."

The outward signs of anger are varied, and can be retained (called "anger in") or projected outwardly (called "anger out"). Anger experts Buss and Durkee (1957) have outlined the following seven subclasses of anger and hostility:

1. Assault: presents as physical violence against others. This outward sign of anger includes getting into fights with others but not destroying objects.
2. Indirect Hostility: presents as both roundabout and undirected aggression. Roundabout aggression, like malicious gossip or practical jokes, is indirect in the sense that the "hated object" is not attacked directly but by devious means. Undirected aggression, like temper tantrums and door-slamming, consists of a discharge of negative affect against no one in particular; it is a diffuse kind of rage that has no target or direction.
3. Irritability: presents as a readiness to explode with negative affect at the slightest provocation. This kind of aggression includes quick temper, grouchiness, exasperation, and rudeness.
4. Negativism: presents as oppositional behavior, usually directed against authority. This kind of aggression involves a refusal to cooperate that may vary from passive noncompliance to open rebellion against rules or conventions.
5. Resentment: presents as jealousy and hatred of others. This kind of aggression refers to a feeling of anger at the world over real or fantasized "mistreatment."
6. Suspicion: presents as projection of hostility onto others. This kind of aggression varies from merely being distrustful and wary of people to beliefs that others are being derogatory or are planning harm against them.
7. Verbal Hostility: presents as negative affect expressed in both the style and content of speech. Style includes arguing, shouting, and screaming. Content includes threats, curses, and being overcritical.

Laboratory findings have shown that chronically angry individuals secrete large quantities of noradrenaline. They seem to be in a chronic state of fight-or-flight, with an emphasis on fight. Noradrenaline (or norepinephrine) is thought to be the main substance released when a person has (or believes he or she has) the effective response for meeting an arousal-inducing situation; the "appropriate" behavior chosen is often fighting. Release of adrenaline (or epinephrine), on the other hand, is thought to be a physiological response to arousal-inducing situations characterized more by an appraised lack of effective responses for meeting the situation; the "appropriate" behavior thus chosen is often flight. Research studies have found noradrenaline release to be more closely associated with "fight" predispositions in individuals, and adrenaline release to be more closely associated with "flight" predispositions.

Moreover, noradrenaline has been found to be produced in large amounts in individuals predisposed to irritation, regardless of the nature of the stressor provoking the irritation. Laboratory studies in recent years have consistently shown that excessive amounts of noradrenaline promote the development of coronary heart disease (known as "CHD") in individuals angrily conditioned. Although there is no definitive answer to the exact course of psychophysiological destruction, excessive amounts of noradrenaline are thought to promote endothelial lesions (i.e., lesions in the lining of the coronary arteries), thus initiating or prematurely hastening the atherosclerotic process (i.e., aging of the arteries). Extremely high levels of circulating catecholamines in the bloodstream, especially noradrenaline, may also produce a direct chemical insult to the heart, predisposing the angry individual to ventricular fibrillation and sudden death. Because noradrenaline causes an increase in the heart rate and cardiac output in preparation for increased physical activity, the heart requires more oxygen to sustain its increased load. Greater oxygen consumption by the heart under "constant" arousal conditions may explain, in part, why chronically angry individuals commonly complain about angina (i.e., chest pain) when they are under stress (Price, 1982).

There are a number of anger and hostility scales available on the market for helping individuals to ascertain if they have an anger problem. One of the most widely used inventories for discovering what individuals do when they are angry is the Buss and Durkee (1957) Hostility Inventory, and one of the most widely used inventories for discovering what provokes anger in individuals is Raymond Novaco's (1975) 90–item Anger Inventory.

Anger Treatments

Because of the potential for self- and other-destruction, high levels of anger need to be managed. In his book *Anger Control*, Raymond W. Novaco, one of the world's leading anger-management experts, recommends a multi-dimensional treatment program for anger management, including CBT, role play provocations, and relaxation therapy.

Novaco (1975) stresses the importance of "cognitive rehabilitation." He says that cognitions about anger provocations have an important role in fomenting, maintaining, escalating, and reinstating the anger process. The results of his research on anger have shown that cognitive control procedures can be effectively used to regulate anger arousal (i.e., provocation). The cognitive control skills that he teaches to clients who are easily provoked include:

- Becoming self-aware about one's own anger provocation stimuli and actively preparing for a provocation by saying to oneself, "I can manage this situation. I know how to regulate my anger."

- Learning how to alternately construe provocations to mitigate the sense of personal threat and reminding oneself to stay positive by saying to oneself, "As long as I keep my cool, I'm in control here. I'm not going to let him (or her) get to me. For a person to be that irritable, he (or she) must be awfully unhappy."

- Instructing oneself to attend to the task dimensions of a provocative situation as a form of actively coping with one's arousal and agitation by saying to oneself, "My muscles are starting to feel tight. Time to relax and slow things down. My anger is a signal of what I need to do. Time to talk to myself. He'd (she'd) probably like me to get really angry. Well, I'm going to disappoint him (her)."

- Rewarding oneself for taking control of a provocative situation by saying to oneself, "It worked! That wasn't as hard as I thought. I guess I've been getting upset for too long when it wasn't even necessary."

Through the effective use of cognitive control and self-talk (as evidenced by the preceding quotes), chronically angry individuals can learn to influence their appraisals of provocation. Having angry individuals discover that there are alternative ways of perceiving and responding to provocations other than those previously conditioned plays a major role in the development of competence in anger management.

Although cognitive reappraisal is critical in managing anger, relaxation therapy (like that outlined in Table 5.2) is important too. Relaxation techniques enable angry individuals to become aware of early signs of tension and agitation. Moreover, relaxation training provides anger-prone individuals with a means of modifying their tension states and reinstating a feeling of mastery over troublesome internal states. With relaxation training, formerly angry individuals learn that they can self-induce relaxation at any time and at any place. This message to the brain is very important because it develops a "new" cognition that the individual is able to control his or her arousal state and not be controlled by it.

PERSONAL FEEDBACK: ARE YOU AN "ANGRY" PERSON?

Participants can now receive feedback on the severity of their outward signs of anger. Please refer to the seven types of anger detailed by experts Buss and Durkee (1957). Within the past month, how often did you find yourself displaying these types of aggression? Would you say that you are conditioned to easy anger provocation, or do you think that you have good anger control? Participants should now be able to conclude:

- If they should seek further advice from a professional about anger management.

CONCLUSION

This session on outward signs of distress was meant to be feedback-oriented and reflective in nature. Participants now have information on their generalized stress responses, given their scores on the SCL and the GHQ. Participants also have feedback and information on the three distress patterns most commonly seen by stress counselors: anxiety, depression, and anger. Perhaps at this stage, participants are in a better position to determine if they need further professional advice on more effective "symptom" management in one or more of these problem areas.

STRESS-COPING SUMMARY POINTS

1. To assess whether they are coping well with stressors, individuals need to regularly monitor their outward signs of distress. The SCL and GHQ serve as useful inventories for providing feedback in this regard.

2. To assess whether they have a particular "stress-coping" problem area, individuals should further reflect on their predispositions for getting unnecessarily anxious, depressed, or angry in high-stress situations. If individuals perceive that their cognitive and behavioral predispositions for stress-coping are uncomfortable or ineffective, they should seek professional assistance on more effective stress-coping.

Appendix 5.1
A Measurement of Your Recent Outward Signs of Distress

Instructions: Over the past two weeks, how often and how intensely have you experienced the following 58 symptoms? For each item, please use this scale:

0 Not at all   1 A Little   2 Quite a bit   3 Extremely

1. Nervousness or shakiness inside

2. Loss of sexual interest or pleasure

3. Feeling critical of others

4. Worried about carelessness or sloppiness

5. Faintness or dizziness

6. Feeling low in energy or slowed down

7. Feeling easily annoyed or irritated

8. Having to do things very slowly to insure correctness

9. Sweating

10. Thoughts of ending your life

11. Temper outbursts you could not control

12. Having to repeat actions (e.g., counting, touching, etc.)

13. Trembling

Appendix 5.1 (continued)

14.	Poor appetite
15.	Having impulses to beat, injure, hurt someone
16.	Having to check and double check what is done
17.	Suddenly scared for no reason
18.	Crying easily
19.	Having to avoid certain things, places, activities because they frighten you
20.	Feeling fearful
21.	Constipation
22.	Heart pounding or racing
23.	Blaming yourself for things
24.	Trouble getting your breath
25.	Feeling lonely
26.	Hot or cold spells
27.	Feeling blue
28.	Lump in your throat
29.	Feeling no interest in things

30. Feeling tense or keyed up
31. Feeling hopeless about the future
32. Headaches
33. Having bad dreams
34. Having trouble remembering things
35. Having difficulty in speaking when you are excited

Source: Derogatis, L. R., Lipman, R. S., Covi, L., Rickels, K., & Uhlenhuth, E. H. (1970). Dimensions of outpatient neurotic pathology: Comparison of a clinical versus an empirical assessment. *Journal of Consulting and Clinical Psychology, 34,* 164–171; Derogatis, L. R., Lipman, R. S., Covi, L., Rickels, K., & Uhlenhuth, E. H. (1974). The Hopkins Symptom Checklist (HSCL): A self-report symptom inventory. *Behavioral Science, 19,* 1–15.

Appendix 5.2
A Measurement of Your Recent Routine

Instructions: Think about how you have been feeling in the past two weeks and compare it with how you normally feel. Please place an X in the appropriate column response for each of the following 30 questions.

1. Have you recently felt that you are constantly under strain?	Not at all	Same as usual	Rather more than usual	Much more than usual
2. Have you recently felt that you think of yourself as a worthless person?	Not at all	Same as usual	Rather more than usual	Much more than usual
3. Have you recently felt that you are able to concentrate on whatever you're doing?	Better than usual	Same as usual	Less than usual	Much less than usual
4. Have you recently felt that you are able to show warmth and affection for others?	Better than usual	Same as usual	Less than usual	Much less than usual
5. Have you recently felt that you are losing sleep because of worry?	Not at all	Same as usual	Rather more than usual	Much more than usual
6. Have you recently felt that life is not worth living?	Not at all	Same as usual	Rather more than usual	Much more than usual
7. Have you recently felt nervous and "hung up"?	Not at all	Same as usual	Rather more than usual	Much more than usual
8. Have you recently felt that you have no energy?	Not at all	Same as usual	Rather more than usual	Much more than usual
9. Have you recently felt that you are managing as well as most people?	Better than usual	Same as usual	Less than usual	Much less than usual
10. Have you recently felt that you are losing confidence?	Not at all	Same as usual	Rather more than usual	Much more than usual

11. Have you recently felt that you are experiencing restless, disturbed nights?	Not at all	Same as usual	Rather more than usual	Much more than usual
12. Have you recently felt that you are able to keep busy and occupied?	Better than usual	Same as usual	Less than usual	Much less than usual
13. Have you recently felt that you are depressed and unhappy?	Not at all	Same as usual	Rather more than usual	Much more than usual
14. Have you recently felt scared or panicky?	Not at all	Same as usual	Rather more than usual	Much more than usual
15. Have you recently felt that life is a struggle?	Not at all	Same as usual	Rather more than usual	Much more than usual
16. Have you recently felt that you are able to get out of the house?	Better than usual	Same as usual	Less than usual	Much less than usual
17. Have you recently felt that you taking things "too hard"?	Not at all	Same as usual	Rather more than usual	Much more than usual
18. Have you recently felt that you are capable of making decisions?	Better than usual	Same as usual	Less than usual	Much less than usual
19. Have you recently felt that you cannot overcome difficulties?	Not at all	Same as usual	Rather more than usual	Much more than usual
20. Have you recently felt that you are not doing things well?	Not at all	Same as usual	Rather more than usual	Much more than usual

21. Have you recently felt that you are not hopeful about your future?	Not at all	Same as usual	Rather more than usual	Much more than usual
22. Have you recently felt that your nerves are too bad to do anything?	Not at all	Same as usual	Rather more than usual	Much more than usual
23. Have you recently felt that you play a useful part in things?	Better than usual	Same as usual	Less than usual	Much less than usual
24. Have you recently felt that you are reasonably happy?	Better than usual	Same as usual	Less than usual	Much less than usual
25. Have you recently felt that your life is entirely hopeless?	Not at all	Same as usual	Rather more than usual	Much more than usual
26. Have you recently felt that everything is "too much"?	Not at all	Same as usual	Rather more than usual	Much more than usual
27. Have you recently felt that you cannot stay alert and awake?	Not at all	Same as usual	Rather more than usual	Much more than usual
28. Have you recently felt that you are not easily getting along with others?	Not at all	Same as usual	Rather more than usual	Much more than usual
29. Have you recently felt that you can continue to enjoy normal daily activities?	Better than usual	Same as usual	Less than usual	Much less than usual
30. Have you recently felt that you are not facing your problems?	Not at all	Same as usual	Rather more than usual	Much more than usual

Source: D'Arcy, C. (1982). Prevalence and correlates of nonpsychotic psychiatric symptoms in the general population. *Canadian Journal of Psychiatry*, 27, 316–324; Goldberg, D. P. (1972). *The Detection of Psychiatric Illness by Questionnaire*. London: Oxford University Press.

Appendix 5.3
A Measurement of Your Recent "Down Moods"

Instructions: Please read the entire group of statements in each group.
Then select the one statement which best describes the way you feel today; that is, right now! Circle the number beside the statement you have chosen. If several statements apply equally, circle each one.

1. 0   I do not feel sad; 1   I feel sad or blue; 2   I am blue or sad all the time and I can't snap out of it; 3   I am so sad or unhappy that I can't stand it

2. 0   I am not particularly pessimistic or discouraged about the future; 1 I feel discouraged about the future; 2   I feel I have nothing to look forward to; 3   I feel that the future is hopeless and that things cannot improve

3. 0   I do not feel like a failure; 1   I feel I have failed more than the average person; 2   As I look back on life, all I can see is a lot of failures; 3   I feel I am a complete failure as a person (parent, husband, wife)

4. 0   I am not particularly dissatisfied; 1   I don't enjoy things the way I used to; 2   I don't get satisfaction out of anything anymore; 3   I am dissatisfied with everything

5. 0   I don't feel particularly guilty; 1   I feel bad or unworthy a good part of the time; 2   I feel quite guilty; 3   I feel as though I am very bad or worthless

6. 0   I don't feel disappointed in myself; 1   I am disappointed in myself; 2   I am disgusted with myself; 3   I hate myself

163

Appendix 5.3 (continued)

7. 0 I don't have any thoughts of harming myself; 1 I feel I would be better off dead; 2 I have definite plans about committing suicide; 3 I would kill myself if I had the chance

8. 0 I have not lost interest in other people; 1 I am less interested in other people than I used to be; 2 I have lost most of my interest in other people and have little feeling for them; 3 I have lost all interest in other people and don't care about them at all

9. 0 I make decisions about as well as ever; 1 I try to put off making decisions; 2 I have great difficulty in making decisions; 3 I can't make any decisions any more

10. 0 I don't feel I look any worse than I used to; 1 I am worried that I am looking old or unattractive; 2 I feel that there are permanent changes in my appearance and they make me look unattractive; 3 I feel that I am ugly or repulsive looking

11. 0 I can work about as well as before; 1 It takes extra effort to get started at doing something; 2 I have to push myself very hard to do anything; 3 I can't do any work at all

12. 0 I don't get any more tired than usual; 1 I get tired more easily than I used to; 2 I get tired from doing anything; 3 I get too tired to do anything

13. 0 My appetite is no worse than usual; 1 My appetite is not as good as it used to be; 2 My appetite is much worse now; 3 I have no appetite at all any more

Source: Beck, A. T., & Beamesderfer, A. (1974). Assessment of depression: The depression inventory. Psychological measurements in psychopharmacology, *Modern Problems in Pharmacopsychiatry*, 7, 151–169.

Scoring Appendix 5.1 and Appendix 5.2

Scoring Appendix 5.1:	Scoring Appendix 5.2:
1. Total your points on all 35 symptoms of Appendix 5.1. The range is from 0-105. What was your total? Mark it here: _____ 2. How "anxious" are you? If you answered "2" or "3" for the following items, circle the item number: 1 5 9 13 17 20 22 24 26 28 30 Of a possible total of 11 circles, how many did you get on "anxiety"? Mark it here: _____ 3. How "depressed" are you? If you answered "2" or "3" for the following items, circle the item number: 2 6 10 14 18 21 23 25 27 29 31 Of a possible total of 11 circles, how many did you get on "depression"? Mark it here: _____ 4. How "angry" are you? If you answered "2" or "3" for the following items, circle the item number: 3 7 11 15 Of a possible total of 4 circles, how many did you get on "anger"? Mark it here: _____ 5. How "perfectionistic" are you? If you answered "2" or "3" for the following items, circle the item number: 4 8 12 16 19 34 Of a possible total of 6 circles, how many did you get on "perfectionistic"? Mark it here: _____	For the 30 questions asked, total the number of Xs that you marked in "column three" or in "column four." Of a possible total of 30, how many did you have in these columns? Mark it here: _____

Source: Goldberg, D. P., Rickels, K., Downing, R., & Hesbacher, P. (1976). A comparison of two psychiatric screening tests. *British Journal of Psychiatry, 129,* 61–67; Derogatis, L. R., Lipman, R. S., Covi, L., Rickels, K., & Uhlenhuth, E. H. (1970). Dimensions of outpatient neurotic pathology: Comparison of a clinical versus an empirical assessment. *Journal of Consulting and Clinical Psychology, 34,* 164–171.

Scoring Appendix 5.3

Total your points for the circled items in Appendix 5.3. If your total score is:	
0-4	You are showing no signs or minimal signs of depression
4-7	You are showing mild signs of depression
8-15	You are showing moderate signs of depression
16+	You are showing severe signs of depression

Source: Beck, A. T., & Beamesderfer, A. (1974). Assessment of depression: The depression inventory. Psychological measurements in psychopharmacology. *Modern Problems in Pharmacopsychiaty, 7,* 151–169.

REFERENCES

Beck, A. T., & Beamesderfer, A. (1974). Assessment of depression: The depression inventory. Psychological measurements in psychopharmacology. *Modern Problems in Pharmacopsychiatry*, 7, 151–169.

Beck, A. T., Emery, G., & Greenberg, R. L. (1985). *Anxiety Disorders and Phobias*. New York: Basic Books.

Buss, A. H., & Durkee, A. (1957). An inventory for assessing different kinds of hostility. *Journal of Consulting Psychology*, 21, 343–348.

Cannon, W. G. (1929). *Bodily Changes in Pain, Hunger, Fear and Rage: An Account of Recent Researches into the Function of Emotional Excitement* (2nd ed.). New York: Appleton.

Chen, P. Y., & Spector, P. E. (1992). Relationships of work stressors with aggression, withdrawal, theft and substance use: An exploratory study. *Journal of Occupational and Organizational Psychology*, 65, 177–184.

Clark, D. M. (1989). Anxiety states: Panic and generalized anxiety. In K. Hawton, P. Salkovskis, J. Kirk, & D. M. Clark (Eds.), *Cognitive Behavior Therapy for Psychiatric Problems: A Practical Guide*. Oxford: Oxford University Press, 53–96.

Clark, D. M., & Ehlers, A. (1993). An overview of the cognitive theory and treatment of panic disorder. *Applied and Preventive Psychology*, 2, 131–139.

Cohen, S., & Hoberman, H. M. (1983). Positive events and social supports as buffers of life change stress. *Journal of Applied Social Psychology*, 13, 99–125.

Cooper, C. L. (1986). Job distress: Recent research and the emerging role of the clinical occupational psychologist. *Bulletin of the British Psychological Society*, 39, 325–333.

Corley, K. C., Mauck, H. P., and Shiel, F. O'M. (1975). Cardiac responses associated with "yoked chair" shock avoidance in squirrel monkeys. *Psychophysiology*, 12, 439–444.

D'Arcy, C. (1982). Prevalence and correlates of nonpsychotic psychiatric symptoms in the general population. *Canadian Journal of Psychiatry*, 27, 316–324.

Derogatis, L. R., Lipman, R. S., Covi, L., Rickels, K., & Uhlenhuth, E. H. (1970). Dimensions in outpatient neurotic pathology: Comparison of a clinical versus an empirical assessment. *Journal of Consulting and Clinical Psychology*, 34, 164–171.

Derogatis, L. R., Lipman, R. S., Covi, L., Rickels, K., & Uhlenhuth, E. H. (1974). The Hopkins Symptom Checklist (HSCL): A self-report symptom inventory. *Behavioral Science*, 19, 1–15.

Derogatis, L. R., Rickels, K., Uhlenhuth, E. H., & Covi, L. (1974). The Hopkins Symptom Checklist (HSCL): A measure of primary symptom dimensions. Psychological measurements in psychopharmacology. *Modern Problems in Pharmacopsychiatry*, 7, 79–110.

Dohrenwend, B. P., Dohrenwend, B. S., Gould, M. S., Link, B., Neugebauer, R., and Wunsch-Hitzig, R. (1980). *Mental Illness in the United States: Epidemiological Estimates*. New York: Praeger.

Frankenhauser, M. (1980). Psychoneuroendocrine approaches to the study of stressful person-environment transactions. In H. Selye (Ed.), *Selye's Guide to Stress Research*. New York: Van Nostrand Reinhold, 46–70.

Friedman, A. S., Granick, S., Utada, A., & Tomko, L. A. (1992). Drug use/abuse and supermarket workers' job performance. *Employee Assistance Quarterly*, 7, 17–34.

Goldberg, D. P. (1972). *The Detection of Psychiatric Illness by Questionnaire*. London: Oxford University Press.

Goldberg, D. P., Cooper, B., Eastwood, M. R., Kedward, H. B., & Shepherd, M. (1970). A standardized psychiatric interview suitable for use in community surveys. *British Journal of Preventive Social Medicine*, 24, 18.

Goldberg, D. P., Rickels, K., Downing, R., & Hesbacher, P. (1976). A comparison of two psychiatric screening tests. *British Journal of Psychiatry*, 129, 61–67.

Henry, J. P., & Stevens, P. M. (1977). *Stress, Health, and the Social Environment: A Sociobiologic Approach to Medicine*. New York: Springer-Verlag.

Kirkcaldy, B. D., & Shephard, R. J. (1990). Therapeutic implications of exercise. *International Journal of Sport Psychology*, 21, 165–184.

Klerman. (1972). As quoted in D. Brand, Beyond the Blues, *Wall Street Journal*, April 7, p. 1.

Lazarus, R. S. (1976). *Patterns of Adjustment*. New York: McGraw-Hill.

Lehmann, H. E. (1972). Epidemiology of Depressive Disorders. In *FIE VE Depression in the 70's*. Amsterdam: Excerpta Medica.

Novaco, R. W. (1975). *Anger Control: The Development and Evaluation of an Experimental Treatment*. Lexington, MA: Lexington Books.

O'Reilly, B. (1994). Depressed? Here's help. *Reader's Digest*, 144, May 11–16.

Ost, L. G. (1987). Applied relaxation: Description of a coping technique and review of controlled studies. *Behavior Research and Therapy*, 25, 397–410.

Price, V. A. (1982). *Type A Behavior: A Model for Research and Practice*. New York: Academic Press.

Selye, H. (1950). *The Physiology and Pathology of Exposure to Stress*. Montreal: Acta.

Selye, H. (1974). *Stress Without Distress*. Philadelphia: Lippincott.

Selye, H. (1983). The stress concept: Past, present, future. In C. L. Cooper (Ed.), *Stress Research*. Chichester: Wiley, 1–20.

Spector, P. E. (1975). Relationships of organizational frustration with reported behavioral reactions of employers. *Journal of Applied Psychology*, 60, 635–637.

Spector, P. E. (1978). Organizational frustration: A model and review of the literature. *Personnel Psychology*, 31, 815–829.

Spielberger, C. D., Gorusch, R. L., & Lushene, R. E. (1970). *The State-Trait Anxiety Inventory*. Palo Alto, CA: Consulting Psychologists Press.

Statistics Canada, Canadian Centre for Health Information. (1987). Causes of death, 1987. *Health Reports*, 1, 7, 100–105.

Statistics Canada, Canadian Centre for Health Information. (1993). Hospital morbidity: 1991–1992. *Health Reports*, 5, 1, 355–360.

U.S. National Center for Health Statistics. (1987). Advance report of final mortality statistics. *1985 Monthly Vital Statistics Report*.

Zung, W. K. (1974). The measurement of affects: Depression and anxiety. Psychological measurements in psychopharmacology. *Modern Problems in Pharmacopsychiatry*, 7, 170–188.

Chapter 6

Assessing the Organization's Outward Signs of Distress

A CASE IN POINT

William Bartell, Human Resource Manager for Wyler Industries Limited, understood the frustration that some of the managers in the Stress-Empowerment sessions were having. Although most managers within the organization committed themselves to visibly "walk" and "talk" stress-empowerment on a day-to-day basis, there was nothing, they argued, to guarantee equal commitment to the program by individual organizational members and their labor representatives. In his second session on Outward signs of distress, William decided to confront this critical macrosystem C-O-P-E-ing issue—one that could cause the minimalization or failure of the stress management program.

THE OPENING ADDRESS: THE IMPORTANCE OF JOINT COMMITMENT TO STRESS EMPOWERMENT PROGRAMS

William began his second session on outward signs of distress:

In talking through the case of Warren Potts earlier on, we managers at Wyler Industries began to empathize with the frustrations and anger of stressed-out organizational members who receive little or no understanding from their supervisors and coworkers when they admit to, or are overtly manifesting, a high-stress state. Despite our wanting to turn an empathetic lease on organizational life by "walking" and "talking" stress-empowerment, some of you admitted in earlier sessions that even though Wyler's health-promotion program is still in its infancy stage, resistance to the notion is already being shown by some organizational members. As I was preparing for this C-O-P-E-ing session, I read an interesting organizational-stress case on an assembly plant in the United States, called ABC Machinery (Ames & Delaney, 1992). Because the problems at ABC Machinery are pertinent to the content of our session today—outward signs of organizational distress and multiparty commitment to reducing stress in the workplace, I'd like to share it with you.

Briefly, ABC Machinery is a diversified corporation and is one of the largest U.S. private employers. The work site of interest to us is a relatively new machinery fabrication plant in a metropolitan area. Almost 5,500 organizational members are employed at this work site. About 90% of these members are paid on an hourly basis and work on an assembly line, while the remaining 10% or so are in salaried positions. The assembly-line members are organized into groups supervised by a foreman. These members are represented by a local branch of a large union, and whenever disciplinary problems arise, a union steward is usually called in to handle the problem. For example, if substance-abuse discipline is invoked by a foreman, the organizational member accused of the infraction will almost always request representation from a steward for consultation or grievance action. Of importance to this case is the fact that both union and management at ABC Machinery are said to be committed to the organization's Employee Assistance Program (EAP), a service which provides professional assistance and rehabilitation to organizational members who have "problems" interfering with productivity (i.e., substance abuse, family problems, and lack of anger control). The stress case of Carla, a first-shift supervisor at ABC Machinery, follows:

Carla's shift begins with the department manager's meeting with all foremen and the general foremen. Each day every problem, large and small, related to employee incidents, quality of work, or line slowdowns is aired and the foreman responsible for the area where it occurred is brought to task. Warnings are given; the air is tense and responsibility for mistakes is passed back and forth among foremen in adjacent line areas. Errors are treated as serious at this meeting; every minute that the line is stopped, thousands of dollars are lost. Explanations for slowdowns such as high absenteeism, inexperienced substitutes, a mechanical failure, or a breakdown in materials transportation system are not well taken. According to Carla, "Fix it fast or perish" is clearly the unspoken demand given to foremen by the department manager at these meetings. The manager in charge gets the same message from higher management. Although there is a no-smoking sign in the conference room, over 50% of the foremen, including Carla, chain-smoke throughout the meeting.

Back on the line again. This day presents Carla with many problems, some of them near-crisis; the line could stop if she doesn't handle them quickly. Today a new model of a machine is coming down the line; it will involve different parts and different tasks. She has only a few minutes to instruct the workers before the shift start-up whistle starts the line moving. To make matters worse, she has counted seven absentees, and substitutes must quickly be transferred in from the substitute pool. She says she knows some of them are inexperienced for the tasks at hand and will have problems adapting to the demands of the day. Within hours the department manager is yelling at Carla on the hotline phone, blaming her area for installing wrong parts into some of the new models, resulting in problems down the line. Carla frantically runs the length of her line segment to get to the source of the problem, only to find that the materials department delivered the wrong parts. Although Carla had been accused of incompetence in the heat of the crisis, no apologies were forthcoming from higher-up managers. Carla lights another cigarette and says, "No one ever apologizes to a foreman."

Perhaps in reaction to her frenetic demands for help in finding the error, or maybe out of habit, one line worker starts shouting at Carla and bangs a steel table with a piece of pipe, disrupting the line routine. Carla says that he is a known troublemaker and a heavy drinker who regularly shows signs of drinking on the job. Normally she ignores his behavior, and takes no formal action, knowing that his removal will bring yet another inexperienced substitute. On this day, she later explains, it has gone too far and she decides to remove him from the line. She felt an example of intolerance for this kind of behavior must be set now, early in her tenure as foreman with this group. "If I don't do something now, more will test me later on."

As is procedure, when disciplinary action is taken, the union steward for the area is immediately summoned by Carla. Over the intense disapproval of the steward, she takes formal action that dismissed the worker for balance of shift for that day with loss of wages. Immediately following the incident, the steward filed a grievance for the worker against Carla's action and then organized the entire work group to file a formal group grievance against her.

Carla [tells the researcher that she] fully expects the grievance procedure to rule in favor of the worker; that is, it will be dismissed and his wages will be reinstated. She says that she knows from past experience that "some kind of a deal will be struck" between her department manager and the steward; a pending safety or housekeeping grievance will be "forgiven" in return for clearing the employee's record. Most likely, she says, the employee will be diverted to a treatment program—with pay—through the EAP. The group grievance filed against Carla, another matter altogether, may involve her in a stressful encounter with her department manager and the steward. (Ames & Delaney, 1992, pp. 183–184)

What this case illustrates quite readily is that Carla and her coworkers are manifesting outward signs of distress. Ineffective stress-coping is evident: cigarette smoking is pronounced (despite company policy), drinking alcohol on the job is "tolerated" to some degree by union representatives and supervisors alike, hostility and aggression are openly vented, and blatant disregard for workers' and supervisors' psychological and physiological well-being present. What's more, it seems that a number of factions within ABC Machinery are responsible for the "stress mess" that they find themselves in. Which factions are contributing to the organization's outward signs of distress and why are the important issues to be discussed in this session. Why health-promotion and health-rehabilitation programs like EAPs are sometimes minimalized, misused, or fail altogether is another topic of focus.

So as not to bias your responses to the inventories you are about to complete, *I would ask that you please turn to the appendix for this session* (i.e., Chapter 6 Appendixes) *and complete as honestly as you can the inventory items that appear before you. Please do not score these inventory items until asked to do so. After you have finished responding, please join us for further discussions of this material.*

MODERN-DAY APPROACHES TO MINIMIZING
OUTWARD SIGNS OF ORGANIZATIONAL DISTRESS

As already noted, the case of ABC Machinery illustrates an organization that is presenting many outward signs of distress. The good news is that an Employee Assistance Program exists here.

For those not familiar with the concept of EAPs, they started appearing in corporate America about 40 years ago when alcohol abuse was first addressed as a major organizational problem. Thus, in their early stages of development, EAPs are usually concerned solely with alcohol abuse problems. More mature EAPs have a much broader agenda which includes counseling, rehabilitation, and referral services for anxiety, depression, anger management, cardiovascular problems, assertiveness training, relaxation training, financial management, family or marital counseling, and so on. Commonly, EAPs are jointly sponsored by an organization's labor and management representatives. Today, they are present in organizations all over the world.

When in place, EAP services are generally available to all organizational members on a self-, supervisor-, or labor representative-referral basis. Generally a referral is made when some recognized "problem" or "potential problem" with productivity is perceived by an individual or someone else of enlightenment within the organization. Importantly, this emphasis on job-behavior symptomology rather than on mental-stability symptomology eliminates what has been referred to as the "witch hunt" approach to stress and strain control within organizations (Googins & Godfrey, 1987).

EAPs that are well received by organizational members are generally found in organizations that have a good degree of trust between organizational members and management and an open organizational climate rather than a closed one. Steps taken with organizational members who refuse to go to an EAP for help when an obvious productivity problem presents, or steps taken with organizational members who do not cooperate with the EAP-advised course of treatment once enrolled, vary from company to company.

Most EAP programs exist under a much larger health-promotion and health-maintenance umbrella within organizations. The latter include wellness and stress management programs, which not only provide information to organizational members on health-reducing risk factors but provide personalized risk-factor calculations, stress-coping strategies, and professional assistance for those who want to be more effective health and stress managers. Moreover, wellness programs often include some type of access for organizational members to physical fitness centers. In short, while EAPs focus on rehabilitation, wellness and stress management programs focus on prevention of stress-related disabilities.

Terborg (1986) identified three categories of organizational activities meant to improve organizational members' physical and mental health and, therefore, help them to better manage their stressors and strains:

Health-protection activities are designed to protect organizational members from work-related diseases, illnesses, and injuries. These activities, often put in place to comply with government health and safety regulations, include such programs in organizations as Workplace Hazardous Materials Information Systems (WHMIS), a standardized system for communicating to organizational members the hazards that they are required to work with.

Health-promotion activities are educational and informational campaigns that include some combination of reading material, lectures, seminars, and films for encouraging the adoption of physical, mental, and behavioral health- and stress-management habits.

Wellness and stress management activities provide some form of day-to-day workplace empowerment to organizational members to help them maintain regimens that optimize productivity on the job as well as promote psychological and physical wellness and stress management on and off the job. Wellness, self-healing, or stress-managing regimens have been found by experts to include physical fitness, proper nutrition, a healthy weight maintenance, relaxation periods, good sleep habits, effective stress-coping efforts, early stress-symptom detection and management, and the moderation or limitation of potentially destructive substances (like alcohol or drugs). Singly or in combination, these proactions are thought to increase an organizational member's capacity to manage stressful situations because they nullify the physiological arousal that typically occurs in stressful situations, bring about a state of relaxation either during or shortly after psychological and physiological arousal (thereby preventing a buildup of tension and frustration), and directly reduce tension, depression, anxiety, and anger (Falkenberg, 1987; Maddi, 1987; Steffy, Jones, & Noe, 1990).

At the present time, few conclusive estimates on EAP, wellness, and stress management program "returns" exist in the organizational or health literature. Part of this scarcity is due to a lack of record-keeping by organizations, and part of this is due to calculation difficulties encountered by organizations. Data collection difficulties result because (Cascio, 1991):

- Health-related costs that actually decrease are often difficult to identify.
- Program sponsors use different methods to measure and report perceived costs and benefits.

- Program effects vary because of *when* they are measured (i.e., immediate or lagged) and because of *how long* they are measured (i.e., for one year, for five years, for ten years, and so on).

- Few assessment studies use control groups (i.e., nonparticipants in the programs under review) besides experimental groups (i.e., participants in the programs under review).

- Data on effectiveness are limited in the choice of variables, on estimates of the economic value of indirect costs and benefits, on estimates of the timing and duration of program effects, and on estimates of the present value of future benefits.

Therefore, at the most basic level of evaluating EAPs, wellness, and stress management programs, organizations tend to maintain some record of the clients who showed interest in the program and to what degree, the number of interactions or referrals handled, and the number of dollars spent to keep the program functional. The returns on the program investment are then based on some assessment of the amount of improvement in productivity, absenteeism, accident rates, medical expenses, insurance premiums, unemployment costs, member morale, and/or job satisfaction.

Despite the paucity of information available, many companies around the world have recognized the need for and have therefore adopted some type of EAP program to help rehabilitate organizational members with alcohol and substance abuse problems. For example, as of 1991, over 70% of Fortune 500 companies (including IBM, Control Data, Xerox, and Kimberly-Clark) had EAPs (EAPA, 1991) of one form or another. In a 1987 survey of smaller U.S. firms, 51% of the companies with 750 or more organizational members had an EAP for alcohol-related problems, 34.7% of the companies with 250–749 members had one, and 14.8% of the companies with fewer than 100 members had one (Kiefhaber, 1987).

Besides EAPs, government-legislated health protection programs are also popular. Using Statistics Canada 1990 data as a case in point (Geran, 1992), over 50% of Canadian working adults polled said that safety and accident prevention programs were available at their work sites.

Far fewer organizations have sophisticated, multifaceted EAP, health promotion, or stress management programs. Using the Statistics Canada 1990 data as a case in point, only 32% of the Canadian working adults polled said that counseling was available for psychological problems, and only 31% said that basic health promotion programs such as fitness classes, nutrition counseling, relaxation training, or smoking cessation were available. These findings mirror an earlier 1985 national survey of U.S. work sites with over 50 employees; only 27% of the organizations reported offering some form of stress management program to their organizational members (Fielding, 1989).

The statistics that are available case-by-case generally indicate good returns on EAP, wellness, and stress management programs for organizations at the macro- and microsystem levels. In well-designed programs where trust, confidentiality, and respect for human dignity exist, 40 to 50% of organizational members eventually choose to participate in the program to some degree (List, 1987). Regarding the return for wellness programs, in particular, British Columbia Hydro calculated the benefit/cost ratio for its plant's program to be well in excess of 2:1; that is, for every dollar that B. C. Hydro spends on their wellness program, they estimate that at least two dollars of benefit is derived (Cascio & Thacker, 1994). Moreover, the U.S.-based AT&T reported multiple returns on its EAP program. After tracking 110 organizational members for 22 months before entering the EAP and for 22 months after their entry, AT&T found that:

1. The location of the EAP within the medical department and the supervisors' use of job performance criteria for referrals resulted in an effective EAP. This combination of factors instilled confidence in organizational members and provided them an opportunity to receive comprehensive diagnosis and treatment for such outward signs of distress as alcohol/drug abuse (42% of the users), psychological ill health (39% of the users), and family/marital or work-related difficulties (19% of the users).

2. The rate of rehabilitation or improvement for all cases was an impressive 86%. (In the case of alcohol abuse, rehabilitation was defined as eighteen months of sustained sobriety.)

3. Other outward signs of distress were significantly decreased, including accidents on and off the job, absenteeism, and visits to the medical department following EAP participation. (For example, 26 accidents resulting in 164 lost work days occurred for the 110 participants before participation in the EAP and 5 accidents resulting in 19 lost workdays occurred after participation).

4. For the organizational members referred by their supervisors as having "poor performance" (and in serious jeopardy of losing their jobs) prior to EAP participation, over 85% of these organizational members were no longer "poor performers" following EAP involvement. In fact, of the 110 members, 41% were promoted during the postinvestigation period.

5. Over a three-and-a-half-year period, five variables for which dollar figures could be determined (i.e., accident rates, incidental absences, disability absences, visits to medical people, and anticipated replacement losses) yielded a net savings from "before EAP involvement" to "after EAP involvement" of $790,000 (1990 U.S. dollars). (Cascio & Thacker, 1994)

Finally, returns on stress management programs for organizational members are equally impressive. In one of the earliest corporate programs dealing specifically with stress management, Equitable Life Assurance established its Emotional Health Program. This comprehensive approach to stress reduction in the workplace was concerned with prevention, treatment, and referral of overstressed organizational members. Staffed by a clinical psychologist, a physician, a psychology intern, and a counselor, it offered a variety of services, including relaxation training, biofeedback, and counseling. Program evaluations completed to date have shown significant reductions in organizational members' stress-related presentations, including anxiety, headaches, and health center visits (Ivancevich et al., 1990).

After a slow beginning, during which compliance rates with program recommendations were low, New York Telephone Company's stress management program now points to increased usage and significant improvements in participants' stress-coping skills, along with reductions in anxiety, depression, and hostility. Finally, the STAYWELL program developed by Control Data (and now marketed to other companies) and the Johnson & Johnson Live for Life health promotion program are examples of comprehensive organizational stress management efforts with high usage records. Evaluations of both these programs suggest positive physical (e.g., lower blood pressure), psychological (e.g., increased job satisfaction), and behavioral (e.g., decreased alcohol usage) outcomes for the program participants (Ivancevich et al., 1990).

Based on a number of independent studies completed during the last decade, study findings seem to suggest that health promotion programs do, in fact, eliminate or reduce health-risk factors, and that these positive changes seem to be long-lasting (Gebhardt & Crump, 1990). One basic macrosystem ingredient needs to be present, however, for positive returns to be realized: health promotion and health rehabilitation must be "talked" and "walked" daily by managerial staff, labor representatives, and organizational members.

MACROSYSTEM FACTORS CAUSING EAP, HEALTH-PROMOTION, AND WELLNESS PROGRAMS TO BE MINIMALIZED

We have just noted the good news about ABC Machinery: That an EAP is in place. Now for the bad news. Despite the potential for "healthy" stress-empowerment at ABC Machinery, there exists at the present time an adversarial, productivity-fixated environment, whereby existing health-promotion policies are "talked" but not "walked" by a number of factions. The ongoing tension between union and management is reflected in the large number of outstanding grievances that are currently on file in this plant: over 3,000. In this sort of negative cultural milieu, where stress levels run excessively high, chances are that the EAP, while in existence, would be minimalized. Minimalization, by definition, means that the values, beliefs, and practices existing within an organization reduce the awareness, acknowledgment, and assessment of the occurrence of distress in the workplace. Consequently, treatment and rehabilitation for organizational members' physical, psychological, and behavioral problems are often needlessly delayed—or are not attended to properly—by managers, union representatives, and organizational members alike.

Ames and Delaney (1992), the experts studying the ABC Machinery case, reported that EAPs and other stress management/wellness programs are likely to be minimized if the organization is faced with such competing macrosystem interests and behaviors as:

1. A "talking" by management about the importance of organizational members' psychological, physical, and behavioral well-being, but a "walking" that indicates that superiors prioritize and reward production agendas and minimize or even punish "competing" human-health agendas.

2. A "talking" by superiors about the importance of organizational members' psychological, physical, and behavioral well-being, but a "walking" that indicates that workplace stress problems and outward signs of distress should be overlooked or "swept under the rug" when production quotas are in danger of not being met.

3. A "talking" by union stewards or other labor representatives about the importance of organizational members' psychological, physical, and behavioral well-being, but a "walking" that advocates antidisciplinary positions on health and safety abuses (such as alcohol and drug usage) in the workplace.

4. A "talking" by union stewards about the importance of organizational members' psychological, physical, and behavioral well-being, but a "walking" that goes counter to this notion if the followership of unionized organizational members is perceived to be in jeopardy.

5. A "talking" by organizational group members about the importance of psychological, physical, and behavioral well-being in the workplace for all members, but a "walking" that goes counter to this notion and may even involve acts of aggression toward supervision, especially when job-security differences of opinion prevail between the parties.

All of the just-noted presentations exist at ABC Machinery, placing the plant at risk for minimalization. Traditionally, a management-supported policy called "shop rules" provides the foreman with specific instructions for what constitutes alcohol-related misconduct. Management policy states that bringing alcohol into the plant, on-the-job drinking, and alcohol-impaired behavior come under scrutiny as "employee misconduct." Rules are enforced through a set of disciplinary procedure steps. Some of the plants at ABC Machinery, including this one, however, discontinued posting "shop rules" because of pressure from the union for more egalitarian treatment of organizational members. Although foremen, certain labor relations personnel, and managers continued to follow the shop rules as policy for alcohol-related issues, the union recognized only the bargaining agreement language.

The union and management's agreed-upon policy for handling substance abuse problems was documented in the national union contract. Alcohol language, in particular, guaranteed treatment and support for organizational members who are alcohol-dependent. The national contract contained language that gave the employer the right to discipline workers for alcohol- or drug-related misconduct, but with an understanding that the union had the right to file grievances against such action. Unfortunately, the contract policy did not provide guidelines for what constitutes alcohol problems that warrant "treatment" or "disciplinary action." Thus, the decision of problem definition was usually taken out of the hands of supervisors and placed in the hands of the EAP (i.e., an EAP professional was asked to make a diagnosis of the "case" in question) or the union (i.e., the grievance system was called into play).

So were the health-maintenance policies at ABC Machinery effective in reducing organizational members' outward signs of stress and strain? To determine organizational members' and supervisors' perceptions to this critical question, Ames and Delaney (1992) surveyed 832 union and 152 salaried organizational members within the plant. Their survey results indicated that the majority of both the hourly and salaried members reported that it is "easy" or "very easy" to bring alcohol into the plant, to have a drink at workstations, and to have a drink during breaks. Most members believed it was "unlikely" or "very unlikely" they would get caught if they drank alcohol inside the plant. Regarding intervention, 69% of the hourly and 48% of the salaried members replied that it is "likely" or "very likely" that a supervisor would do nothing or just talk to the organizational member and not take other action if someone was seen drinking on the job occasionally. Most replied that they "disagreed" or "strongly disagreed" that their union, including their EAP representatives, did a good job of preventing drinking at work. A large percentage "agreed" or "strongly agreed" that receiving disciplinary action for drinking only means that it will probably be reversed later through grievance procedures.

The general plant survey corroborated evidence from interviews held with supervisors at ABC Machinery. In response to the earlier question, the company alcohol policy was found to be confusing and (in the main) ineffective, and the EAP was minimalized. The extent to which ambivalent policy and interacting organizational agendas influenced supervisors' perceptions on drinking norms, practices, and action is illustrated in Carla's further comments about workers drinking alcohol under her supervision:

Now on the first shift you have your very senior people that are longtime drinkers and probably alcoholics; you don't bother them because they know how to cover their drinking. You still know they drink, though, because you can smell it on them and you know they keep a bottle. But some days I couldn't tell one way or another, because they never did anything different from day to day. But not second shift. People on my second shift teams who drank stopped at bars on the way to work or signed out for lunch and came back in screwed up. They can't hide it as well as the first shift drinkers, and they become abusive sometimes and stress-out earlier in the day. Friday nights are the worst because on Fridays five or six of them will drink in groups, sometimes in the open, because they know I can't throw all of them out and be short that many people on the line. I know the decision-making on whether they can do their work or not is up to me, but unless they are obviously drunk, I have to see the bottle or see them take a drink to make it (disciplinary action) stick. (Ames & Delaney, 1992, pp. 184–185)

Ames and Delaney concluded that the EAP at ABC Machinery was, indeed, minimalized. The alcohol policy language in the bargaining unit contract set the stage for the EAP to be used as a means of circumventing the disciplinary process. If an organizational member were channeled into treatment by the union steward or an EAP representative, disciplinary action for alcohol-related misconduct was almost always automatically dismissed. In this particular plant, some organizational members had been channeled through EAP-directed treatment programs up to three times. Some organizational members suggested that these members had no real intention of being rehabilitated—they just wanted to be paid while they were off work. Moreover, the less-than-effective supervisors' actions on alcohol problems in the workplace, as illustrated by Carla's avoidance behavior, were caused by the interactive processes of

- Ambiguous union-management alcohol policies;
- A difficult position for EAP staff (under pressure from the union and management, the EAP staff had to make a decision on the seriousness of the individual's drinking problem and counsel him or her on available treatment sources within or outside the plant);
- The union's own agenda of taking a firm stance against disciplinary action for drinking on the job;
- Management's agenda of allowing leniency on drinking infractions if production was threatened; and
- Organizational members' abusing the EAP by enrolling for treatment (up to three times) to avoid disciplinary action and to receive paid time off for detoxification, treatment, and recovery.

Given this situation, it is clear why there were so many outward signs of distress presenting at ABC Machinery. Moreover, there appeared to be few forces for organizational change. Ames and Delaney reported that during their investigations into the attitudes of members, only a handful of "enlightened" union and management organizational members cognizant of the systematized and double-standard nature of the diversionary practices in their company were found. These members openly expressed their deep concern about the contingencies and paradoxes that restricted personal-control maintenance and, thus, escalated outward signs of distress for many organizational members. But they felt powerless to move the adversarial management-union mountain when the majority of organizational members were blind or accepting of such destructive forces.

These kinds of competing forces that cause high stress for organizational members result in many forms of outward signs of distress, and minimalize EAPs' existence in companies around the world. Discernible differences between managements', labor representatives', and organizational members' goals, agendas, and views on health and safety issues are found in many large and small organizations. These differences not only affect the form and process of health-maintenance and stress-intervention efforts but enhance the development of overly liberal or ambivalent workplace norms, which can be destructive. Moreover, enforcement by supervision of health-maintenance company policy can be hampered by the politics, trade-offs, and other practicalities of labor relations culture, particularly when there exists an adversarial-type of climate. The "bottom line," posit Ames and Delaney (1992), is this: Competing macrosystem issues such as these need to be identified and understood in terms of their interactional impact on workplace stress-tolerance norms and on resulting outward sign presentations. Without this knowledge and the willingness of management and labor leaders to cooperate in making a "stress-moderated" work environment, a lack of endorsement of health-promotion programs by many and a minimalized usage of health-rehabilitation programs by the majority will likely result.

MICROSYSTEM FACTORS INFLUENCING ORGANIZATIONAL SIGNS OF DISTRESS: STRESS-COPING EFFORTS AND LIFESTYLE

When management and union representatives work cooperatively to reduce pathological stress in the workplace, individual organizational members' stress-coping efforts and their lifestyles often become key "make-it" or "break-it" factors for stress-disabling conditions. As was the case at ABC Machinery, when management and union representatives do not work cooperatively to reduce pathological stress AND when individual organizational members engage in "unhealthy" stress-coping cognitions and behaviors, the organizational health picture becomes bleak rather quickly.

Throughout our stress-empowerment sessions, we have spent considerable time talking about the deleterious effects of chronic work distressors and poor organizational climate on organizational members' physiological, psychological, and behavioral well-being. We have talked about how organizational members' negative life events such as having to deal with a close friend's or a family member's death can precipitate psychological and somatic distress symptoms. And while we have noted the positive impact of workplace empowerment on organizational members' well-being and reduced outward-sign presentations, we have spent relatively little time talking about the importance of individuals' stress-coping behaviors, lifestyles, and health habits for reducing outward signs of distress. It is time now for this discussion.

Stress-Coping Styles and Outward Sign Reduction

Throughout our sessions, we have talked about the stress process as being a sort of dynamic relationship existing between an individual and his or her internal and external environment. The stress-strain (outward sign) relationship, in particular, we have noted, implies a two-way dynamic in which the individual can impose a particular interpretation on his or her environment, and the ever-changing environment can help shape an individual's interpretations of stressors that present.

To more fully understand individuals' interpretations, say experts, one must conceptually distinguish between primary and secondary appraisals. Primary appraisals pose the question to the individual, "Is there a problem?" Secondary appraisals then pose, "If there is a problem, *what* can I do about it?" It is at this juncture that stress-coping comes into play (Dewe & Guest, 1990).

As noted earlier, "coping" in the stress literature refers to an individual's efforts to master life conditions or life demands that tax or exceed one's adaptive life resources (see Chapter 2). These efforts can be cognitive (i.e., perceptual) and behavioral. Whether these efforts result in successful stress-reduction outcomes, such as reduced outward-sign presentation, is another question. Coping efforts, then, can be conceptually distinguished from the success of these efforts.

In recent years, experts have attempted to measure individuals' stress-coping efforts, but this objective has been difficult to meet, in part, because "coping" can occur at both the conscious and unconscious psychological levels. Moreover, because "coping" is not a fully conscious process, self-reports—which provide the usual means for assessing individuals' stress appraisals—are liable to some degree of error, omission, and distortion (Dewe & Guest, 1990).

Accepting that there is no perfect measurement for stress-coping efforts, researchers have, nonetheless, attempted to assess stress-coping efforts in the workplace. Most have started from Folkman and Lazarus's (1980) conceptual basis of individual appraisal and have differentiated two main kinds of workplace stress-coping efforts:

1. *Control* or *direct action* or *problem-focused* efforts that attempt to tackle the source of job stress. Behaviorally working overtime to meet an impending deadline might serve as such an example.
2. *Escape* or *palliative* or *emotion-focused* efforts that attempt to deal with the emotional discomfort caused by job stressor(s). Cognitively reducing the importance of an imposed deadline rather than working overtime to meet it might serve as such an example.

In recent years, workplace stress-coping efforts have been described along variations on the Cannon-Selye "control-escape" theme. Pearlin and

Schooler (1978), for example, identify coping efforts that attempt to change the stressful situation by altering the meaning of the situation or by controlling the feelings of discomfort brought about by the situation. Latack (1986), whose work is cited often in the organizational stress literature, distinguishes three work stress-coping efforts which are used by organizational members, singly or in combination:

1. *Control-coping* efforts consist of both actions and cognitive reappraisals that are proactive, "take-charge" in tone.
2. *Escape-coping* efforts consist of both actions and cognitive reappraisals that suggest an escapist, "avoidance" mode.
3. *Symptom-management* efforts consist of individuals' strategies for managing outward signs of distress.

The kinds of cognitions and behaviors commonly assessed along these three lines are summarized in Table 6.1 (Latack, 1986).

Often, notes Latack, organizational members use all three types of stress-coping styles to either maintain or regain a sense of personal control in the workplace. The symptom-management efforts generally are called into place to ameliorate some of the psychosomatic discomforts that are being experienced. In terms of adaptive resource requirements, control-coping behaviors imply a level of energy, optimism, and positive affect (PA) on the part of the organizational member that escape-coping efforts do not.

In her industrial investigations on the usefulness of these three efforts for bringing about stress reductions for individuals, Latack found that control coping, in particular, was generally negatively correlated with stress symptoms such as psychosomatic illness and propensity to leave the organization, while escapist coping was positively related to these outward signs of distress (Latack, 1986).

More recently, Leiter (1991) emphasized the importance of the interaction between organizational members' stress-coping efforts and the efforts of the organizational macrosystem in reducing widespread distress symptomology. Cognitive and action control coping, affirms Leiter, presumes to some extent a favorable, open, and trusting organizational climate. An assertive, controlling approach to job-related problems in the absence of a supportive relationship with one's supervisor and the empowering resources to get one's job done effectively and safely may only lead to additional stressful incidents and related outward signs of distress for organizational members. Leiter's position echoes that posited by Pearlin and Schooler (1978), Ames and Delaney (1992), Connor and Worley (1991), and others. Individual or microsystem coping behaviors alone are ineffective at addressing most forms of occupational stress. Managers, labor leaders, and organizational members need to work cooperatively to proact against excessive job stress.

Table 6.1
Common Stress-Coping Efforts for Organizational Members

Control Coping	Escape Coping	Symptom Management
Get together with my supervisor to discuss this.	Avoid being in this situation if I can.	Get extra sleep or nap.
Try to be very organized so that I can keep on top of things.	Tell myself that time takes care of situations like this.	Drink a moderate amount (i.e., 2 drinks) of liquor, beer, or wine.
Talk with people who are involved (other than supervisor).	Try to keep away from this type of situation.	Drink more than a moderate amount (i.e., over 2 drinks) of liquor, beer, or wine.
Try to see this situation as an opportunity to learn and develop new skills.	Remind myself that work isn't everything.	Take tranquilizers, sedatives, or other drugs.
Put extra attention on planning and scheduling.	Anticipate the negative consequences so that I'm prepared for the worst.	Do physical exercise (jogging, exercycle, dancing, or other participative sports).
Try to think of myself as a winner--as someone who always comes through.	Delegate work to others.	Practice transcendental meditation.
Tell myself that I can probably work things out to my advantage.	Separate myself as much as possible from the people who created this situation.	Use biofeedback training.
Devote more time and energy to doing my job.	Try not to get concerned about it.	Use relaxation training.
Try to get additional people involved in the situation.	Do my best to get out of the situation gracefully.	Seek company of friends.
Think about the challenges I can find in this situation.	Accept this situation because there is nothing I can do to change it.	Seek company of family.
Try to work faster and more efficiently.	Set my own priorities based on what I like to do.	Eat or snack.
Decide what I think should be done and explain this to the people who are affected.		Watch television.
Give it my best effort to do what I think is expected of me.		Attend sporting, cultural or community events.
Request help from people who have the power to do something for me.		Take it out on family or friends.
Seek advice from people outside the situation who may not have power but who can help me think of ways to do what is expected of me.		Pursue hobbies or leisure time activities not covered above.

Table 6.1 (continued)

Work on changing policies which caused this situation.		Go buy something; spend money.
Throw myself into my work and work harder, longer hours.		Take time off work.
		Change physical state in a manner not covered above (get hair done, get a message, take a sauna, engage in sexual activity).
		Take a trip to another city.
		Daydream.
		Seek professional help or counseling.
		Turn to prayer or spiritual thoughts.
		Complain to others.
		Smoke cigarettes, cigar, or pipe.

Source: Latack, J. C. (1986). Coping with job stress: Measures and future directions for scale development. *Journal of Applied Psychology, 71,* 377–385.

Experts Brief and Folger (1992) hold similar views about the meshing of individuals' stress-coping efforts and the macrosystem's reinforcement of healthy or destructive cognitions and behaviors. They have described two kinds of macrosystem normative situations which tend to reinforce "ineffective" forms of individual stress-coping, leading to widespread workplace substance abuse, aggression, and low tolerance for others' points of view:

1. In *precipitating work situations,* cues that instigate individuals' predispositions to think, feel, and behave in "ineffective" stress-coping ways are elicited. The armed services may serve as such a case in point. Because military life dictates that organizational members play a "masculine" role to be successful—a role which includes drinking, cigarette smoking, and aggressing as ways in which performance can be legitimized—this requirement provides a precipitating work situation for organizational members who are predisposed to having substance abuse or anger-control problems. Consequently, "predisposed" members often become attracted to, selected in, and have little desire for leaving the military. Other traditional male-

oriented work environments—mining, manufacturing, and railroading—have through similar "masculine" role expectations reinforced and, consequently, faced similar organizational distress problems.

2. In *weak work situations*, the work culture does not offer strong policies or restrictions against destructive stress-coping attitudes and behaviors but instead has weak, unstructured, and/or ambiguous policies regarding such. ABC Machinery may serve as such a case in point. Although policies on smoking and alcohol drinking on the job were in place, a lack of adequate controls on such behaviors—by management, the union, and the organizational members themselves—effectively minimalized such policies.

To reinforce effective cognitive and behavior stress-coping, Brief and Folger (1992) advocate *strong work situations* for reducing organizational signs of distress. Strong work situations provide salient cues that guide organizational members away from ineffective or destructive stress-coping efforts by having a fairly high degree of structure and definition. Thus, health-promoting and health-rehabilitating policies are not only developed and communicated thoroughly to organizational members but their usage is monitored and rewarded regularly. A strong work situation at ABC Machinery would have had well-defined and interactively consistent company, union, and member policies against drinking alcohol on the job. All factions would have endorsed early constructive rehabilitation through the EAP for organizational members seen to have obvious problems in this regard.

Lifestyle and Outward Sign Reduction

The range of lifestyle, health-habit, and symptom-management options available to organizational members for ameliorating or preventing outward signs of distress is large. Engaging in physical exercise programs, regularly performing relaxation training, and limiting or moderating substance intake all fall within this range.

In recent years, experts have attempted to determine which activities within this range are most beneficial for preventing stress-disabling conditions and which are less beneficial, or even destructive. At first inspection, it might seem relatively easy for experts to determine whether regular participation in a program of vigorous physical exercise, or if regularly engaging in relaxation therapy, for example, reduces stress-disabling conditions. But, as noted earlier for stress-coping efforts and for program assessments, problems in determining the impact of lifestyle, habits, and symptom management on stress symptomology reduction have been reported in the literature.

Assessment problems arise from a number of complications, including a lack of experimental and control groups, differing definitions provided by experts as to symptom management and lifestyle options, poor compliance by participants assigned to certain health-maintenance regimens under investigation, imprecisions or biases in self-report outcomes, and individual variations to suggested therapeutic processes for reducing outward signs of distress (Kirkcaldy & Shephard, 1990).

Despite these technical difficulties, there is now clear evidence that regular, moderated physical activity of any form (i.e., that causing perspiration but not musculoskeletal injury) is a critical lifestyle factor of particular benefit to organizational members' physical and psychological health. Moreover, in the long run, exercise is more pleasant and less labor-intensive than many alternative forms of psychotherapy.

The psychological benefit of moderate bouts of physical activity may be attributable to an increase in arousal and/or the secretion of mood-altering, neurotransmitting beta-endorphins (which produce pleasant moods). Consequently, individuals who engage in regimens of moderate exercise often report reduced levels of anger, hostility, tension, and anxiety. In moderated regimens involving teams or other individuals, the psychological gains probably arise gradually through positive changes in an individual's body image and through the social benefits accrued from interpersonal involvement. Gradual physical gains—such as increased physical performance, decreased fatigue, and a reduced risk of ischemic heart disease accrue as additional dividends of moderated exercise regimens (Kirkcaldy & Shephard, 1990).

Moderated exercise regimens need to be differentiated from rigorous exercise regimens. Overly intensive or excessive bouts of physical activity can lead to a physical exercise psychological "addiction," musculo-skeletal injury, and heart attack (in predisposed individuals) (Kirkcaldy & Shephard, 1990).

In a 1990 study which investigated the impact of broader lifestyle and health habits on the outward signs of distress reported by 3,337 organizational members in 58 organizations, Steffy, Jones, and Noe (1990) found that maintaining both a healthy lifestyle and good health habits has a strong negative outcome on strain responses reported. "Healthy lifestyle" meant acquiring exercise, nutrition, sleep, and relaxation behaviors that contribute to one's overall physical and mental health. "Good health habits" meant moderating or limiting the intake of substances that, if used excessively, could be harmful to one's physical and/or mental health (i.e., alcohol, substances, and cigarettes.) Their study findings showed that at a general level, organizational members who exercised moderately, had good nutrition, ingested "safe" limits of alcohol and/or coffee and/or tobacco, got eight hours of sleep at least four times a week, used relaxation techniques when stressed, and got physical check-ups regularly had significantly lower levels of job tension, job dissatisfaction, and psychosomatic distress than their colleagues who engaged in less health-maintaining regimens. The lifestyle and health habit factors found to contribute to decreased signs of distress in organizational members are summarized in Table 6.2.

Table 6.2

Lifestyle and Health Habit Factors Reducing Outward Signs of Distress

Lifestyle Factors	Health Habit Factors
Drinking less than three cups of caffeinated drinks (coffee, tea, soda pop) a day	Not driving after consuming two or more drinks of alcohol
Exercising moderately and participating in recreational activities	Moderating or limiting beer drank during a typical week
Exercising to the point of perspiration at least three times a week	Moderating or limiting wine drank during a typical week
Using stress-management techniques regularly	Moderating or limiting liquor drank during a typical week
Staying in good physical condition	Moderating or limiting cigarettes smoked during a typical day
Staying within healthy body weight limits	Moderating or limiting alcoholic drinks to relax and unwind on the weekend
Eating a balanced diet regularly	Moderating or limiting alcoholic drinks to relax and unwind after work
Getting a thorough physical examination each year	Moderating or limiting pipe and cigar smoking
Getting approximately 8 hours of sleep at least four times a week	
Taking relaxation breaks routinely during the day	
Relaxing and "coming down" regularly at the end of the work day	

Source: Steffy, B. D., Jones, J. W., & Noe, A. W. (1990). The impact of health habits and lifestyle on the stressor-strain relationship: An evaluation of three industries. *Journal of Occupational Psychology*, 63, 217–229.

ORGANIZATIONAL FEEDBACK: DO YOU AND YOUR COLLEAGUES TRY TO CONTROL JOB STRESS OR ESCAPE FROM IT?

Participants can now receive feedback on whether they tend to control job stress when it presents—or escape from it. *Please now score your responses to the "Assessing Your Behavior at Work When You Face Difficult Situations Inventory"* (Appendix 6.1).

Participants should now have two scores in their possession: a "controller" score and an "escaper" score. Your stronger tendency when stressed at work is your larger column score. A tie score means that you have a tendency to vacillate between the two coping styles when stressed. What are you—a controller or an escaper? Do you fight against stress, or do you flee from it? Considering that your PA/NA ratios were earlier compared to a normative value of 1.64 (see pages 63 and 64), to what degree does your "controller/escapist" ratio meet or exceed 1.64?

If you were to give this inventory to work groups who seem to exhibit high signs of distress, do you think that the members of those work groups would be predominantly controllers or escapers?

Given their responses to these questions, participants should now be able to conclude:

- If their own stress-coping efforts are cognitively and behaviorally more "controlling" or "escaping"; and

- If their own work groups have members who are cognitively and behaviorally more "controlling" or "escaping."

ORGANIZATIONAL FEEDBACK: DO YOU AND YOUR COLLEAGUES MAINTAIN HEALTHY LIFESTYLES AND HEALTH HABITS?

Participants can now receive feedback on whether they tend to maintain healthy lifestyles and health habits. *Please now score your responses to the "Assessing Your Lifestyle and Health Habit Predispositions Inventory"* (in Appendix 6.2).

Participants should now have one score in their possession that ranges from 0 to 20. The higher the score, the healthier your lifestyle and health habits appear to be. The lower the score, the more destructive and potentially disabling your lifestyle and health habits appear to be. Which end of the continuum does your score fall closer to—the potentially destructive end (i.e., closer to 0) or the self-healing end (i.e., closer to 20)?

If you were to give this inventory to organizational members who seem to exhibit high signs of distress, do you think that their lifestyles and health habits would likely be destructive or self-healing?

Given their responses to these questions, participants should now be able to conclude:

- If their own lifestyle and health habit predispositions are self-healing or self-destructive; and

- If their own work groups have members whose lifestyles and health habits are predominantly self-healing or self-destructive.

ANSWERS TO QUESTIONS OFTEN ASKED ABOUT DEVELOPING EAP, WELLNESS, AND STRESS MANAGEMENT PROGRAMS

Managers who are considering developing EAP, wellness, or stress management programs for their organizations often have some important questions to ask. Some of the more frequent ones will be attended to now.

Questions on EAPs

Regarding EAPs, managers often ask, How many different kinds of EAP models are there, and is one model more effective in reducing outward signs of distress in the workplace than others?

There are four basic EAP models that have been developed as methods for delivering counseling and well-being rehabilitation services, including the:

In-house model. Here, the professional assistance staff are employed by the organization. The organization directly supervises the program's personnel, sets policies, and designs all procedures. Offices can either be in-house or on premises outside.

Out-of-house model. Here, the organization contracts a vendor to provide an employee assistance staff and services. The organization might set specific policies and procedures in the contract or allow the vendor to use its own. The vendor provides services either in its offices, in the organization's offices, or in some combination of the two.

Consortium model. Here, several organizations pool their resources to develop a collaborative program to maximize resources. This model tends to work very well for organizations having fewer than 2,000 organizational members. Services can be provided on-site or on outside premises.

Affiliate model. Here, a vendor subcontracts a local professional rather than use salaried staff. This arrangement allows the vendor to reach organizational members in a location in which the vendor might not have an office. This model is generally used in conjunction with a model that has paid staff (Masi & Friedland, 1988).

Is one model preferred by organizations? Apparently not. A study completed by Straussner (1988) found that top management in organizations surveyed believed that in-house models provided good service at lower costs and allowed for increased control over resources, greater identification of distressed organizational members, increased supervisory and medical referrals, and more positive acceptance by union representatives. Out-of-house programs, on the other hand, were viewed as providing better accountability and having lower legal liability and greater ease of start-up and implementation. The study findings did reveal, however, that the con-

sortium and affiliate models were less acceptable to top management because they were more complex to run, had more difficult decision-making
processes, allowed for less control over subcontracted professionals, and
offered less accountability and decreased responsiveness. The "bottom line"
of Straussner's study seems to be that any organization considering the
development of an EAP should review its own characteristics. In most cases,
a consultant with expertise in the design and implementation of EAPs can
help match company characteristics on size, geographic location, diversity,
employee population, values, and goals with a particular EAP model that
can best suit the organization's needs.

Questions on Wellness Programs

Managers often want to know what objectives organizations should aim
for in setting up wellness programs, given that so many options are available.

As stressed throughout this session, the process of corporate health promotion begins by management and unions jointly promoting health awareness among their members. That is, members throughout the organization
need to have a basic knowledge of the present and future consequences of
their living self-destructive rather than self-healing lives. Stress-coping efforts, lifestyles, and health habits fall into this knowledge base. As noted
earlier, wellness programs differ from EAPs in that wellness programs focus
on prevention of stress-disabling conditions, whereas EAPs focus on rehabilitation. Reed (1984) suggests the following four objectives for well-
designed organizational wellness programs, some of which have been
amended slightly:

1. Educate organizational members about health-risk factors—lifestyles,
coping efforts, and health habits that may increase their chances of developing a serious illness. For heart disease, for example, some of the risk
factors associated with it include high blood pressure, cigarette smoking,
high cholesterol levels, diabetes, a sedentary lifestyle, obesity, and a hard-
driving and impatient personality. Some of the risk factors associated with
cancer include being exposed to carcinogens (like cigarettes) and repressing
negative emotions. Smoking, stress-excesses, and poor nutrition are associated with many diseases.

2. Identify the health-risk factors that each organizational member faces.

3. Help organizational members eliminate or reduce these risk factors by
adopting healthier lifestyles and health habits, as well as good stress-
management techniques. Moreover, provide them with an organizational
climate that is strong rather than precipitating or weak, and one that is
stress-empowering rather than stress-escalating.

4. Help organizational members maintain their healthy lifestyles through
self-monitoring means and system rewards. The central theme of health

promotion policies should be positive and empowering. "No one takes better care of you than you do" is a theme that works well for this purpose.

Questions on Stress-Management Programs

Managers often want to know, if we have a stress-management program in our organization, should we have supervisors "volunteer" organizational members to attend sessions or should we allow organizational members to "volunteer themselves"?

Again, a distinction needs to be made between EAP referrals and health-promotion program participation. When productivity is at risk, the supervisor should take it upon himself or herself to reinforce company policy in this regard. As Brief and Folger have suggested, strong work situations work best in rehabilitating organizational members who are a health-and-safety risk to themselves and others.

When it comes to stress management session participation, allowing organizational members to volunteer themselves seems to work best. Often the cycle seen in program adoption is that of any product adoption: early adopters who attend the stress management sessions initially are impressed with what the stress management program has to offer; they share this perception with other colleagues, who then become interested and volunteer themselves to attend following sessions; positive word continues to spread throughout the organization, until eventually even the late adopters show interest in the program. Two observations are certain when it comes to stress-management program development:

- When supervisors, superintendents, managers, union representatives, and chief executive officers (CEOs) become earlier rather than late adopters, the adoption process seems to be catalyzed.
- Allowing organizational members to volunteer themselves to attend stress management sessions is the best approach to getting session registrations and "psychologically ready" participants.

The latter point needs further clarification. Stress management programs, by their nature, involve significant self-mirror gazing and self-introspection periods by participants. Therefore, psychological readiness for such involvement by participants is critical. When organizational members are not psychologically ready to self-introspect, the process can be personally damaging and organizationally expensive. The U.S. case of *McLaren v. Webber Hospital Association* (1978) serves as a useful reminder that stress can be induced by even a well-intentioned program if organizational members are forced to attend or forced to participate beyond their psychological "comfort zones." In the aforementioned case, a sensitivity group training seminar held for executive development triggered an episode of psychiatric illness, which led to the organizational member's compensation claim for mental disability being awarded. Enough said about this important topic.

Along somewhat similar lines, organizations should take care not "to volunteer" an organizational member for a stress management or wellness program because the supervisor or someone else in the organization knows that he or she had a "past" alcoholism or stress-related problem. In recent weeks, Imperial Oil Ltd.'s substance abuse policy was ruled discriminatory by a board of inquiry set up under the Ontario Human Rights Commission because of privacy invasion. The "bottom line" of the Commission's decision was that Canadian companies have a legitimate interest in making sure alcohol-imbibing organizational members do not cause accidents on the job. BUT they do not have the right to ask organizational members about past alcoholism. If organizational members remain sober and productive, the company is at risk of a lawsuit or stress claim if they challenge the member adversely (Gibb-Clark, 1995).

Finally, the question is often asked, Should supervisors and organizational members attend the same stress management session?

Given that large amounts of personal data are generally shared among the participants attending, not all organizational members feel comfortable participating in this fashion with their supervisor(s) or immediate group members present. Therefore, all organizational participants should be given the choice of attending the sessions with or without their supervisors and/or peers.

CONCLUSION

This session on outward signs of organizational distress began with the case of ABC Machinery, an organization that seemed plagued by distressed organizational members. A closer look at the interaction of certain macro- and microsystem factors revealed that much of the strain presenting was understandable. An alcohol policy was in place but was not adhered to by management, union representatives, or individual organizational members. Thus, the returns that could have resulted from the health-promotion policy and the organization's EAP program were minimalized.

This session closes on an optimistic note. Studies have shown that stress reduction and distress symptomology can be brought under control with strong work situations and open, empowering organizational climates. In companies where managers, union representatives, and organizational members work together to uphold the principles of stress management and well-being maintenance for all organizational members, the benefits are reaped. Outward signs of distress are brought within reasonable limits, morale throughout the organization is solid, and productivity is raised to impressive levels.

STRESS-COPING SUMMARY POINTS

1. In developing health-rehabilitation and health-promotion EAPs, wellness, and stress management programs, managers, labor representatives, and organizational members need to work together to set policies that are reasonable, clear, and consistent with the organizational members' and the organization's needs. Once a policy is in place, all of the just-cited parties need to daily "walk" the health-empowerment "talk" rather than deviate from it.

2. Moreover, individual organizational members throughout the organization need to be their own health- and stress-control boards, both on and off the job. This objective includes maintaining effective stress-coping efforts, healthful lifestyles, and good health habits. The two inventories provided in this session serve as useful feedback devices for organizational members in this regard.

3. Managers and labor representatives contemplating developing an EAP, wellness, or stress-management program for their plants might ask organizational members to complete (anonymously) the two inventories provided in this session to get some baseline data on the organization's outward signs of distress and the organizational members' current abilities to cope with, or manage, their presenting job stressors. Organizations already having such programs might find such data to be useful in determining the existing program's overall effectiveness.

Appendix 6.1
Assessing Your Behavior at Work When You Face Difficult Situations

Instructions: For the 22 items below, indicate whether you engage in the following activities when you are facing difficult situations at work. Simply circle the "yes" or the "no" to each question asked. Please be honest in your responses. DO YOU TEND TO:		
1. Get together with your supervisor to discuss the difficulties you are having?	YES	NO
2. Try to be very organized so that you can keep "on top of things"?	YES	NO
3. Talk with people who are involved in the situation to get their views on the matter?	YES	NO
4. Try to see this situation as an opportunity to learn and develop new skills?	YES	NO
5. Put extra attention on planning and scheduling?	YES	NO
6. Try to think of yourself as a "winner"--as someone who always comes through?	YES	NO
7. Avoid being in this situation if you can?	YES	NO
8. Try to remind yourself that work isn't everything?	YES	NO
9. Try to delegate your work to others?	YES	NO
10. Devote more time and energy to doing your job?	YES	NO
11. Tell yourself that time takes care of situations like this?	YES	NO
12. Try to keep away from this type of situation?	YES	NO

13. Anticipate the negative consequences so that you are prepared for "the worse"?	YES	NO
14. Separate yourself as much as possible from the people who created this situation?	YES	NO
15. Try not to be concerned about the situation?	YES	NO
16. Try to get additional people involved in the situation?	YES	NO
17. Think about the challenges you can find in this situation?	YES	NO
18. Do your best to get out of the situation gracefully?	YES	NO
19. Accept this situation because there is nothing you can do to change it?	YES	NO
20. Request help from people who have the power to do something for you?	YES	NO
21. Work on changing policies which have caused this situation?	YES	NO
22. Set your own priorities based on what you like to do?	YES	NO

Source: Adapted from Latack, J. C. (1986). Coping with job stress: Measures and future directions for scale development. *Journal of Applied Psychology*, 71, 377–385.

Appendix 6.2
Assessing Your Lifestyle and Health Habit Predispositions

Instructions: For the lifestyle and health habit questions below, answer "yes" or "no" in the space to the right of the question. Please be honest in your responses. DO YOU:	
Lifestyle Questions	**Health Habit Questions**
Drink less than three cups of caffeinated drinks (coffee, tea, soda pop) a day?	Not drive after consuming two or more drinks of alcohol?
Exercise moderately and participate in recreational activities?	Moderate or limit the beer drank during a typical week?
Exercise to the point of perspiration at least three times a week?	Moderate or limit the wine drank during a typical week?
Use stress-management techniques regularly?	Moderate or limit the liquor drank during a typical week?
Stay in good physical condition?	Moderate or limit the cigarettes smoked during a typical day?
Stay within healthy body weight limits?	Moderate or limit the alcoholic drinks to relax and unwind on the weekend?
Eat a balanced diet regularly?	Moderate or limit the alcoholic drinks to relax and unwind after work?
Get a thorough physical examination each year?	Moderate or limit pipe and cigar smoking?
Get approximately 8 hours of sleep at least four times a week?	Moderate or limit illegal substances (such as cocaine)?
Take relaxation breaks routinely during the day?	
Relax and "come down" regularly at the end of the work day?	

Source: Steffy, B. D., Jones, J. W., & Noe, A. W. (1990). The impact of health habits and lifestyle on the stressor-strain relationship: An evaluation of three industries. *Journal of Occupational Psychology, 63,* 217–229.

Scoring Appendix 6.1

Are you a "controller" or an "escaper"? To find out which is your stronger style, total your score for each tendency, as shown in the two columns to the right. The higher score is your stronger predisposition. A tie score indicates a predisposition to vascillate between the two styles of stress-coping.	**Controller?** Total your "yes" responses to questions: 1, 2, 3, 4, 5, 6, 10, 16, 17, 20, 21 Total Score _____	**Escaper** Total your "yes" responses to questions: 7, 8, 9, 11, 12, 13, 14, 15, 18, 19, 22 Total Score _____

Source: Latack, J. C. (1986). Coping with job stress: Measures and future directions for scale development. *Journal of Applied Psychology*, 71, 377–385.

Scoring Appendix 6.2

Give yourself 1 mark for each question you responded "yes" to in Appendix 6.2 The range is 0-20. The higher the score, the healthier your lifestyle and health habits appear to be. The lower your score, the more destructive your lifestyle and health habits appear to be.

REFERENCES

Ames, G., & Delaney, W. (1992). Minimization of workplace alcohol problems: The supervisor's role. *Alcoholism: Clinical and Experimental Research*, 16, 180–189.

Brief, A. P., & Folger, R. G. (1992). The workplace and problem drinking as seen by two novices. *Clinical and Experimental Research*, 16, 190–198.

Cascio, W. F. (1991). *Costing Human Resources: The Financial Impact of Behavior in Organizations* (3rd ed.). Boston: PWS-Kent.

Cascio, W. F., & Thacker, J. W. (1994). *Managing Human Resources*. Toronto: McGraw-Hill Ryerson, Ltd., 569–606.

Connor, P. E., & Worley, C. H. (1991). Managing organizational stress. *Business Quarterly* (Summer), 1–7.

Dewe, P. J., & Guest, D. E. (1990). Methods of coping with stress at work: A conceptual analysis and empirical study of measurement issues. *Journal of Organizational Behavior*, 11, 135–150.

Employee Assistance Professionals Association (EAPA). (1991) Arlington, VA: Resource Center.

Falkenberg, L. E. (1987). Employee fitness programs: Their impact on the employee and the organization. *Academy of Management Review*, 12, 511–522.

Fielding, K. (1989). Work site stress management: National survey results. *Journal of Occupational Medicine*, 31, 990–991.

Folkman, S., & Lazarus, R. S. (1980). An analysis of coping in a middle-aged community sample. *Journal of Health and Social Behavior*, 21, 219–239.

Gaeta, E., Lynn, R., & Grey, L. (1982). AT&T looks at program evaluation. *EAP Digest* (May-June), 22–31.

Gebhardt, D. L., & Crump, C. E. (1990). Employee fitness and wellness programs in the workplace. *American Psychologist*, 45, 262–272.

Geran, L. (1992). Occupational stress. *Canadian Social Trends*, Statistics Canada.

Gibb-Clark, M. (1995). Imperial oil alcoholism ruling backed: Firms have right to prevent work accidents, but not to probe employee's past, lawyers say. *The Globe and Mail* (July 1), p. B1.

Googins, B., & Godfrey, J. (1987). *Occupational Social Work*. Englewood Cliffs, NJ: Prentice-Hall, Inc.

Ivancevich, J. M., Matteson, M. T., Freedman, S. M., & Phillips, J. S. (1990). Worksite stress: Management interventions. *American Psychologist*, 45, 252–261.

Kiefhaber, A. (1987). *The National Survey of Worksite Health Promotion Activities*. Washington, DC: U.S. Department of Health and Human Services. Office of Health Promotion and Disease Prevention.

Kirkcaldy, B. D., & Shephard, R. J. (1990). Therapeutic implications of exercise. *International Journal of Sport Psychology*, 21, 165–184.

Latack, J. C. (1986). Coping with job stress: Measures and future directions for scale development. *Journal of Applied Psychology*, 71, 377–385.

Leiter, M. P. (1991). Coping patterns as predictors of burnout: The function of control and escapist coping patterns. *Journal of Organizational Behavior*, 12, 123–144.

List, W. (1987). Employee fitness pays dividends. *The Globe and Mail* (May 15), p. D18.

Maddi, S. S. (1987). Hardiness training at Illinios Bell Telephone. In J. P. Opatz (Ed.), *Health Promotion Evaluation*. Birmingham, MI: Institute of Wellness, 43–53.

Masi, D. A., & Friedland, S. J. (1988, June). EAP actions and options. *Personnel*, 61–67.

McLaren v. Webber Hospital Association, 386 A.2d 734 (Maine 1978).

Pearlin, L. I., & Schooler, C. (1978). The structure of coping. *Journal of Health and Social Behavior*, 19, 2–21.

Reed, R. W. (1984). Is education the key to lower health care costs? *Personnel Journal* (January), 40–46.

Steffy, B. D., Jones, J. W., & Noe, A. W. (1990). The impact of health habits and lifestyle on the stressor-strain relationship: An evaluation of three industries. *Journal of Occupational Psychology*, 63, 217–229.

Straussner, S. L. A. (1988). Comparison of in-house and contracted-out employee assistance programs. *Social Work* (January-February), 53–55.

Terborg, J. R. (1986). Health promotion at the worksite: A research challenge for personnel and human resources management. In K. H. Rowland & G. R. Ferris (Eds.), *Researching Personnel and HRM*. Greenwich, CT: JAI Press, 225–267.

Part IV

The Personality
Predisposition Issue

Chapter 7

Understanding the Difference between Self-Healing and Self-Destructive Personality Predispositions

A CASE IN POINT

William Bartell, Human Resource Manager for Wyler Industries Limited, felt that by the end of the last session on outward signs of distress, many participants expressed high interest in receiving feedback on their *Person*-ality predispositions, the third segment of the C-O-*P*-E model. Participants' curiosities focused on whether their longer-term, habituated cognitions and behaviors placed them closer to the "self-healing" end of the health-distress continuum or closer to the "self-destructive" end. Despite the pervasive level of psychological readiness apparent in the room, a few participants expressed concerns about getting feedback that might *not* be positive, and that could, therefore, distress them more. William said that while he understood and respected these concerns, he genuinely felt that a self-introspection session such as they were about to begin might, indeed, provoke some mild psychological pain in the short term but lead to mental- and physical-health gains over the longer term. His response seemed to bring some relief. William ended the outward signs of distress session by telling the participants to participate in the Personality predisposition sessions only if they felt psychologically ready and comfortable to do so.

THE OPENING ADDRESS: SELF-HEALING AND SELF-DESTRUCTIVE PERSONALITY PREDISPOSITIONS

William began his first session on personality predispositions:
It is probably clear by now that it is not just environmental stressors that create pathological levels of distress for individuals and organizations.

Rather, as suggested by Lazarus, excessive stress levels result from the *interactions* between "objective" characteristics in the work and home environments, organizational members' personality predispositions (i.e., their enduring cognitive and behavioral traits), and their appraisals of stressors in these two arenas. Though stress is transactional, recent research has shown that individuals with good stress-coping skills seem to be able to reduce their appraisals of distress across situations and life stages because they perceive that, *intrinsically*, they have the requisite adaptive life resources to handle taxing life events. Thus, by their very nature, "good stress-copers" remain "self-healers" over the longer term, often having a good quality of life and adequate years of life. Individuals with poor stress-coping skills, on the other hand, seem not to be able to reduce their appraisals of distress across situations or life stages because they perceive that, *intrinsically*, they do not have the requisite adaptive life resources to handle taxing life events. Thus, by their very nature, "poor stress-copers" become "self-destructive" or "disease-prone" over the longer term, often impairing their quality of life and/or the number of years of life.

This session and the next one on personality predispositions, the third segment in the stress-C-O-P-E-ing model, are meant to provide participants with feedback about the "healthfulness" or "destructiveness" of their habituated thoughts, feelings, and behaviors. While we looked at participants' positive affect (PA) and negative affect (NA) predispositions in an earlier session (see Chapter 3) and appraised participants' stress-coping efforts in our last session (Chapter 6), there has been additional information on stress-coping reported in recent years. These two sessions on Personality predispositions focus on this critical health- and life-saving information.

So as not to bias your responses to the inventories you are about to complete, *I would ask that you please turn to the appendixes for this session* (i.e., Chapter 8 Appendixes) *and complete as honestly as you can the inventory items that appear before you. Please do not score these inventory items* (in Chapter 8) *until asked to do so. After you have finished responding, please join us for further discussions of this material.*

A SHORT HISTORY OF THE QUESTS FOR THE MENTAL, PHYSIOLOGICAL, AND ORGANIZATIONAL HEALTH "GRAILS"

The Mental Health Quest

After the release of Lazarus's transactional model of stress and strain in the mid-1960s, and throughout the 1970s, some mental health experts suggested that when individuals are asked to rate the stressfulness of a recent life event (as in the SRRS; see Chapter 3), they base their judgments, at least in part, on the degree of negative affect and resulting tension experienced. Other mental health experts suggested that when individuals are asked to rate the stressfulness of a recent life period, they base their judgments, at least in part, on the breadth and severity of stress symptomology experienced (as in the SCL and the GHQ; see Chapter 5). By the end of the 1970s, many experts concluded, therefore, that a strong case could be made for assessing individuals' overall stress-coping effectiveness by measuring both their appraised degree of negative affect and the intensity of symptomology experienced.

By the end of the 1970s, and particularly with the advent of the term "burnout" and the recognition that some organizational members in a highly distressful work environment do not burn out, mental health experts began to question why it is that some individuals cope well with taxing life events, while others seem not to cope so well. Because by their very nature individuals differ in their predispositions to experience distress, Freudenberger (1974), Latack (1984), and others have argued that greater clarification of the role of personality attributes is needed to determine how it is that some individuals stay relatively "self-healing," while others seem to self-destruct or become "disease-prone." Thus, starting in the late 1970s and continuing through the present, mental health experts around the world have searched, in earnest, for the personality components contributing to the "mental-health grail."

The Physiological Health Quest

In the early 1960s, astonished by the billion-dollar losses to society and organizations from cardiovascular disease, physiological and medical experts around the globe devoted much energy to discovering factors that contribute to early onset of this disabling and often fatal disease. By the start of the 1970s, epidemiological research had uncovered a number of physiological, lifestyle, and habitual factors associated with increased risks of myocardial infarctions (i.e., heart attacks), including high concentrations of serum cholesterol, elevated blood pressure, cigarette smoking, and, to a lesser degree, obesity and diabetes, a lack of moderated physical exercise, and a family history of heart disease. Despite these advancements in knowledge, physiological and medical experts concluded that whether viewed singly or in combination, the just-cited risk factors failed to identify new cases of heart disease in the population at highest risk in the 1970s: middle-aged men. Therefore, experts (particularly those in the United States) turned their attention to the personality-predisposing risk factors leading to "premature" cardiovascular disease (i.e., before age 55) (Stambler, Berkson, & Lindberg, 1972; Jenkins, 1976). And so it was that starting in the mid-1970s and continuing through the present, physiological and medical experts have searched, in earnest, for the personality components contributing to the "cardiovascular health grail."

A similar search history exists for cancer, another major disabling and often fatal disease draining societies and organizations. By the late 1970s, epidemiological research revealed that externally imposed carcinogens (i.e., cancer-producing agents) and lifestyle/habit-induced risk factors (such as cigarette smoking and alcohol drinking), singly or in combination, could not fully account for humans' cancer onsets. In fact, in 1981, the National Cancer Institute's statistics showed that diet and tobacco-ingestion habits account for about 30% of cancer causes, reproductive/sexual behavior accounts for about 7% of cancer causes, occupational hazards account for about 4%, alcohol-ingestion accounts for about 3%, geophysical variables account for about 3%, environmental pollution accounts for about 2%, and industrial products account for about 1%. Independent laboratory investigations reported that, at most, 40% of the total variance for cancer incidence could be accounted for by environmental and/or lifestyle/habit factors (*Journal of the National Cancer Institute*, 1981; Schmidt, 1984; Grossarth-Maticek et al., 1982). Therefore, some experts posited, other personality risk factor(s) not previously studied needed to be investigated. Therefore, starting in the late 1970s and continuing through the present, cancer experts (particularly those in Europe), have searched, in earnest, for the personality components contributing to the "cancer-prevention grail."

The Organizational Health Quest

By the late 1970s, organizational experts, too, became discouraged by the lack of variance accounted for by macrosystem variables when assessing organizational members' job satisfaction and other organizational health measures. Despite warnings from experts in the 1930s about the likely impact of organizational members' dispositional influences on job satisfaction (Fisher & Hanna, 1931), the bulk of organizational health research prior to and including the early 1970s focused on situational determinants (like role ambiguity, role conflict, and role overload/underload) (Fried & Ferris, 1987). Then Schneider and Dachler (1978) shook the organizational world with the news that organizational members' job satisfaction levels, in particular, seemed to stabilize over a sixteen-month period, implying that job satisfaction (and likely other organizational health outcomes) could be caused by factors *intrinsic* to organizational members besides factors *extrinsic* to them. In 1985, Staw and colleagues reported stability of organizational members' job satisfaction levels over a five-year period—even when their employers or occupations changed. The following year, Staw and colleagues reported that individuals' job satisfaction dispositions measured during adolescence were predictive of their job satisfaction many years later (George, 1992), indicating that job satisfaction not only resides, in part, *within* individuals but seems to remain stable from one life stage to another. Finally, in a study of monozygotic twins reared apart, researchers Arvey and colleagues (1989) concluded that 30% of the observed variance in organizational members' job satisfaction could be explained by genetic factors. Thus, by the end of the 1980s, a growing body of evidence suggested that likely up to 70% of the variance in organizational members' job satisfaction and other organizational-health measures could be explained by the *interaction* of personality AND situational factors (George, 1992). Thus, starting in the late 1970s and continuing through the present, organizational experts around the globe have searched, in earnest, for the personality components contributing to the "organizational-health grail."

Summary

Unsurprisingly, the accumulated findings over the last twenty years indicate that the somewhat independent searches for mental, physiological, and organizational health uncovered similar sets of personality-predisposing "self-healing" and "disease-prone" factors. These will now be discussed in some detail.

RECENT DISCOVERIES OF PERSONALITY PREDISPOSITIONS ASSOCIATED WITH MENTAL HEALTH AND MENTAL ILL HEALTH

The notion that some mental diseases are not only caused by stress but may be related to certain aspects of personality has been considered over centuries by physicians relying on their own personal experience and insights. Early theories of the relationship between personality and mental health came, in fact, from the ancient Greeks, who believed that the proportions, or balance, of the four bodily fluids—blood, black bile, yellow bile, and phlegm—determined both an individual's temperament and mental health. Accordingly, an oversupply of blood led to a sanguine and ruddy personality, an oversupply of black bile led to depression and degenerative disease, an oversupply of yellow bile led to an angry personality, and an oversupply of phlegm led to a cold personality. Eventually, the bodily fluid explanation of personality and mental health lost favor within the medical community, and with its disappearance went the personality "risk" factors that influenced medical practice for over 2,000 years.

Then, with the ground-breaking release of Hans Selye's (1950) physiological research findings on human stress in the 1950s, with Lazarus's (1960) description of the important role of stress appraisal in the 1960s, with Freudenberger's (1974) delineation of burnout in the 1970s, and with Latack's (1984) reporting of the importance of controller and escapist stress-coping in the mid-1980s, the notion of a critical relationship between stress and personality resurfaced. Today, experts in the psychology, medical, physiological, and organizational sciences agree that to study stress and personality separately is a grievous error.

The Personality Predispositions Associated with Mental Health

The question that has confronted experts in recent years is: Can it be said that self-healing personalities are resistant to the mental destruction of stress and strain over the longer term—and if so, what components of personality are responsible for such mental resiliency?

The answer to the latter question seems to be, yes. Like the Greek physicians centuries ago, current researchers believe that certain enduring cognitive and behavioral factors in individuals can make them seemingly resilient to destruction. Experts believe that individuals predisposed to NOT becoming mentally disabled or diseased do so because of a combination of health-maintaining factors, including but not limited to genetics, temperament, cognitions related to previously appraised life events, early socialization, moderated energy usage, a healthy lifestyle, good habits, time for relaxation and energy-refueling, and a broad range of controlling and palliative stress-coping efforts (Friedman & VandenBos, 1992). Called by many names in the health and organizational literature, including the "self-healer," "the assertive Type B," and "the autonomous personality," individuals who are so predisposed appear to be good stress-copers, and, therefore, good stress managers.

A large part of the self-healing process is due to the unique information processing that goes on within the minds of "health-maintenance" individuals. Their reaction to taxing work and home stressors is distinct. For example, when self-healing personalities encounter psychosocial environments that are a poor match for their personal needs (of, say, a power, affiliation, or achievement nature), their cognitions about such life situations are appraised as being "eustressfully challenged" rather than "distressfully threatened." As a result, these adaptive individuals often develop healthy and changed cognitions to allow them to more easily accept and assimilate their "challenging" experiences into previously gathered information sets. In short, self-healing personalities tend to have an unending need to learn and to grow personally from their taxing life events rather than to become distressed, stifled, or destroyed by them. Moreover, self-healers seem to have an abundant supply of optimism that gets them through most naturally occurring or uncontrollable life disasters and negative life events. Thus, over the course of their lives, self-healing personalities become cognitively and behaviorally habituated to self-mastery and self-aspiration and emotionally habituated to positive affects.

In the past few years, mental health experts' attention has turned to identifying the cognitive elements of mental well-being. Accordingly, Friedman and VandenBos (1992) and Kobasa (1979) have described the mind-set of self-healers as "enthusiastic" and "stress-hardy." "Enthusiastic" means "having a godly spirit within." "Stress-hardy" means "experiencing stress without falling ill."

Mental and physiological health experts Chesney and Rosenman (1983) have painted a similar positive picture of the self-healing, assertive Type Bs' mind-behavior patterns by suggesting that the former are not provoked to become excessively competitive, aggressive, or impatient when taxing demands present but instead maintain an optimistic, moderated, task-and-emotion-balanced style of responding.

Similarly, Grossarth-Maticek and Eysenck (1991) paint the picture of the autonomous individual with the same positive brush strokes. Autonomous types, they note, are characterized by their ability to correct exaggerated expectations by recognizing the actual consequences—costs and benefits—of their behavior. In this way, autonomous individuals can regulate their "nearness to" or "distance from" particular persons or things in the light of probable consequences resulting from this two-sided evaluation. Autonomous individuals are not naive or unrealistic about the returns on their investments. Moreover, they do not expect satisfaction of their most important emotional needs from other people or things in a passive, helpless, and dependent position, but are able to achieve the desired consequences through their own well-planned activities, positive or corrective self-evaluations, and moderated behavior patterns. Thus, they are able to correct or abandon "extreme" object-dependent patterns of behavior in the light of the resulting consequences and, as a result, learn new and autonomous behavior patterns. These alternative patterns of behavior, as long as they are experienced as need-satisfying, are seen to be a more acceptable type of behavior than "object-dependent" relationships—whether these objects be money, people, things, or activities.

In contrast, individuals who cannot—for whatever reason—reach this degree of autonomy but who remain in an "object-dependent" relationship, in general, experience great anxiety about being abandoned by a so-called "symbiotic" object- or person-relationship (that is, "symbiotic" by their own appraisals). Thus, nonautonomous individuals' cognitions and behaviors make for a lifetime of self-appraised unhappiness and anger (Grossarth-Maticek & Eysenck, 1991).

Experts Friedman and VandenBos (1992) suggest that there are a number of manifest behaviors that distinguish self-healing, assertive Type B, autonomous individuals from disease-prone types. Self-healers' constellation of verbal and nonverbal traits includes a natural smile (that is, the individual's eye movements, eyebrows, and mouth are synchronized, not forced, into producing a warm, inviting smile); a calm and conscientious appearance, not prone to fidgeting or aggressive gestures; "balanced" body movements and speech, with body gestures that tend to move away from the body and with vocal tones that sound "at peace" and moderated; and an emotionally

intact but not over-controlled mind, as reflected in few speech disturbances—even in stress-producing situations.

Moreover, from an interpersonal perspective, self-healers attract others
to them because they seem to make the best out of a not-so-perfect situation, and they have a remarkable sense of bringing the best out in others.
They have an optimistic growth orientation, are spontaneous and creative,
are good problem solvers, have a sense of humor that is philosophical
rather than hostile, and are generally concerned with issues of beauty, justice, ethics, and understanding. Self-healers have few stress-related mental
and physical disorders because they derive much eustress from their home
lives, their leisure pursuits, and their jobs. Moreover, they are habituated
to healthy lifestyles. They build into their daily regimens the time and the
means for emotionally refueling, self-introspecting, and relaxing (i.e.,
"down-time"). Although they are achievement-oriented and like to do their
jobs competently, they are not obsessed with perfection. They realize that
energy must be appropriately allocated for tasks at work and at home and
for emotional refueling with significant others. Because self-healers invest
much time and energy in both their tasks and emotions, they develop emotionally "healthy" relationships with their spouses, their children, their
friends, and their coworkers. The latter provide a kind of social network
and means of "venting" during periods of high life stress (Friedman &
VandenBos, 1992).

Kobasa (1979) discovered that besides setting up good stress-venting social networks, the cognitions of hardy types deescalate the psychological
noise associated with stressful life events rather than escalate it. In this
sense, self-healers are truly copers rather than victims of stress. There are
three life-saving cognitions, in particular, that seem to keep them mentally
and physically healthy:

- They perceive that they have a great sense of control over what occurs in their
  lives;
- They feel committed to the various areas of their lives, including work and nonwork activities; and
- They view change as a challenge rather than as a threat.

First, as noted, self-healers try to control what they can control in their
lives—without infringing on others' rights to do the same. Because of this
belief, they remain healthier than those who feel powerless to control their
lives, or who feel that they have to control everybody else's lives besides
their own. Self-healers maintain decisional control by seeing themselves as
having the capability to autonomously choose among various courses of
action about how to handle stressors. Moreover, they work on developing
a wide-ranging repertoire of suitable responses for dealing with stressors
and make a conscious effort to maintain (sometimes against the odds) a

positive motivation to achieve and to self-actualize in spite of temporary setbacks.

Second, as noted, self-healers feel committed to the various areas of their lives. Thus, with all sorts of activities and interactions available for "energy-refueling," these extraverted individuals remain healthier than those who are introverted, alienated from others, and unidimensionally fixated on either task perfection or on relationship perfection.

Third, as noted, self-healers appraise change as "a challenge." Thus, they remain healthier than those who view change as "a threat" and who, consequently, misuse or overuse their sympathetic systems, as described by Cannon, or their parasympathetic systems, as described by Selye (see Chapter 5). As change seekers, self-healers value a life filled with interesting experiences for personal growth, but unlike disease-prone types, they do not engage in irresponsible, energy-draining adventurousness. Moreover, self-healers have a tendency to be cognitively "flexible" and "elastic" rather than "rigid" and "inelastic." This flexibility allows them to more adequately integrate and more effectively appraise the demands of new (and sometimes initially intimidating) life situations. Finally, self-healers, in being enjoyably challenged by all that life has to offer, have an uncanny ability to persist in their life journeys for truth and justice, even when newly appraised information may be (uncomfortably) incongruous with information previously collected in earlier life stages (Kobasa, 1979).

To understand the mind-set of autonomous self-healers more clearly, mental health experts McCrae and Costa (1989) have recently suggested that the five-factor model of personality (which is widely accepted in mainstream personality psychology) needs to be considered. Briefly, the five-factor model of personality is a version of trait theory, which maintains that the many ways in which individuals differ in their enduring emotional, cognitive, and behavioral styles can be characterized along a mental-health continuum ranging from low-to-high degrees of the following five traits:

- N or *neuroticism* includes the predisposition to experience negative affects such as anxiety, anger, and depression, and other cognitive and behavioral manifestations of emotional instability. Self-healing personalities tend to be lower on this dimension.

- E or *extraversion* includes sociability, activity, dominance (rather than submissiveness), and the tendency to experience positive affect. Self-healing personalities tend to be higher on this dimension.

- O or *openness to experience* is seen in imaginativeness, aesthetic sensitivity, depth of feeling, curiosity, and need for variety. Self-healing personalities tend to be higher on this dimension.

- A or *agreeableness* encompasses sympathy, trust, cooperation, and altruism. Self-healing personalities tend to be higher on this dimension.

Table 7.1
Adjectives That Define the Five Personality Factors and the Self-Healing
Personality

Factor (Higher or Lower)	Descriptor Continuum
N	Calm-Worrying Even tempered-Temperamental Self-satisfied-Self-pitying Comfortable-Self-conscious Unemotional-emotional Stress-Hardy-Stress-vulnerable
E	Reserved-Affectionate Loner-Joiner Quiet-Talkative Passive-Active Sober-Fun-loving Unfeeling-Passionate
O	Down-to-earth-Imaginative Uncreative-Creative Conventional-Original Prefer routine-Prefer variety Uncurious-Curious Conservative-Liberal
A	Ruthless-Soft-hearted Suspicious-Trusting Stingy-Generous Antagonistic-Acquiescent Critical-Lenient Irritable-Good-natured
C	Negligent-Conscientious Lazy-Hardworking Disorganized-Well-organized Late-Punctual Aimless-Ambitious Quitting-Persevering

Source: McCrae, R. R. (1991). The five-factor model and its assessment in clinical settings. *Journal of Personality Assessment, 57*, 399–414.

- C or *conscientiousness* includes organization, persistance, scrupulousness, and a "healthy" (but not obsessive) need for achievement. Self-healing personalities tend to be higher on this dimension.

Adjectives that further define the five traits associated with self-healing predispositions are shown in Table 7.1 (McCrae, 1991).

Besides the five-factor model, the Myers-Briggs type indicator, or MBTI, has become a recent popular device for ascertaining self-healing personality predispositions by delineating how individuals process information or react to stimuli in their environment (Myers & McCaulley, 1985). Although the less controversial five-factor model is not based on any single theory of personality but has been shown to encompass traits that operationalize a number of theoretical perspectives, the more controversial MBTI is based on one of the classic statements of personality theory (i.e., Jungian theory) and purports to measure sixteen distinct "types" of personality, based on some combination of the following four information-processing predispositions:

Extraversion-Introversion (E-I). Extraverts (E) are aroused by external information and stimuli, whereas introverts (I) are aroused by internal information and stimuli.

Sensing-Intuitive (S-N). Sensing (S) individuals have strong preferences for focusing on environmental stimuli received in a direct, factual, realistic way, whereas intuitive (I) types rely less on sensory stimuli and more on internally generated, "sixth-sense" kinds of "creative" stimuli.

Thinking-Feeling (T-F). Thinking (T) types rely on cognitive processes to put their life experiences into order—preferring to link ideas according to abstract concepts and logic, whereas feeling (F) types have a strong preference for organizing their life experiences and ideas around previously developed personal values and beliefs.

Judging-Perceptual (J-P). Judging (J) types prefer to make decisions, bring closure to issues, and complete tasks according to routine, whereas perceptual (P) types prefer to gather much information before making decisions, avoid closure, and keep decision-making options open in case some new, useful information comes along.

Since 1962, the MBTI has increasingly become widely used in clinical and industrial settings for a variety of purposes—not only to help individuals become "self-aware" about their self-healing information-processing predispositions but to develop teams in organizations, to develop leaders, to counsel marriage partners, to help individuals manage stress, and to select individuals for jobs. In fact, in North America alone, millions of working adults have completed this inventory to receive their prevailing four-letter "Type" reading. It is not uncommon for participants to wear pins advertising their Type within their seminars, and type clubs have even recently emerged. Despite its popularity, personality psychologists have been less enthusiastic about the MBTI than industrial consultants, suggest that the Jungian concepts that are supposed to underlie the MBTI have been distorted, that the sixteen so-called "unique" psychological Types have not been differentiated into those that are "self-healing" and those that are "self-destructive," and that the validity of sixteen distinct Types is questionable and counter to the normal-distribution-of-trait philosophy of personality assessment. Because of such claims, in 1991 the National Research Council (NRC) in the United States, a panel of the National Academy of Sciences comprised of fourteen psychologists, examined the MBTI and research findings pertaining to its reliability, validity, and usage. The panel concluded that while the MBTI gives participants valuable insights into their extraversion (E)-introversion (I) tendencies, its ability to give reliable sensing (S), intuitive (N), thinking (T), feeling (F), judging (J), or perceptual (P) tendency readings is weaker. The panel concluded that when the MBTI is used as a self-awareness tool (with continuous dimension scores rather than a four-letter "Type") and applied to choosing an occupation, marital counseling, or stress management, its use is consistent with its strengths. However, as a selection device for hiring and promoting organizational members or as an instrument for forming effective work teams, its usefulness is not consistent with its strengths—and is likely to be challenged in the court system as an "inappropriate use" of the MBTI (Zemke, 1992).

In North America, men are said to "cluster" on the ISTJ and ESTJ Types, whereas women are said to be distributed among the 16 Types formed by the various four-letter combinations. Older individuals have been found to prefer judging (J) lifestyles, women have been found to prefer feeling (F) stimuli and situations, and more formally educated individuals have been found to prefer intuitive (N) stimuli and situations. Occupational Type trends across cultures are reportedly stable, with some variation within each culture as to the degree of Type rather than kind. In the male-dominated management field, for example, the average Type profile for Chinese managers is reportedly ISTJ, whereas that for European managers is reportedly ESTJ. Within cultures, male-dominated occupations like business, mining, construction, and mechanics tend to attract predominantly thinking (T) rather than feeling (F) information processors, whereas in the health professions like counseling and education, the feeling (F) rather than the thinking (T) information processors tend to predominate (McCrae & Costa, 1989; Davey, Schell, & Morrison, 1993).

Because of the potential usefulness of the MBTI in stress management sessions as a means of ascertaining mental-health predispositions, in 1989 McCrae and Costa investigated how the "continuous" MBTI scores of 267 men and 201 women, aged 19 to 63, correlated with their scores on the NEO-PI, an instrument known to assess the traits of the five-factor model. The correlation findings between these two sets of scores are presented in Table 7.2 (McCrae & Costa, 1989, p. 30). Note that the MBTI scores are given in the direction of the second letter; that is, higher scores indicate introversion (I), intuition (N), feeling (F), and perception (P).

The following findings from Table 7.2 are worthy of note:

- Both men and women who received high neuroticism (N) scores on the NEO-PI tended to have high introversion (I) scores on the MBTI.
- Both men and women who received high extraversion (E) scores on the NEO-PI tended to have high extraversion (E) scores on the MBTI.
- Both men and women who received high openness (O) scores on the NEO-PI tended to have high intuitive (N) and perceptual (P) scores on the MBTI.

Table 7.2
Correlations of Self-Reported NEO-PI Factors (N, E, O, A, C) with MBTI
Continuous Scales (EI, SN, TF, JP) in Men and Women

	Neuroticism (N)	Extraversion (E)	Openness (O)	Agreeableness (A)	Conscientious (O)
Men					
EI	.16**	-.74***	.03	-.03	.08
SN	-.06	.10	.72***	.04	-.15*
TF	.06	.19**	.02	.44***	-.15*
JP	.11	.15*	.30***	-.06	-.49***
Women					
EI	.17*	-.69***	-.03	-.08	.08
SN	.01	.22**	.69***	.03	-.10
TF	.28***	.10	-.02	.46***	-.22**
JP	.04	.20**	.26**	.05	-.46***

* $p < .05$; ** $p < .01$; *** $p < .001$
Source: McCrae, R. R., & Costa, P. T., Jr. (1989). Reinterpreting the Myers-Briggs type
    indicator from the perspective of the five-factor model of personality. *Journal of Person-
    ality, 57,* 17–40.

• Both men and women who received high agreeableness (A) scores on the NEO-
  PI tended to have high feeling (F) scores on the MBTI.
• Both men and women who received high conscientious (C) scores on the NEO-
  PI tended to have high thinking (T) and judgmental (J) scores on the MBTI.
• Some significant gender differences were observed. Women with high neuroticism
  (N) scores on the NEO-PI also tended to have high feeling (F) scores on the MBTI,
  but this finding did not hold for men. Men with high extraversion (E) scores on
  the NEO-PI also tended to have high scores on the feeling (F) and perceptual (P)
  dimensions of the MBTI, whereas women with high extraversion (E) scores on
  the NEO-PI also tended to have high scores on the intuitive (N) and perceptual
  (P) dimensions.

Thus, if one were attempting to generalize these MBTI and NEO-PI findings to the notion of a "self-healing" personality, it would seem that "self-
healing" men and women tend to have higher E (extraversion) scores rather
than I (introversion) scores. Beyond this conclusion, however, the study
results using these two key inventories seem to provide few other "self-
healing" personality consistencies because of the gender differences noted
and because of certain trait contradictions. Note, for example, that while
men and women with high scores on the valued open (O) dimension were
found to have high scores on intuition (N) and perception (P), those with

high scores on the valued conscientious (C) dimension were found to have high scores on the thinking (T) and judgmental (J) dimensions. So which trait package is it more "self-healing" to have—an intuitive (N)-perceptual (P) trait package or a Thinking (T)-judgmental (J) one? The latter question is one that has intrigued mental-health experts in recent years and, as yet, has not been answered.

The Personality Predispositions Associated with Mental Ill Health

All human beings are capable of experiencing bouts of anger, worry, sadness, and guilt, and the extent to which "normally predisposed" human beings do so varies widely within the population. The predisposition to experience pronounced negative affect and related predispositions such as poor impulse control and irrational thinking corresponds to the basic dimension of personality called neuroticism (N). It is the first factor in the five-factor model, and was discussed earlier.

Even though negativism is a dimension of "normal" personality, experts have recently preferred to use the term negative affect (NA) to differentiate the mild or mood-induced forms of negativism from the more pronounced, or trait, forms of neuroticism (N). Moreover, "psychologically well-adjusted" and "emotionally stable" are terms used by mental health experts to describe individuals very low in N, such as the self-healers.

For years, the neuroticism (N) dimension has been prevalent in psychological inventories specifically designed to assess individuals predisposed to mental ill-health or abnormal cognitions. The Eysenck Personality Questionnaire, the Minnesota Multiphasic Personality Inventory (MMPI), the Millon Clinical Multiaxial Inventory (MCMI), and the NEO-PI (for assessing the five personality factors) all include N assessments.

There is a growing body of evidence suggesting that neuroticism (N) is, in large part, genetically determined, and like other personality traits, is very stable in adulthood. Intervening stressful life-events seem to have little influence on the long-term stability of N. That is, individuals high in neuroticism (N) are prone to worry and stress, regardless of the presence of threatening stimuli. They are prone to feelings of depression even in the absence of losses (such as the death of a loved one). Given identical environmental circumstances, individuals high in neuroticism (N) will perceive much more life stress than those who are low in N. Therefore, posit present-day mental-health experts, if two individuals differ in their levels of perceived stress, one cannot assume that the individual who reports more distress is actually under more stress. He or she may simply be more N-predominant, or distress-prone, and from situation to situation and from one life stage to another appraise "stress" as occurring, regardless of the life circumstances or stressors presenting (McCrae, 1990).

McCrae has further posited that if neuroticism (N) affects only subjectively based appraisals of stress, it would be a small problem, contributing only random error to measurement. But because personality predispositions exert a pervasive influence on individuals' cognitions, feelings, and behaviors, neuroticism (N) contributes systematic bias that can seriously confound research applications in the area of stress management. Specifically, neuroticism (N) has been shown to influence individuals' perceptions of stress (i.e., they are highly stressed), their ways of coping (i.e., they tend to be poor stress copers), their satisfaction with social supports (i.e., they think that there is never enough support or that others have "the problem"), their psychological well-being (i.e., their well-being levels are self-reportedly low), and their somatic complaints (i.e., their somatic complaints are self-reportedly high but not necessarily with presenting disease). Thus, N needs to be taken into serious consideration by stress management counselors and consultants.

For the latter reasons, stress experts tend to currently believe that the degree of neuroticism (N) presenting in clients needs to be assessed before stress treatment interventions of either a macroorganizational or microsystem nature are developed. For if the "real" problem is in the stressed client's personality, changing conditions in the environment or macrosystem will not help in the long run. Instead, psychotropic medications for stressed individuals or training in relaxation or meditation may be more fruitful ways to reduce such organizational members' chronic distress levels (McCrae, 1991).

Within recent years, McCrae and others have further posited that besides neuroticism (N), the other four factors in the five-factor model need to be assessed to ascertain individuals' other predisposing traits of mental ill health. Whether the MMPI, the MCMI, the NEO-PI, or some other well-designed, reliable, and valid instrument of personality assessment is used is somewhat immaterial, for it is apparent from the findings in Table 7.3 (McCrae, 1991, p. 407), shown below, that scales from both the MMPI and the MCMI—which have been used worldwide by clinicians to assess psychiatric disorders—are saturated by high neuroticism (N) and low extraversion (E), in particular.

Although there are several statistically significant correlation coefficients shown in Table 7.3 between the MMPI/MCMI scales and the personality dimensions of openness (O), agreeableness (A), and conscientiousness (C), these coefficients seem to be much smaller in magnitude than those for N and E (McCrae, 1991).

Recent evidence indicates that two of the latter "interpersonally related" personality variables—A and C—may be useful in identifying physiologically "disease-prone" types like the cardiovascular-prone type As (i.e., who seem to have prevailing high C scores) and the cancer-prone type Cs (who seem to have prevailing high A scores).

Table 7.3
Correlations of the NEO-PI Factors with Scales from the MMPI and MCMI

	N	E	O	A	C
MMPI Scales					
Hs	.35***	-.16**	-.01	.04	-.02
D	.34***	-.43***	-.03	.16**	.01
Hy	-.09	.01	.07	.20***	.11
Pd	.21***	.05	.24***	-.21***	-.28***
Mf	.31***	.09	.31***	.31***	.03
Pa	.07	-.01	.23***	.12*	.08
Pt	.63***	-.30***	.02	-.05	-.21***
Sc	.39***	-.28***	.12*	-.11	-.25***
Ma	.09	.34***	.13*	-.32***	-.19**
Si	.47***	-.63***	-.15*	-.02	.05
MCMI Scales					
Anxiety	.47***	-.28***	-.12	.15*	-.11
Somatoform	.50***	.01	-.27***	.19**	-.04
Hypomania	.15*	.54***	.10	-.11	-.04
Dysthymia	.47***	-.36***	-.03	.19***	-.11
Alcohol Abuse	.34***	.21**	-.05	.00	-.08
Drug Abuse	.01	.47***	.09	-.16*	-.08
Psychotic Thinking	.32***	-.36***	-.11	-.02	-.09
Psychotic Depression	.52***	-.32***	-.06	.07	-.10
Psychotic Delusion	-.09	-.13	-.13	-.18*	.27***

Note: N = 274 for MMPI and N = 207 for MCMI; * p < .05; ** p < .01; *** p < .001.
Source: McCrae, R. R. (1991). The five-factor model and its assessment in clinical settings. Journal of Personality Assessment, 57, 399–414.

Because the MBTI has no measure of neuroticism (N), it has up to now not been particularly useful as a mental ill-health assessment tool. However, because of its widespread popularity in industry and in some counseling programs, in 1986 experts Linton, Kuechenmeister, and Kuechenmeister (1986) wanted to determine if the MBTI inventory could be used to ascertain proneness to mental ill-health. Accordingly, they sought to answer three questions:

1. How frequently do various MBTI Types appear in a specific psychiatric patient population?

2. What, if any, is the relation between MBTI Type and psychiatric symptoms?

3. Given knowledge about the relationship between MBTI Types and psychiatric symptoms, can an accurate clinical diagnosis be predicted?

Linton, Kuechenmeister, and Kuechenmeister (1986) used the MBTI to assess information-processing Type and the MMPI to assess extreme psychiatric symptomology. Study participants were 200 patients (78 males and 122 females) admitted to an open psychiatric ward in a general hospital, and ranging in age from 17 to 67 years (with a mean age of 38). Only patients who were able to read and respond to the inventory items were included in the study; no other selection criteria were used. The researchers compared the percentage of hospitalized patients having each MBTI Type with the percentage having that Type in the nonpatient (i.e., "normal") population. Their results are summarized in Table 7.4 (p. 40).

In comparing their patients' data with that of nonpatients, these experts (Linton, Kuechenmeister, & Kuechenmeister, 1986) found

• An incidence of Introversion (I) in the patient population nearly twice that of the nonpatient population;

• An incidence of the introverted, sensing, feeling, judgmental (ISFJ) Type in the patient population three times that found in the female nonpatient population and six times that found in the male nonpatient population;

• A predominance of the ISFJ Type in the patient population;

• A predominance of ISFJ Types in all psychiatric disorder groups (i.e., adjustment disorders, depression disorders, psychotic disorders, and schizophrenic disorders), except for the anxiety disorder group, in which the ESFJ Type predominated; and

• A marked difference between males and females in the incidence of various other Types in the patient population.

These researchers also found that age correlated in a negative direction with intuition (N). This finding, they noted, is significant because it would appear that allowing for creative expression, which is what high-intuitives do, may be an effective stress-reducing and mental-ill-health prevention mechanism for many individuals. The time that young high-intuitives (or low-sensing Types) might become highly distressed and thus seek psychiatric treatment is when they are rebellious and "locked into" highly structured and "conditionally loving" home and school environments. The time that older, low-intuitives (or high-sensing Types) might become highly distressed and thus seek psychiatric treatment is when they experience a rapidly changing world requiring many cognitive and behavioral changes

Table 7.4
Percentage of Respective Population (Patient/Normal) for Each MBTI Type

MBTI Type	Males	Females	Genders Combined
ISTJ	13/9	8/5	10/7
ISFJ	30/5	32/10	31/7
INFJ	1/1	7/2	5/2
INTJ	0/3	2/1	1/2
ISTP	8/7	3/2	5/4
ISFP	13/6	4/6	8/6
INFP	4/3	6/4	5/4
INTF	1/4	4/1	3/3
ESTP	1/10	4/4	3/7
ESFP	3/8	6/12	5/10
ENFP	0/5	7/9	4/7
ENTF	1/5	0/3	1/4
ESTJ	14/18	4/13	8/16
ESFJ	6/9	12/21	10/15
ENFJ	4/2	2/4	3/3
ENTJ	1/4	0/2	1/3

Patients: Female N = 122, Male N = 78; Normals: Female and Male N < 1000.
Source: Linton, P. H., Kuechenmeister, C. A., & Kuechenmeister, S. B. (1986). Personality
type and psychiatric symptom formation. *Research Communications in Psychology, Psychiatry, and Behavior,* 11, 37–49.

from them—at a time when structure, stability, and personal control are needed the most by their "Type."

In responding to the question of why the predominance of the ISFJ Type in the patient population, Linton, Kuechenmeister, and Kuechenmeister (1986) outlined a number of reasons which suggest a personality-environmental kind of "misfit." First, they noted, introverted (I) Types have little interest in their "outer worlds" but prefer to place much of their attention on their "inner world" of concepts, ideas, and values. Thus, introverts are less communicative than extraverts, so in times of distress, the former are likely to withdraw from others and remain in isolation, focusing inwardly on their problems. Second, sensing (S) Types use their five senses to gather facts; thus, they put much faith in what they appraise as being "actual" or "realistic." Thus, even when their appraisals of life events are unrealistic or different from those of the majority, strong sensing Types remain committed to their beliefs. Third, feeling (F) Types like to please others and to be pleased in return. In order to stay "eustressed," feeling Types need a steady stream of affection, praise, and sympathy. Because SFs attempt to shape their lives to support the idealized values about which they feel most deeply, they often become disappointed—and highly distressed—to discover that no one in the world can sate their high needs for affection and affiliation. Fourth, judging (J) Types like to live a planned, orderly life, wanting to control and regulate which way their lives (and sometimes others' lives) go. Once judging Types make a decision, their minds are unlikely to change. Thus, even if judging Types could bring themselves to discover that a past decision made by them was inappropriate, they would bullishly stick to their already-made resolutions rather than make a change (which is what allows "well-adjusted" individuals to easily adapt and remain low to moderately stressed).

In short, said this team of researchers, because of their predispositions, ISFJs seem to particularly suffer from pathological levels of mental distress when they become "locked into" emotional relationships with someone of very different personality traits and values. The difficulty arises from the ISFJ's strong need to give and receive affection only in terms of an idealized, highly valued, "real" experience, although the "real" experience may be partly or wholly romantic. Adding to the stress and strain difficulty is the ISFJ's inability or lack of desire to change; that is, to learn new ways of relating to others in his or her environment.

Linton, Kuechenmeister, and Kuechenmeister concluded their study by noting:

Our results suggest that the measure of the stylistic attribute of human temperament, personality "type," is associated with specific psychiatric symptoms and syndromes. There is also evidence that some personality "types" are more vulnerable to psychiatric illness in certain situations where they show "poorness of fit." Whether it is a cause or a result, the "type" of preference manifested by psychiatrically ill patients remains the subject of further research, but the link between personality "type" and mental illness seems to be well established. (1986, pp. 47–48)

THE METHODOLOGICAL DIFFICULTIES OF DISCOVERING PERSONALITY PREDISPOSITIONS ASSOCIATED WITH PHYSIOLOGICAL ILL HEALTH

Physiological experts over the past twenty years have had considerable difficulty unraveling the mysteries behind personality predispositions and physiological ill health. Part of the difficulty has been that researchers cannot use "conventionally sound" experimental methodology to assess personality-physiological disease presentations. That is, researchers cannot randomly assign certain personality-predisposed individuals or MBTI Types

or five-factor Types to "eustressful" or "distressful" life situations and then
follow these Types' physiological health for years, documenting presenting
symptomology along the way. Given this methodological shortcoming,
most of what researchers have discovered about personality predisposition
and physiological disease-proneness has come from inferences drawn from
various kinds of theoretical assumptions and "after disease presents" empirical evidence.

As for mental ill health, more than any other personality factor, the
pattern of association between neuroticism (N) or negative affect (NA) and
physiological disease-proneness has been well documented across recent
prospective studies (Eysenck, 1987a, 1987b) and through a complex statistical technique called meta-analysis (a sophisticated kind of statistical
averaging) (Friedman, 1991; Booth-Kewley & Friedman, 1987).

OVERVIEW OF THE "PHYSIOLOGICALLY DISEASE-PRONE" COGNITIVE-BEHAVIORAL PROFILE

It should be emphasized that the findings that prevail in the 1990s on
the physiologically disease-prone personality have been challenged and cri-
tiqued many times over by experts around the world. The findings that
have remained in considerable favor have shown that there are groups of
adults who are disease-prone by virtue of their inability to express "appropriately and assertively" their negative emotions (Kissen & Eysenck, 1962),
their failure to cope with interindividual stress in an "appropriate" fashion
(Eysenck, 1985), and their overreaction to environmental stressors by way
of anger and aggression or by way of excessive emotional dependency on
others (Friedman & Booth-Kewley, 1982).

There is a sort of consensus among experts that, unlike self-healers or
assertive Type Bs, physiologically disease-prone adults lack adequate degrees of "autonomous self-regulation" and positive affect (PA). They are
characterized, instead, by large degrees of "outside control" and negative
affect (NA). The NA predominance is catalyzed, in part, by genetics and,
in larger part, by "discomforting" early childhood conditioning and socialization (Price, 1982; Grossarth-Maticek & Eysenck, 1991).

Thus, for disease-prone Types, a lack of autonomous self-regulation becomes associated in early childhood with a strong dependence on particular
"objects" in the child's environment, including unrealistically high or unrealistically low task or emotional goals, obsessions with task- or emo-
tional-fulfillment at any cost, and specific negative thoughts about oneself
and one's potential to self-master and self-actualize without the assistance
or presence of "particular objects." The latter negative self-evaluations follow the child into early adulthood and through later life stages.

Because of their chronically negative affect cognitions, physiologically
disease-prone adults suffer from bouts of anxiety and depression as they

move from one life stage to another. Then, once in a depression, these adults tend to further increase their distress levels and NA by dramatically inhibiting "healthful tendencies" to guide their behavior in light of probable, realistic, and possibly eustressful consequences. Their "ill-health tendencies," instead, guide their behavior in light of improbable, often unrealistic, catastrophic consequences. Over time, these psychological noise-escalating predispositions result in pathological levels of stress and strain, with eventual physiological disease presentations. Finally, because of their "object-dependent" predispositions, physiologically disease-prone adults tend to attribute "their health problems" to others in their work and/or home environment rather than own them. Thus, disease-prone individuals, because of this external locus of control orientation, often are found to be their own worst enemies when it comes to treatment.

DETAILS OF THE TYPE A AND TYPE C COGNITIVE-BEHAVIORAL PROFILES

Individuals who are cardiovascular disease-prone, in particular, have been labeled in the psychophysiological literature the "Type As," with a recent correction and heavy emphasis on "angry Type As." Individuals who are cancer-prone, in particular, have been called in the psychophysiological literature the "Type Cs," with a recent distinction between the "emotionally dependent" and "rationally dependent" Type C.

Although "angry Type As" and "emotionally or rationally dependent Type Cs" seem to have similar self-destructive cognitive predispositions, their outward appearances and manners of coping with environmental stressors vary considerably. Thus, from a stress management perspective, it becomes important to discuss these differences (Price, 1982; Grossarth-Maticek & Eysenck, 1991).

Starting in early childhood, both Type As and Type Cs are conditioned by significant others (like parents or guardians) to become person- or object-dependent and, thus, to become "regulated" from the outside rather than from the inside. Through the child's being repeatedly "encouraged" (through verbal, nonverbal, or behavioral means) to make his or her need-satisfactions and problem-solving capabilities dependent on the behavior of particular persons (like parents/guardians) or on objects (like marks in school or success in sport), the psychopathological behavior patterns of Type As and Type Cs become indelibly marked at an early age. Certainly by age 5, the Type A and Type C child's need-satisfactions become contingent upon playing this external locus-of-control role—which makes "autonomous self-regulation" virtually impossible.

In later childhood, adolescence, and through later life stages, Type A and Type C individuals live the conviction that they, themselves, are incapable of achieving need-satisfying situations and need-satisfying reactions through their own adaptive resources. Thus, they hold to the conviction that they are incapable of finding life significance of "their own making." Thus, desired "persons" or "objects" become, increasingly, all-powerful as a condition for their well-being, while the contribution of their own autonomous behavioral patterns for the achievement of personal satisfaction becomes, increasingly, unimportant.

Particulars of the Type C Stress-Coping Style

It is this continued "passivity" of coping with life's stressors which constitutes the essential personality and behavioral predispositions of emotionally dependent Type Cs. Their childhood emotional dependence on "important others" leads in adulthood to Type Cs' fulfilling their emotional needs within a "symbiotic framework" series of relationships. But "true symbiosis" does not exist, for the emotionally dependent Type C adult sees some all-powerful and all-needs-satisfying "chosen other" (such as friend, lover, spouse, or boss) as determining his or her behaviors and emotional reactions to situational outcomes. If "the chosen other" declines or fails to satisfy the Type C's needs and wishes, then hopelessness, agitation, helplessness and anxiety result. Ironically, although unsated, the Type C's dependency on "chosen others" escalates with time.

What is more, unsated Type Cs seem not to learn from their painful relationship outcomes the importance of their own self-healing cognitions and behaviors but enter instead into a habit of chronic self-blame, self-denigration, and negative escapist stress-coping. They rarely, if ever, place themselves in a position of correcting their feelings of low self-worth; therefore, Type Cs actually set themselves up for a lifetime of "eustress" failure. Through a lifetime of blocked needs and negative feelings about themselves, non-refueled Type C adults often become exhausted. Their inability to make themselves independent and self-autonomous leads to increasing passive acceptance of a "miserable" life situation; to overuse of the parasympathetic stress-response system, as described by Selye; to hopelessness, despair, depression; and, inevitably, (say some experts) to cancer. Finally, because emotionally-dependent Type Cs seem not to take full ownership of their problems, treatment interventions typically come later rather than sooner.

Particulars of the Type A Stress-Coping Style

In the coronary-prone Type A child, early childhood reactions to stressors are somewhat different from those of Type Cs. Whereas the same nonautonomous pattern of thinking is conditioned early on, Type A children, and later Type A adults, react to rejection by emotionally important others or to losses of emotionally important objects with anger, which may be suppressed. Angry Type As, unable in their minds to put an end to the needed associations or to the needed objects, experience a lifetime of self-appraised pain, frustration, and disappointment.

In an external locus of control orientation, these emotionally unfulfilled Type As convince themselves that "the desired person(s)" or "the system" that could reasonably sate their needs is responsible for their experienced stress, strain, and pain. Unable to take ownership of their problems (as self-healers normally would) but instead continually projecting the blame onto others, angry Type As' voluntary admission for stress treatment typically comes later rather than sooner.

Because blame is attributed to others or to macrosystems, revenge against these objects by angry, poorly adjusted Type As is not uncommon. Moreover, because of their inability to change their previously conditioned "tried-and-true habits" of stress-coping, which include keeping perfectionistically task-busy to avoid thinking about the problem, becoming psychologically or physically controlling over others as a means of remaining personally in control, and competing against or aggressing toward others if they are seen as "standing in the way" of task achievement or need fulfillment, pronounced Type As (like pronounced Type Cs), often unconsciously, set themselves up for failure. Unable to get their own way or to regain a sense of personal control, angry Type As seem to chronically vacillate between periods of depression and anxiety (though they may not openly admit it).

Because of their inability to "need-fulfill" or to "energy-refuel" over the longer term, an overwhelming feeling of "entrapment" in Type As leads to escalating levels of anger and hostility. Some of this anger is kept within (called "anger-in") and some of it is released (called "anger-out")—but not necessarily consciously. Accordingly, for angry Type As, the sympathetic stress-response system (as described by Cannon) is chronically being misused and over-used. Because of a life history of anger-retention (i.e, anger-in) and low positive affect, angry Type As age their cardiovascular systems prematurely. Sooner rather than later, say many experts, cardiovascular disease presents.

Additional Recent Points about Type As' and Type Cs' Health Risks and Personality Predispositions

Because of their distinct response patterns to stressors, Eysenck and his colleagues suggest that Type As should be "innoculated" against getting cancer prematurely and Type Cs should be "innoculated" against getting cardiovascular disease prematurely (Price, 1982; Grossarth-Maticek & Eysenck, 1991). Whether this assertion is indeed the case remains open for discussion and research investigation.

The five-factor model constellations which best describe angry Type As and emotionally dependent Type Cs are also still in question. Evidence to date (Eysenck & Fulker, 1983; Byrne & Rosenman, 1986; May & Kline, 1987) suggests that it is likely that "interpersonally distressed" Type As have high N (neurotic), low O (openness), low A (agreeableness), and high C (conscientious) predispositions, whereas "interpersonally distressed" Type Cs have high N (neurotic), low O (openness), high A (agreeableness) predispositions.

Finally, some recent study findings are indicating that "non-disease-prone Type As" may exist, characterized by high positive affect (George, 1992), but this predisposition has not been consistently reported in the psychophysiological literature.

CONSISTENTLY REPORTED RESEARCH FINDINGS ON TYPE As

On face, Type As tend to walk fast, talk fast, think fast, have relatively loud voices, are job- and task-fixated, use sarcasm, have forced rather than natural smiles, and talk over others if others take too long to come to the point. There is very little lag time between their processing of stimuli and their responses to them. They tend to be very action-oriented. Moreover, because of their reliance on the sympathetic system, it is not uncommon for Type As to appear, on face, to be somewhat anxious, hyperactive, and ready to begin a "fight or flight." A listing of prevailing Type A personality traits cited in the research literature from 1959 through 1979 is shown in Table 7.5 (Price, 1982, p. 113).

As is obvious from Table 7.5, primary personality traits associated with Type As include competitive achievement-striving (i.e., they are determined to win "at any cost"), a heightened sense of time-urgency (they often talk of "being on time" or "beating the clock" in order to optimize their task achievements for the day), and easily aroused impatience and anger (i.e., they are often seen as being easily agitated by things or people blocking their need-fulfillment and/or task-progress) (Friedman & Rosenman, 1974).

Type A mind-behavioral predispositions are especially common among those in highly urbanized settings, where a demanding environment catalyzes both the genetic predispositions and the hyperactive stress responses of individuals attracted to this type of setting. The Type A predisposition is said to characterize approximately half of present-day employed males and females (Thurman, 1984; Haynes et al., 1978). Type A women, like their Type A male counterparts, typically boast of having large incomes, white-collar, executive, or administrative positions, and considerable formal education (Thoreson & Low, 1990).

A variety of epidemiological and physiological research has reported that hyperactive Type As may be twice as likely as moderated, assertive Type Bs to suffer from premature cardiovascular disease (Jenkins, 1976). Age is

Table 7.5
Type A Characteristics and Frequency of Citation in the 1959–1979 Literature

Characteristic Cited	Frequency of Citation
Competitiveness	72
Time urgency	62
Aggressiveness	44
Drive	41
Achievement-striving	33
Preoccupation with deadlines	28
Ambitious desire for advancement	26
Accelerated pace	25
Impatience	24
Hostility	19
Motor mannerisms	18
Hyperalertness	14
Speech mannerisms	13
Struggle	13
Hard-driving	12
Restlessness	12
Job commitment	12
Involved in too much	11
Extremely conscientious	11
Seek recognition	10
Coping style to gain control	7
Job success/High productivity	3
Chronic conflicts; challenge	2
Neglect of non-job activities	2

Source: Price, V. A. (1982). What is Type A? A cognitive social learning model. *Journal of Occupational Behavior*, 3, 109–129.

also a factor in Type A presentation. Recent research findings suggest that the Type A Behavior pattern in adults begins to diminish gradually after age 55–60, either because of insights about the self-destructiveness of this lifestyle pattern or because of a declining life-energy pool (Moss et al., 1986).

The anger-driven Type A pattern has been known to wreak havoc on work and home relationships. Because pronounced Type As' anger fuses detonate easily, and because their need to be overtly "in control" of themselves, their environment, and others in it is often excessive, extensive laboratory research indicates that Type As have a difficult interpersonal style and are prone to interpersonal conflicts. With little provocation, they become impatient, irritable, and hyperreactant. They want to win at any cost rather than lose to "the competition."

Despite the odds for failure, apparently Type A/A marriages or living arrangements can be successful—as long as both adult parties commit themselves to abide by a joint "business kind" of relationship with well-defined terms and conditions. In arrangements where one spouse is Type A and the other is non-Type A, there are reported elevated levels of distress for the non-Type A. Reports indicate that the non-Type A partner often chooses to leave the "nonsymbiotic" relationship as a means of preventing energy burnout or, choosing to stay, eventually burns out (Haynes, Eaker, & Feinleib, 1983; Becker & Byrne, 1984; Burke & Weir, 1980; Baron, 1989; Miller, Lack, & Asroff, 1985).

When stressed, angry Type As seem to become even more undesirable to be around; they either withdraw from contact with others—a behavior that triggers bouts of depression—or they become more aggressive to get their own way. Needless to say, strong Type As tend not to be good stress-copers. They are forever expending excessive amounts of life-energy on "less-than-deserving" life demands and are forever saving little life-energy for personal or emergency situations. Angry Type As' exaggerated need to work at or over capacity, with few fuel reserves, eventually leads to exhaustion and eventual cardiovascular destruction.

Evidence indicates that not only do strong Type As have a difficult time breaking away from their task-obsessions and task-perfections, but when they engage in leisure-time activities, they play as hard and as obsessively as when they work, finding pure relaxation for relaxation's sake more a bore than a pleasure (Tang, 1986). Because of their addictions to nor-adrenaline-releasing competitions, pronounced Type As often report being "addicted" to the endorphin highs associated with their work and leisure-time competitive activities. It is not surprising, therefore, that as a result of their competitive need to win "at any cost," pronounced Type As have a history of sport injury-proneness.

The "irrational" cognitions that seem to drive Type As and keep them "pumped-up" for hyperactivity and fight-or-flight responses are summarized in Table 7.6 (Thurman, 1984).

If Type As find their cognitions—which to them are perfectly rational, reasonable, and worthy of keeping (Westra & Kuiper, 1992)—to be challenged or taxed, they reportedly try to maintain or regain control using a narrow range of direct-action, problem-focused efforts (Carver, Coleman, & Glass, 1976; Pittner & Houston, 1980; Burke, 1981; Hart, 1988). If emotion-focused, palliation efforts are relied on, they seem to be used pri-

Table 7.6
Irrational Beliefs Associated with the Type A Behavior Pattern

Quantity of output is more important than quality of output.
Faster is always better.
It is horrible when things are not done on time.
Winning or losing a competition is a reflection of one's worth as a person.
One is only as good as their accomplishments.
Most events that slow one down are avoidable.
No endless string of accomplishments ensures that one will like oneself.
Nonachievement-oriented activities are a waste of time.
One can have complete control over one's life if one just tries hard enough.
Speeding up the pace of one's activities is the best way to keep or regain control.
Being perfectionistic is the best way to ensure high quality achievements.
Openly expressing anger and hostility makes other people pay for getting in my way.

Source: Thurman, C. W. (1984). Cognitive-behavioral interventions with type A faculty. *The Personnel and Guidance Journal, 62,* 358–362.

marily by female Type As and only in conjunction with direct-action efforts (Greenglass, Burke, & Ondrack, 1990). Unlike the broad range of socially oriented palliation-and-control efforts relied on by self-healers under stress, female Type As, in particular, reportedly prefer to confine themselves to negative affect and introverted (I) palliation efforts, including denying that they have a problem, isolating themselves from others, projecting the problem onto others, self-denigrating (i.e., putting themselves down), and cognitively avoiding the problem by keeping busy (Greenglass, 1988).

Recently, Denollet and De Potter (1992) have raised concerns about a consistent pattern of stress-coping styles for male Type As. Their 1992 study of 166 men with coronary heart disease who completed an outpatient rehabilitation program in Belgium revealed four likely subgroups of Type As and stress-coping styles, some more effective at moderating and relieving stress than others:

1. The *high negative affectives* were characterized by high negative affect and social inhibition (i.e., they lacked assertiveness and were introverted) and by a low level of self-deception (i.e., they were low on the nonconscious, self-deceptive component of personality that underlies defensiveness). These men reported high levels of transient distress, disability, chronic tension, anger, and cardiovascular disease. They appraised themselves as having a low level of psychological well-being, and they had the highest ratings of any subgroup on Type A behavior. These particular find-

ings, noted the researchers, support the notion that high-NA Type As are chronically poor stress-copers, and that they, in part, are the reason for their own elevated stress levels—remaining hypervigilant and constantly scanning their world for signs of impending trouble or competitive-arousal.

2. The *low negative affectives* were characterized by low negative affect, low social inhibition (i.e., they were extraverted and assertive), and low self-deception. These men reported moderate levels of stress in their lives and had moderate ratings on Type A behavior. Of the four groups studied, this group appeared to be the most hardy and self-healing in nature, utilizing most fully both escapist and controlling stress-coping efforts.

3. The *defensive inhibitors* were characterized by low negative affect and high self-deception and social inhibition (i.e., they were introverted and lacked assertiveness). They reported low levels of distress and had the lowest ratings on Type A behavior. However, they had significantly higher ratings of "anger-in" than the other three groups, and like the introverted, high-NAs, they seemed to be at high risk for developing cardiovascular disease. Some of these anger-inhibited individuals displayed high levels of agreeableness (A) as well as tension in assertion situations, suggesting that they may tend to avoid interpersonal conflicts by utilizing the self-effacing solution of moving toward others rather than fighting with them.

4. The *defensive repressors* were characterized by low negative affect and social inhibition (i.e., they were extraverted and assertive) and by a high level of self-deception. They reported low levels of distress and had moderate ratings of Type A behavior. Because anger-repressors fail to detect their outward signs of somatic distress, they may be particularly at risk for "silent" myocardial ischaemia and may fail to seek appropriate medical treatment and follow-up.

Denollet and De Potter (1992) also reported that, following coronary crises, the high-NA types were less likely to return to work as early as the low-NA types. Moreover, the high-NAs appraised themselves as being the least well-off at a fifteen-month follow-up investigation and were the most likely to report anginal pain and to use sleeping pills for anxiety reduction over the longer term.

CONSISTENTLY REPORTED RESEARCH FINDINGS ON TYPE Cs

On face, Type Cs have softer voices and more moderated behavioral patterns than Type As. In fact, they appear to be much more Type B-ish in character than Type A-ish. According to behavioral oncologists, emotionally dependent Type Cs (who may even be a kind of nonassertive Type B) suppress their negative emotions and/or have an inability to express their negative emotions, particularly anger and frustration. Other characteristics of emotionally dependent Type Cs include their appearing to be overly patient, conflict-avoidant, and group harmonizing in work and nonwork environments. They are often seen by others as being "socially desirable" and "as complying" with authorities (Baltrusch, Stangel, & Waltz, 1988).

Grossarth-Maticek and Eysenck (1990) have suggested a second "strain" of the Type C which appears, on face, to be overly rational and antiemotional. Until further data are analyzed and reported in the literature, the presence of a rationally dependent Type C predisposition remains tentative.

The emotionally dependent Type C's stress-coping style is generally characterized as abrogating one's own needs in favor of others' needs and as suppressing one's negative emotions by being overly cooperative, unassertive, appeasing, and accepting of others' points of view. This pattern, concealed behind a facade of pleasantness, appears to be effective as long as one's environmental and personal homeostasis remain intact (Baltrusch, Stangel, & Waltz, 1988). However, studies have shown that the chronic blockage of the expression of one's own needs and the chronic blockage of negative affect have destructive psychophysiologic consequences. Not only does the Type C individual suffer from bouts of hopelessness, helplessness, and depression because of an inability to handle interpersonal conflicts at work and at home, but their parasympathetic stress-response systems are put into heavy use, resulting in high plasma cortisol levels and immune deficiencies (Baltrusch, Stangel, & Waltz, 1988).

Using a cognitive diathesis-stress theory framework, Grossarth-Maticek and Eysenck (1991) posit that Type Cs' depression bouts are caused, in large part, by their own self-defeatist attitudes. That is, Type Cs come to believe that highly desired relationship outcomes are unlikely to occur, or that highly aversive relationship outcomes are likely to occur, and that no response in their limited stress-coping repertoire—which is highly negatively palliative in nature—will change the likelihood of these outcomes. Cancer patients have been clinically observed to utilize this type of self-defeatist coping strategy as a means of coping with their anxiety (Baltrusch, Stangel, & Waltz, 1988).

A summary of Type C personality predispositions reported in the psychophysiological literature is given in Table 7.7 (Baltrusch, Stangel, & Waltz, 1988, p. 19).

RECENT DISCOVERIES ABOUT PERSONALITY PREDISPOSITIONS ASSOCIATED WITH ORGANIZATIONAL HEALTH

Although research studies on organizational health have involved outcome variables of considerable range (i.e., job satisfaction, productivity, absenteeism, turnover, and accident-proneness), in recent years pervasive-

Table 7.7
Summary of Type C Characteristics

Genetic and Early Childhood Factors:
- Genetic Predispositions - Unfavorable family interaction patterns (i.e., lack of closeness to parents during childhood and youth) - Early losses and separations
Behavioral Features:
- Overcooperative - Appeasing - Unassertive - Over-patient - Overly rational and anti-emotional (?) - Avoidance of conflicts; exhibits "harmonizing behavior" - Unexpressive of negative emotions, in particular anger - Compliant with external authorities - Defensive response to stress (i.e., high on social desirability and anxiety)
Medical Findings:
- Type C is a prognostic indicator in patients with malignant melanoma, significantly associated with thicker and more invasive tumors - Breast cancer patients score higher than healthy controls on measures of social desirability, emotional suppression, and state anxiety - Significantly higher suppression of anger using the Courtauld Emotional Control Scale in cancer patients, compared to healthy persons

Source: Baltrusch, H. J. F, Stangel, W., & Waltz, M. E. (1988). Cancer from the biobehavioral perspective: The type C pattern. *Activas Nervosa Superior*, 30, 18–20.

ness of "prosocial or helping behavior" in organizations has received considerable attention. By definition, prosocial or helping behavior is that performed by organizational members with the intent to aid or benefit another member or the organization as a whole. Since organizational effectiveness and survival in a continually changing external environment are dependent on the performance of prosocial behaviors—given that appropriate "survival" measures cannot be stipulated ahead of time—organizational members' tendencies to spontaneously help coworkers with work-related problems or to make constructive suggestions for greater organizational efficiency and/or effectiveness are critical.

Although there has been considerable debate about whether personality and members' prosocial behavior propensities are associated, a 1990 review of the literature (and more recent research findings) indicates that organizational members having high self-esteem and self-induced competence, an internal locus of control, high moral development and ethics, prevailing positive affect, and low needs for approval from others are the most likely to spontaneously perform prosocial behaviors (George, 1992). This description, as detailed earlier, applies most aptly to the self-healing, autonomous, hardy, assertive Type B personality.

In a recent meta-analytic study investigating the five-factor model of personality and three performance outcomes (i.e., job proficiency, training proficiency, and personnel data such as salary level) for five occupational groups, low negative affect (NA) and conscientiousness (C) were found to predict the three performance outcomes for all five occupations. Depending on specific job requirements, other personality variables were also shown to be important productivity-enhancing factors. For example, for the two occupational groups involving interpersonal interactions (i.e., management and sales), extraversion (E) was found to be a valid predictor for successful job performance (George, 1992).

CONCLUSION

This session looked at the important role that personality predispositions have on individuals' mental, physiological, and behavioral well-being. As a result of the studies and findings reviewed here, it is now probably quite clear to participants that organizations who are able to attract and retain mentally and physiologically healthy members benefit several-fold. For organizations with members having temporary or longer-term stress-coping difficulties, managers and labor representatives need to work together to provide organizational members at all levels with stress management information sessions, self-awareness and self-introspection sessions led by qualified professionals, and rehabilitative programs for dealing with stress and strain health presentations. The latter steps are not only positive and proactive but go a long way to preventing workplace disabilities and workplace disability claims.

For participants who have not yet fully grasped the characteristics of the self-healing, autonomous, hardy, assertive Type B personality predisposition, Kobasa offers an interesting example of how one such executive who is asked to complete a job transfer copes with the event, perceiving it as a "challenge" rather than as a "threat":

Whether hardy or not, the executive will anticipate and experience the changes that the transfer will bring about—learning to cope with new subordinates and supervisors, finding a new home, helping children and [spouse] with a new school and neighborhood, learning new job skills, and so on. The hardy executive will approach the necessary readjustments in his[her] life with (a) a clear sense of his[her] values, goals, and capabilities, and a belief in their importance . . . and (b) a strong tendency toward active involvement with his[her] environment. . . . Hence, the hardy executive does more than passively acquiesce to the job transfer. Rather, he[she] throws himself[herself] actively into the new situation, utilizing his[her] inner resources to make it his[her] own. Another important characteristic . . . is an unshakable sense of meaningfulness and ability to evaluate the impact of a transfer in terms of a general life plan with its established priorities. . . . For him[her] the job transfer means a change that can be transformed into a potential step in the right direction in his[her] overarching career plan, and also provide his[her] family with a developmentally stimulating change.

An internal (rather than external) locus of control allows the hardy executive to greet the transfer with the recognition that although it may have been initiated in an office above him[her], the actual course it takes is dependent upon how he[she] handles it.

For all of these reasons, he[she] is not just a victim of a threatening change but an active determinant of the consequences it brings about. (1979, p. 9)

STRESS-COPING SUMMARY POINTS

1. Before intervening in the macrosystem or organizational members' microsystems as a means of curbing pathological stress levels, managers, labor leaders, and organizational members alike need to understand more fully the personality predispositions contributing toward mental health and ill health, physiological health and ill health, and organizational health and ill health.

2. Content issues around this important issue of mind-body-behavior health include understanding the role of Negative Affect (NA) and Positive Affect (PA); the Five Factors of Personality; the usefulness of the NEO-PI, the MBTI, the MMPI, and other well-designed and validated inventories in assessing Personality Predispositions; and the cognitive-behavioral and stress-coping differences between "self-healing" and "disease-prone" personalities, including the angry Type As and the emotionally dependent Type Cs.

REFERENCES

Arvey, R. D., Bouchard, T. J., Segal, N. L., & Abraham, L. M. (1989). Job satisfaction: Environmental and genetic components. *Journal of Applied Psychology*, 74, 187–192.

Baltrusch, H. J. F., Stangel, W., & Waltz, M. E. (1988). Cancer from the biobehavioral perspective: The Type C pattern. *Activas Nervosa Superior*, 30, 18–20.

Baron, R. A. (1989). Personality and organizational conflict: Effects of the Type A behavior pattern and self-monitoring. *Organizational Behavior and Human Decision Processes*, 44, 281–296.

Becker, M. A., & Byrne, D. C. (1984). Type A behavior and daily activities of young married couples. *Journal of Applied Social Psychology*, 14, 82–88.

Booth-Kewley, S., & Friedman, H. S. (1987). Psychological predictors of heart disease: A quantitative review. *Psychological Bulletin*, 101, 343–362.

Burke, R. J. (1981). Interpersonal behavior and coping styles of Type A individuals. *Psychological Reports*, 51, 971–977.

Burke, R. J., & Weir, T. (1980). The Type A experience: Occupational and life demands on administrators and spouse well-being. *Human Relations*, 33, 253–278.

Byrne, D. G., & Rosenman, R. H. (1986). Type A behavior and the experience of affective discomfort. *Journal of Psychosomatic Research*, 30, 663–672.

Carver, C. S., Coleman, A. E., & Glass, D. C. (1976). The coronary-prone behavior pattern and the suppression of fatigue on a treadmill test. *Journal of Personality and Social Psychology*, 33, 460–466.

Chesney, M. A., & Rosenman, R. H. (1983). Specificity in stress models: Examples drawn from Type A behavior. In C. L. Cooper (Ed.), *Stress Research*. New York: John Wiley & Sons, 21–34.

Davey, J. A., Schell, B. H., & Morrison, K. (1993). The Myers-Briggs personality indicator and its usefulness for problem solving by mining industry personnel. *Group and Organization Management*, 18, 50–65.

Denollet, J., & De Potter, B. (1992). Coping subtypes for men with coronary heart disease: Relationship to well-being, stress, and Type A behavior. *Psychological Medicine*, 22, 667–684.

Eysenck, H. J. (1985). Personality, cancer and cardiovascular disease: A causal analysis. *Personality and Individual Differences*, 5, 535–557.

Eysenck, H. J. (1987a). Anxiety, "learned helplessness" and cancer—a causal theory. *Journal of Anxiety Disorders*, 1, 87–104.

Eysenck, H. J. (1987b). Personality as a predictor of cancer and cardiovascular disease, and the application of behavior therapy in prophylaxis. *The European Journal of Psychiatry*, 1, 29–41.

Eysenck, H. J., & Fulker, D. (1983). The components of type A behaviour and its genetic components. *Personality and Individual Differences*, 4, 499–505.

Fisher, V. E., & Hanna, J. V. (1931). *The Dissatisfied Worker*. New York: Macmillan.

Freudenberger, H. J. (1974). Staff burn-out. *Journal of Social Issues*, 30, 159–165.

Fried, Y., & Ferris, G. R. (1987). The validity of the job characteristics model: A review and meta-analysis. *Personnel Psychology*, 40, 287–322.

Friedman, H. S. (1991). *The Self-healing Personality: Why Some People Achieve Health While Others Succumb to Illness*. New York: Holt.

Friedman, H. S., & Booth-Kewley, S. (1987). Personality, Type A behavior and cardiovascular disease: The role of emotional expression. *Journal of Personality and Social Psychology*, 53, 783–792.

Friedman, H. S., & Rosenman, R. H. (1974). *Type A Behavior and Your Heart*. New York: Alfred A. Knopf.

Friedman, H. S., & VandenBos, G. R. (1992). Disease-prone and self-healing personalities. *Hospital and Community Psychiatry*, 43, 1177–1179.

George, J. M. (1992). The role of personality in organizational life: Issues and evidence. *Journal of Management*, 18, 185–213.

Greenglass, E. R. (1988). Type A behavior and coping strategies in female and male supervisors. *Applied Psychology: An International Review*, 37, 271–288.

Greenglass, E. R., Burke, R. J., & Ondrack, M. (1990). A gender-role perspective of coping and burnout. *Applied Psychology: An International Review*, 39, 5–27.

Grossarth-Maticek, R., & Eysenck, H. J. (1990). Personality, stress and disease:

Description and validation of a new inventory. *Psychological Reports*, 66, 355–373.

Grossarth-Maticek, R., & Eysenck, H. J. (1991). Creative novation behavior therapy as a prophylactic treatment for cancer and coronary heart disease: Part I—Description of treatment. *Behavioral Research Therapy*, 29, 1–16.

Grossarth-Maticek, R., Kanazir, D. T., Schmidt, P., & Vetter, H. (1982). Psychosocial and organic variables for lung cancer, cardiac infarction, and apoplexy. Paper presented at Plenary Session of XIII European Conference on Psychosomatic Research, Noordwijkerhout, September 19–25.

Hart, K. E. (1988). Association of Type A behavior and its components to ways of coping with stress. *Journal of Psychosomatic Research*, 32, 213–219.

Haynes, S. G., Eaker, E. D., & Feinleib, M. (1983). Spouse behavior and coronary heart disease in men: Prospective results from the Framingham Heart Study. *American Journal of Epidemiology*, 118, 1–22.

Haynes, S., Feinleib, M., Levine, S., Scotch, N., & Kannel, W. (1978). The relationship of psychosocial factors to coronary heart disease in the Framingham Study, II: Prevalence of coronary heart disease. *American Journal of Epidemiology*, 107, 384–402.

Jenkins, C. D. (1976). Recent evidence supporting psychologic and social risk factors for coronary disease: Part II. *New England Journal of Medicine*, 294, 987–994, 1033–1038.

Journal of the National Cancer Institute (1981), p. 66.

Kissen, D. M., & Eysenck, H. J. (1962). Personality in male lung cancer patients. *Journal of Psychosomatic Research*, 6, 123–127.

Kobasa, S. C. (1979). Stressful life events, personality, and health: An inquiry into hardiness. *Journal of Personality and Social Psychology*, 37, 1–12.

Latack, J. C. (1984). Career transitions within organizations: An exploratory study of work, nonwork and coping strategies. *Organizational Behavior and Human Performance*, 34, 296–322.

Lazarus, R. S. (1966). *Psychological Stress and the Coping Process*. New York: McGraw-Hill.

Linton, P. H., Kuechenmeister, C. A., & Kuechenmeister, S. B. (1986). Personality type and psychiatric symptom formation. *Research Communications in Psychology, Psychiatry, and Behavior*, 11, 37–49.

May, J., & Kline, P. (1987). Extraversion, neuroticism, obsessionality, and the Type A behavior pattern. *British Journal of Medical Psychology*, 60, 253–259.

McCrae, R. R. (1990). Controlling neuroticism in the measurement of stress. *Stress Medicine*, 6, 237–241.

McCrae, R. R. (1991). The five-factor model and its assessment in clinical settings. *Journal of Personality Assessment*, 57, 399–414.

McCrae, R. R., & Costa, P. T., Jr. (1989). Reinterpreting the Myers-Briggs type indicator from the perspective of the five-factor model of personality. *Journal of Personality*, 57, 17–40.

Miller, S. M., Lack, E. R., & Asroff, S. (1985). Preferences for control and the coronary-prone behavior pattern: "I'd rather do it myself." *Journal of Personality and Social Psychology*, 49, 492–499.

Moss, G. E., Dielman, T. E., Campanelli, P. C., Leech, S. L., Harian, W. R., Von

Harrison, R., & Horvath, W. J. (1986). Demographic correlates of 51 assessments of Type A behavior. *Psychosomatic Medicine*, 48, 564–574.

Myers, I. B. (1987). *Introduction to Type*. Palo Alto, CA: Consulting Psychologists Press.

Myers, I. B., & McCaulley, M. H. (1985). *Manual: A Guide to the Development and Use of the Myers-Briggs Type Indicator*. Palo Alto, CA: Consulting Psychologists Press.

Pittner, M. S., & Houston, B. K. (1980). Response to stress, cognitive coping strategies, and the Type A behavior pattern. *Journal of Personality and Social Psychology*, 39, 147–157.

Price, V. A. (1982). What is Type A? A cognitive social learning model. *Journal of Occupational Behavior*, 3, 109–129.

Schmidt, P. (1984). *Autoritarismus, Entfremdung und psychosomatische Krebsforschung: Explikation der drei Forschungsprogramme durch eine allgemeine theorie und empirischche Tests mittels Strukturvergleichung*. Habilitationsschrift: University of Giessen.

Schneider, B., & Dachler, H. P. (1978). A note on the stability of the job descriptive index. *Journal of Applied Psychology*, 63, 650–653.

Selye, H. (1950). *The Physiology and Pathology of Exposure to Stress*. Montreal: Acta.

Stambler, J., Berkson, D. M., & Lindberg, H. A. (1972). Risk factors: Their role in the etiology and pathogenesis of atherosclerotic disease. In R. W. Wissler & J. C. Geer (Eds.), *Pathogenesis of Atherosclerosis*. Baltimore: Williams and Wilkins.

Tang, T. L.-P. (1986). Effects of Type A personality and task labels (work vs. leisure) on task preference. *Journal of Leisure Research*, 18, 1–11.

Thoreson, C. E., & Low, K. G. (1990). Women and Type A behavior pattern: Review and commentary. In M. J. Strube (Ed.), Type A behavior [Special Issue]. *Journal of Social Behavior and Personality*, 5, 117–133.

Thurman, C. W. (1984). Cognitive-behavioral interventions with Type A faculty. *The Personnel and Guidance Journal*, 62, 358–362.

Westra, H. A., & Kuiper, N. A. (1992). Type A irrational cognitions and situational factors relating to stress. *Journal of Research in Personality*, 26, 1–20.

Zemke, R. (1992). Second thoughts about the MBTI. *Training: The Human Side of Business* (April), 43–47.

Chapter 8

Assessing One's Own Personality Predispositions

A CASE IN POINT

William Bartell, Human Resource Manager for Wyler Industries Limited, knew that many of the participants were anxious to get their personality predisposition "readings" at the soon-to-start second session on *Personality predispositions*, the third segment of the C-O-*P*-E model. Given the content of the first session on Personality predispositions, many participants left the room wanting desperately to be more "self-healing" in character than "disease-prone."

William could not help but think to himself after everyone had gone that maintaining a "self-healing" framework of cognitions and behavior is likely what Nature had in mind for survival. For those who deviate (for whatever reason) from a "self-healing" path, professional treatment interventions are currently available. Unfortunately, William thought, "disease-prone" Types are notorious for their not wanting to change. So, short of an outbreak of cardiovascular disease or cancer, how could he convince the participants who received "disease-prone" feedback that they should consider moving toward the "self-healing" direction?

THE OPENING ADDRESS: SELF-HEALING AND SELF-DESTRUCTIVE STRESS-COPING PREDISPOSITIONS

William began his second session on personality predispositions:
Some of you may have left the room after our first session on personality predispositions thinking that individuals are "pure" self-healing or "pure" disease-prone Types. However, nothing could be further from the truth.

Present-day experts tell organizational members to more accurately think about personality predispositions in terms of "degree of self-healer" or "degree of disease-proneness" residing in individuals at any point in time.

You may recall that this "degree of" approach was taken earlier when participants assessed their degrees of positive affect (PA) and negative affect (NA) residing within. You may also recall that it is because of the "degree of" issue that the MBTI had been criticized by the U.S. panel of psychologists in 1991 as being unrealistic in its approach of placing respondents in one of sixteen "pure" information-processing Type categories. It is also because of the "degree of" issue that McCrae and his colleagues suggested that participants view their "continuous" scores on the MBTI rather than their four-letter "pure" Type reading.

Today, before placing clients along a health-disease continuum, clinicians view clients not as "pure" Type As or "pure" Type Bs but as having obtained some degree of Type A and Type B patterning. That is, clients are seen as scoring somewhere along a continuum of A1–A2–B–X, where A1 represents extreme Type A patterning, A2 represents moderate Type A patterning, B represents high to low Type B patterning, and X represents indeterminate patterning (Suinn, 1982). Similarly, under Grossarth-Maticek and Eysenck's assessment schema, a client is not a "pure" Type C but a scorer along a Health-Disease continuum involving six personality pattern Type anchors (Grossarth-Maticek & Eysenck, 1990).

Before discovering where along such a continuum participants' personality predispositions scores lie, we need to consider two important issues: personality predisposition score applications, and clients' motivations to "predisposition change."

On the first issue, experts believe that in order for organizations to reduce pathological levels of stress and strain systemwide, organizational members need to understand their own personality predispositions and have some understanding of the predispositions of others with whom they interact frequently (i.e., their bosses, their coworkers, their spouses). This knowledge not only helps organizational members to monitor and manage their own stress levels better but helps them to appreciate when others who are "closer to" or "further from" their habituated patterns are showing signs of being overstressed.

On the second issue, although there has been a sort of hard-sell going on in these stress-empowerment sessions for a "self-healing" predisposition, experts caution that not everybody is motivated to become more "self-healing." Pronounced Type As, in particular, are strongly resistant to changing their ways of thinking and doing things. In fact, Friedman, Thoreson, and Gill explicitly stated in 1981 that a significant change toward "self-healingness" in pronounced Type A clients under 35 years of age is "almost impossible to effect" (Friedman, Thoreson, & Gill, 1981, p. 94), especially if these clients are not in a diagnosed disease-state already (Friedman, 1978). Roskies and her colleagues (1978) noted, more optimistically, that Type A-predisposed individuals who are health conscious and physically fit—and who want to stay that way—can become motivated to modify their "disease-prone" cognitions and behaviors in a more "self-healing" direction.

Although pronounced Type As' drives to achieve, to compete and win, to gain recognition, and to successfully handle responsibility are in serious danger of being thwarted by the very behaviors that they habitually display in response to organizational-, home-, and leisure-time challenges, Deszca and Burke (1981) posit that Type As' tenacity to stay "Type A" results from a number of factors, including believing:

- That it takes Type A behavior to rise up the hierarchy of large-scale organizations, even though recent data suggest that assertive patterned Bs have a better chance of getting there;

- That significant others (i.e., bosses, coworkers, and spouses) will not respect Type As if they move toward a self-healing direction;

- That beneficial task outcomes will come to an end if Type As move away from their task-obsessive and perfectionistic habits; and

- That society—which values hard work and good performance—will start to view Type As "as lazy" rather than "as productive" if they move away from their "quantity-fixated" work styles and move toward a "quality-oriented" work style.

Like pronounced Type As, there are likely skeptics among you participants who feel that Type As have the right ideas about life. Although I respect your judgment, I would like to share with you now a "real" story that happened to a consultant who helped design these stress-empowerment sessions. Her story illustrates quite clearly that what's perceived to be "a cup of tea" for stressed-out (and often short-lived) pronounced Type As "ain't necessarily" what's perceived to be a "cup of tea" for stressed-out non-Type As. It further illustrates that even when faced with a life-threatening situation, pronounced Type As are resistant to change their "tried-and-true" aggressive way of doing things.

Forgive me for using some poetic justice as I relate this story to you, but my memory fails me at times and a few of the details could be off "just a tad." I will tell this story from the consultant's point of view:

It had been a stormy day yesterday. Though only October, the snow hit hard, closing schools and crippling businesses. Today, the skies were forecasted to be blue and sunny. I looked forward to the drive up North to visit one of the mines active in stress management and wellness. I had only a few hours to get to my 9 A.M. meeting, but I knew that the drive would be worthwhile. Besides seeing some good friends who had "championed" the wellness program at the mine, I would be meeting the physician who cared for many of the clients who were found in our sessions to be "stress-suffering."

My drive was relatively uneventful for the first hour or so. After all, there is little life that is awake at 5 A.M., and even less that is roaming about in minus-twenty degree temperatures. I remember thinking that the physician who was involved with the wellness program at the mine must be a "self-healer." Although his high-school daughter was killed tragically by a crazed man one afternoon as she walked out of her house, this doctor was committed to making himself well again, to helping his family through the tragedy of their loved one's untimely death, and to helping others in industry to not only de-stress but to find peace and harmony within themselves.

Then, all of a sudden, a truck trailer "whited-out" my windshield, and all that I could do was steer into a blanket of white, not knowing if I was on the road—or off. Once the windshield cleared, I could see myself heading totally out of control to the right of the road and into one of many rock outcrops. "Pick a small one," I told my car, which was just a few months old and not yet adapted to Northern Ontario's winters and possible "rock encounters." The car did as it was told. Once stopped, I walked out, totally relieved to see that I was still alive and uninjured—and that my car could likely be salvaged.

Several kind drivers stopped to see if I was okay, and within an hour or so an Ontario Provincial Police (OPP) officer was on the scene to file an accident report and to call a tow truck so that my car could be hauled back to town for repairs. What followed in the next few minutes as we waited for the tow truck was totally revealing. I have shared this story time and time again with my clients, and I'd like to share it with you now.

Initially, the officer asked me what I was doing on the roads so early in the morning, so I quickly filled him in about my scheduled early-morning stress management meeting. He found it interesting what I did for a living, adding that he saw himself as being "highly stressed" lately because of a recent incident that he investigated. I told him to feel free to talk about the incident if he wanted to. Without delay, he began to share his story. What he shared went something like this.

There were three young men from the Toronto area who had headed up north. Two of the men apparently saw themselves as being quite well adjusted. Both were very assertive (Type As?), one significantly more than the other. The main purpose for coming to the northern woods was to help de-stress their nonassertive (Type C?) friend, who was really depressed because of "yet another" relationship that hadn't "panned out." Briefly, the two seemingly well-adjusted men decided that the best way to get their nonassertive friend out of his depression was to do what they did to get relieve stress: get drunk, tell good jokes, and go moose hunting.

Apparently the depressed man resisted the hunting trip idea when his friends first suggested it, but the two very assertive friends kept insisting that they all go. The depressed man reluctantly agreed, and the three arrived up north late Friday evening.

Immediately, the two very assertive men "set up shop" and began to drink beer—lots of it. The nonassertive man said that he was "not into" drinking because it only deepened his depression. Although at first his two drinking buddies left him alone, the drunker they got, the more adamant they became that their depressed friend should join them. Finally, they went into the tent and dragged their friend outside. One of the assertive men held the depressed man's head back while the other poured alcohol down his throat.

Several hours later, the two very assertive men fell asleep after telling "some good jokes" and having a fun time in front of the campfire. The third man—who formerly was a nondrinker—apparently cried himself to sleep.

The next morning, the two assertive men, despite a lingering hangover, were ready to start their moose hunt. The depressed man was slow to awaken, but when he did, he seemed more interested in "grabbing a bite" to eat than in hunting moose. He suggested that some toast "or something" might help settle his stomach. But his very assertive friends were totally excited about their moose expedition, cleaning their rifles and giggling like small children about the fun that they would have once on "the hunt." The depressed man remained silent.

When it was time to depart into the woods, the depressed man told his friends that he was vehemently against hunting moose. The two very assertive men teased him about getting excited about hunting beaver instead of moose. After the depressed man told them that he didn't like their laughing at him, they retorted, "Hey, man, we're laughing WITH you, not AT you."

Then, the depressed man picked up his rifle. Seeing this, one of the assertive men asked, "Are you ready to go now?"

"I am," replied the depressed man, "but we're not going to hunt by your rules." Stunned, the two very assertive men put their rifles on the ground and looked at each other with blank stares. Then, the depressed man pointed his gun into their faces. "Go into the woods," he said. "I will count to ten slowly, and then come in after you. Today, I am the hunter, and you are the bounty. If I find you and kill you, I win. If you find me and kill me, you win."

"Lighten up," suggested one very assertive partner, but with this utterance the depressed man cocked his rifle. In seconds, the two very assertive men ran into the woods.

On their way into the bush, the two very assertive men apparently agreed to stay close to each other to corner the hunter, restrain him, and then take him for medical help. The more aggressive man of the two agreed to risk himself as "the bait." "He's such a wimp," suggested the more aggressive one, "that I'm sure we can capture him in no time."

Shortly thereafter, the hunter came upon the more aggressive man, who placed himself visibly in front of some bushes as bait.

"What is it you want?" asked the hunter.

"To live," replied the more aggressive man.

"Tell me why you should live" replied the depressed man.

"Because I've a lot of living left to do—which is more than you can say about yourself!" yelled the more aggressive man. And with that, the depressed man retorted, "Damned right. I haven't had a really good life, but now things will change. I am not going to let people step on me anymore. I am in control now."

Shortly afterward, the depressed man pointed his rifle at the more aggressive man, saying, "You do not deserve to live." He opened shot, and the once-aggressive man fell to the ground. Then the hunter turned away from the "wounded carcass" and walked into the woods. After a few minutes had passed, the assertive man strayed out of the bushes, leaned over his blood-drenched friend to see if he could be revived, said a prayer over his dead body, and thought through his own survival strategy. He decided to quietly make his way to the highway where he could be rescued by some passerby.

Not too long afterward, however, the hunter found the assertive man resting under a tree. "What is it you want?" asked the hunter.

"To live," replied the assertive man.

"Tell me why you should live," replied the depressed man.

"Because I've a lot of living left to do—and so do you! Let me help you," replied the assertive man.

And with that, the depressed man retorted, "Damned right. I haven't had a really good life, but now things will change. I am not going to let people step on me anymore. I am in control now." Shortly afterward, the depressed man pointed his rifle at the assertive man, saying, "You, too, deserve to live." And with that, he pointed his rifle at the assertive man, shot him once in the leg, and took off into the woods. Not too long afterward, the wounded man heard another shot being fired, but he did not go into the woods to investigate. Instead, according to his survival plan, he tied his leg to prevent bleeding to death, dragged himself through the woods and positioned himself visibly along the roadside to be saved.

The OPP officer who was sitting beside me in the car was the first passerby who found the assertive man lying by the roadside. The officer took the particulars of the incident quickly, arranged to have the wounded man taken to hospital, and called a police search for the missing "hunter." The search party found the hunter deep in the woods, dead from an apparent self-inflicted gunshot wound.

When I finish telling this story to my stress management participants, I usually ask them to tell me what they have learned from this story. "Don't think that your stress-coping strategy will work for everyone else," and "Get your visibly distressed friends professional help rather than doing the 'de-stress' job yourself" are the two themes that commonly emerge from our discussions.

I usually close the session by saying, "Aggressive Type As are hard to change," and "Don't ever underestimate the amount of anger that can be released all at once in highly suppressed Type Cs!"

The purpose of this personality predisposition session is twofold: to give participants personality predisposition scores so that they can ascertain where along a health-disease continuum their scores lie and to briefly review treatment strategies for disease-prone individuals who ask to be rehabilitated.

PERSONAL FEEDBACK: WHERE ALONG THE HEALTH-DISEASE CONTINUUM DO YOUR PERSONALITY PREDISPOSITION SCORES PLACE?

Participants can now receive feedback about where on the health-disease continuum their personality predispositions scores place. *Please now score your responses to the Slocum and Hellriegel short inventory on type, the five-factor model type inventory, and the personality-physiological predispositions inventory* (Appendix 8.1, Appendix 8.2, and Appendix 8.3, respectively).

Assessing Information-Processing Predispositions

Because stress-assessment is based, in large part, on individuals' gathering and evaluating environmental stimuli, experts have been keen to give clients measures of their information-processing predispositions. As noted in our last session, the Myers-Briggs Type Indicator (MBTI) is an instrument often used for this purpose (Briggs & Myers, 1976; Myers, 1962). Other inventories purporting to give similar information include the Gray-Wheelwright Test (Wheelwright, Wheelwright, & Buehler, 1964) and an information-processing Type short-form developed by Hellriegel and Slocum (1983). The latter was provided for feedback purposes in Appendix 8.1.

After scoring their responses to the items in Appendix 8.1, participants should have four "degree of" scores before them: a sensing (S) score, an intuition (N) score, a thinking (T) score, and a feeling (F) score. (For descriptions of these, see Chapter 7).

Where are your highest scores? What do these scores indicate about your information-gathering and information-evaluating predispositions? Considering that Linton's 1986 research team (Linton, Kuechenmeister, & Kuechenmeister, 1986) found "SF" types to be particularly predisposed to mental ill health (see Chapter 7), do your scores indicate that you may ever be "at risk," given distressing environmental conditions? Participants should now be able to conclude:

• If their scores indicate a stronger predisposition for sensing (S) or intuition (N);
• If their scores indicate a stronger predisposition for thinking (T) or feeling (F); and
• If, given earlier study findings, their scores place them closer to the "self-healing" or the "disease-prone" end of the health-disease continuum.

Assessing Five-Factor Model Predispositions

To give participants insights into their five-factor model predispositions, an inventory based on McCrae's (1991) work was developed by the author and is presented in Appendix 8.2.

After scoring their responses to the items in Appendix 8.2, participants should have five "degree of" scores before them: a neuroticism (N) score, an extraversion (E) score, an openness (O) score, an agreeableness (A) score, and a conscientious (C) score. (For descriptions of these, see Chapter 7). The scores are simply feedback, whereby higher numbers might indicate higher trait predispositions; for example, a high score on N might indicate a neurotic tendency.

Where are your highest scores on these five factors? Considering that self-healers are typically lower N, higher E, higher O, higher A, and higher C, where along the health-disease continuum do your scores place you?

Participants should now be able to conclude:

- If they have a higher or lower degree of possible neuroticism (N), extraversion (E), openness (O), agreeableness (A), and conscientiousness (C); and
- If, given earlier study findings, their scores place them closer to the "self-healing" or the "disease-prone" end of the health-disease continuum.

Assessing Personality-Physiological Predispositions

Giving participants feedback on their personality-physiological predispositions is easier for coronary-proneness as compared to cancer-proneness because many more inventories exist for the former as compared to the latter.

First, regarding accurate assessment of Type A patterning, both interview methods and self-report inventories exist. Reviews completed over the past twenty years have consistently indicated that the structured interview (SI) is the more accurate way of assessing coronary-proneness, or Type A patterning. However, this method requires a professional who is trained to accurately "read" clients' verbal and nonverbal cues in order to place them appropriately along the A1–A2–B–X continuum (Rosenman et al., 1964).

Because of the expense and relative inconvenience of engaging in SI assessments, clinicians and stress management experts have, instead, chosen to rely on clients' self-report scores obtained from the popular Jenkins Activity survey (JAS) (Jenkins, Rosenman, & Zyzanski, 1974; Jenkins, Zyzanski, & Rosenman, 1979), the Framingham Type A scale (Haynes et al., 1978), the Bortner scale (Bortner, 1969), or the activity scale of the Thurstone Temperament Schedule (MacDougall, Dembroski, & Musante, 1979). Although all of the latter inventories purportedly assess the degree of primary Type A predispositions presenting in clients—competitive achievement striving, a heightened sense of time-urgency, and easily aroused impatience and anger—experts disagree about the predispositions which are the most coronary-destructive and about which of the just-cited instruments best "predicts" coronary-proneness (Suinn, 1982).

If inventory usage by clinicians is any settlement of the instrument-usefulness debate, then the JAS is clearly the winner of the contest. However, Byrne, Rosenman, Schiller, and Chesney (1985) caution clinicians accepting the consistently reported accuracy of the SI in predicting coronary-proneness that, if the JAS or any other self-report inventory is alternatively chosen, clinicians should be aware of obtaining false cardiovascular-risk readings for clients. In trying to convince clinicians of this occurrence, this team of researchers reported that in terms of classification overlap with the SI:

- The JAS and the SI agree on clients' classification of A1 patterning only 31% of the time;
- The JAS and the SI agree on clients' classification of A2 patterning only 36% of the time; and

- The JAS and the SI agree on clients' classification of Type B patterning an improved 73% of the time.

Within the past decade, experts from Europe have suggested that not only is measuring "just Type A disease-proneness" a rather narrow focus but that inventories could be developed to more broadly assess physiological disease-proneness. Accordingly, Grossarth-Maticek, Eysenck, and Vetter developed and released for usage an inventory that assesses personality predispositions along a broader health-disease continuum. Based in large measure on the results of their 10- and 20-year prospective design research studies involving over 15,000 male and female adults (Eysenck, 1987; Grossarth-Maticek, Eysenck, & Vetter, 1988), the Grossarth-Maticek and Eysenck inventory assesses both Type A and Type C risk propensities as well as Type B propensities. It was included in Appendix 8.3 (Grossarth-Maticek & Eysenck, 1990).

The inventory in Appendix 8.3 provides six "degree of" scores for clients, corresponding to six primary Type patterns that are anchored along the health-disease continuum. These six Type patterns are described below (Grossarth-Maticek & Eysenck, 1990).

- *Type 1s* are predisposed to be emotionally dependent, cancer-prone Type Cs. Their mind-behavior patterns indicate that they are overly cooperative, appeasing, unassertive, overpatient, conflict-avoidant, harmony-seekers, overly compliant, and defensive. They seem unable to deal with interpersonal stress, are hopeless- and helpless-prone, are depression-prone, and are likely to suppress their negative emotions.
- *Type 2s* are predisposed to be more hyperactive and coronary-prone. They are Type A-patterned.
- *Type 3s* are predisposed to be more psychopathic in thought and behavior, but they are unlikely to die prematurely of cancer or of coronary disease.
- *Type 4a,bs* are predisposed to be autonomous, assertive, and self-healing. They are Type B–patterned.
- *Type 5s* are likely predisposed (the data are not yet conclusive) to be cancer-prone. They appear to be a second strain known as the rationally dependent Type C.
- *Type 6s* are likely predisposed (the data not yet conclusive) to be antisocial, criminal, and possibly drug addictive.

Given these six pattern predispositions, the health-disease continuum looks like this, with the positioning of Types 1, 5, 2, and 6 being interchangeable since they are all disease-prone: Type 4a,b–Type 3–Type 6–Type 1–Type 5–Type 2.

Given the data analyzed by Grossarth-Maticek and Eysenck to date, Types 4 and 3 appear to experience life relatively disease-free. Theoretically, such an outcome is to be expected for the self-healing Type 4a,b.

Theoretically, such an outcome is more mysterious for Type 3. Perhaps, suggest these researchers, it is the very act of antisocial behavior that not only constitutes the behavioral expression of emotion for Type 3 but that makes them resilient to disease during their lifetimes.

Accepting the fact that any self-report inventory will have disease-proneness detection errors, and accepting that the inventory in Appendix 8.3 has not been fully validated, participants can now receive feedback on their likely (self-reported) personality-physiological predispositions.

After scoring Appendix 8.3, participants should have seven Type scores before them, two for Type 4 (which are typically within a few marks of each other). The Type scores are derived such that higher numbers indicate higher trait predispositions. If, for example, "Type 1" turned out to be a participant's highest score, then according to this reading, that participant would be said to have a prevailing cancer-prone predisposition. The next highest score would indicate the participant's next strongest predisposition, and so on down the list of six. A tie score would indicate equal Type predispositions.

On which Type is your highest score? On which Type is your second-highest score? Participants should now be able to conclude:

- If, given earlier study findings, their scores place them closer to the "self-healing" or the "disease-prone" end of the health-disease continuum.

CLINICAL INTERVENTIONS FOR REHABILITATING CLIENTS

Mental Health Issues

In earlier sessions, we discussed the various assessment tools and clinical interventions for three frequently presenting mental health problems: anxiety, depression, and anger (see Chapter 5). In the last stress session, we looked at how experts clinically assess clients for psychiatric disorders using the MMPI, the MCMI, the NEO-PI, and the MBTI instruments.

Since in these stress-empowering sessions we do not have the capability to provide participants with accurate readings on any of the more severe forms of mental ill health, I suggest that if participants have been receiving consistent readings on the inventories discussed thus far that a possible mental health problem may exist, participants should seek professional advice from a family physician, a psychologist, or a psychiatrist.

It should be obvious by now that personality predisposition feedback is useful for individuals to assess their possible term degrees of "self-healingness" and "disease-proneness." Perhaps less obvious, such data are also useful for clinicians in understanding their clients and in planning clients' treatment interventions.

McCrae (1991) cautions that while no one self-report instrument or clinicians' ratings can be assumed to be "perfectly" accurate, it is ultimately the responsibility of the clinician to understand the client as fully and completely as possible by using not just one assessment tool but a series of assessment tools. That is clearly the approach that we have taken in these stress-empowerment seminars. Of the mental-health instruments available to clinicians, the NEO-PI has been reported by them to be particularly useful in understanding and in helping their clients (Muten, 1991; McCrae, 1991). By attending to each of the personality factors assessed by the NEO-PI, clinicians can notice strengths and weaknesses in clients that would otherwise have been overlooked (McCrae, 1991). These strengths and weaknesses can also be considered when developing the most expeditious and comprehensive treatment strategy for clients' rehabilitation. The treatment characteristics associated with clients' standings on the five-factor model traits are summarized by Miller and presented in Table 8.1 (Miller, 1991, pp. 418–419).

Like the tale told earlier about the hunters in the woods, participants may have noticed that Table 8.1 illustrates that what's perceived to be "a cup of tea" for some rehabilitating clients "ain't necessarily" what's perceived to be a "cup of tea" for other rehabilitating clients. Miller says that not only do NEO-PI scores provide a detailed, rather accurate portrait of clients' needs, feelings, proximate motives, and preferred interpersonal styles, but that they can also be linked to clients' prognoses. Specifically, Miller (1991) suggests that

- Neuroticism (N) influences the intensity and duration of the clients' distress;
- Extraversion (E) influences the clients' enthusiasm for treatment;
- Openness (O) influences the clients' reactions to the therapist's interventions;
- Agreeableness (A) influences the clients' reactions to the person or therapist; and
- Conscientiousness (C) influences the clients' willingness to do the work of psychotherapy.

Physiological Health Issues

As noted repeatedly, disease-prone individuals are often resistant to changing their ways of thinking and behaving. Let's face it, many are just not interested in living a "self-healing" lifestyle. Given this reality, clinicians have been attempting to determine the best way of converting present-state disease-sufferers and future-state disease-sufferers into "self-healers." While there still are no conclusive findings in this regard, two approaches, in particular, seem to work well for clinicians:

- The first approach is to instill fear in young clients (under age 50) about the dangers of maintaining a disease-prone life path and to work on actively rehabilitating cardiac-diseased or cancer-diseased clients who are motivated to change; and

Table 8.1
Treatment Characteristics Associated with Standing on Five Factors

Factor	Presentation	Problems	Opportunities	Pitfalls
High N	Variety of painful feelings.	Full gamut of neurotic misery.	Psychological pain motivates compliance.	Existence likely to remain distressed.
Low N	Emotional blandness, especially if low E.	Situational problems.	Wants and can benefit from advice and values clarification.	Emotional blandness may be perceived by others as being defensive.
High E	Needs to talk; needs people.	Excitable; if also high N, unstable mood, interpersonal conflict.	Comfortable with less structured approaches; optimistic, energetic.	Need to talk can blunt treatment focus.
Low E	Reluctant to talk. Can feel overwhelmed by people.	Somber. If also high N, depression, withdrawal, apathy.	Comfortable with structured approaches.	Lacks enthusiasm for interaction with therapist.
High O	Likes variety, novelty; curious.	Problems vary but framed in abstract, imaginative terms.	Prefers imaginative approaches.	Excessive curiosity can scatter resources.
Low O	Discomfort and perplexity in reaction to novel experiences.	Problems vary but framed in conventional, concrete terms.	Responds well to practical approaches: education, support, behavior therapy.	Rigidity and lack of curiosity can be wrongly seen as being resistant.
High A	Genuinely compassionate and generous. Sees the sweet side of life.	Easily exploited, naive, gullible. If high N, oversensitive to criticism.	Treatment alliance easily formed.	Accepts advice without questions. Need to please counsellor interferes with honest speaking.
Low A	Wants to be admired, to be "somebody." Sees the bitter side of life.	Unpopular, overly competitive; lacks social support. Envious, suspicious, holds grudges.	Assertiveness and clear thinking about self-interest facilitate problem-solving.	Anger, skepticism toward counsellor; difficult to form treatment alliance.

Table 8.1 (continued)

High C	Loves accomplishment	Overwork.	Works hard to benefit from treatment. Willing to tolerate discomfort and frustration.	Possibly none.
Low C	Loves leisure.	Low achievement, impulsivity, half-hearted problem solving.	Possibly none.	Unlikely to do homework; likely to reject therapy that requires hard work or pain.

Source: Miller, T. R. (1991). The psychotherapeutic utility of the five-factor model of personality: A clinician's experience. Journal of Personality Assessment, 57, 415–433.

- The second is to educate adults, en masse, about the benefits of adopting a "self-healing" life path and to work on actively rehabilitating cardiac-diseased or cancer-diseased clients using group-support therapy. (Friedman, 1978; Roskies, 1980)

Although many questions remain about the process and content of effective disease-rehabilitation programs, mental and physiological experts seem convinced that a regimen involving some combination of relaxation training therapy and cognitive-behavioral therapy (CBT) pays off for many clients. In fact, studies have consistently shown that just using relaxation therapy or just placing clients through psychoanalytic treatment seems not to work so well.

Researchers have found that the muscle relaxation-CBT combination is likely effective because muscle relaxation training de-stresses clients "on the spot" and helps them to regain a sense of personal control, and because CBT complements the latter by removing clients' irrational beliefs that "feed" distress cycles and replaces those with rational beliefs that promote self-healing cycles. Table 8.2 (Thurman, 1984) provides Type A irrational beliefs which, through CBT, are sought to be replaced by the rational counterchallenges listed.

For Type A pattern modification and rehabilitation, in particular, clinicians suggest that the numbers of therapy sessions involved vary from 6 to 60. What is less apt to vary are the content issues which are dealt with in coronary-relieving CBT sessions. The latter commonly include one or more of the following (Deszca & Burke, 1981; Levenkron et al., 1983): anxiety, depression, and anger management; the importance of relaxation and relaxation therapy; the importance of the mind-body-behavior "well-being"

Table 8.2
Type A Irrational Beliefs and Rational Counterchallenges

Type A Irrational Belief	Rational Counterchallenge
Quantity of output is more important than quality of output.	The quality of one's output is more related to success than the quantity of one's work.
Faster is always better.	Many things need to be done slowly in order to be done well.
It is horrible when things are not done on time.	It is inconvenient when people or things are late, not the end of the world.
Winning or losing a competition is a reflection of one's worth as a person.	The outcome of a competition reflects relative performance, not relative human worth.
One is only as good as their accomplishments.	Worth as a human being is defined more by who one is than by what one does.
Most events that slow one down are avoidable.	Situations that cause delay are an inescapable part of life.
No endless string of accomplishments ensures that one will like oneself.	Numerous accomplishments are no guarantee that one will like who they are.
Nonachievement-oriented activities are a waste of time.	Activities do not have to result in achievement to be worthwhile.
One can have complete control over one's life if one just tries hard enough.	Total effort will not bring total control.
Speeding up the pace of one's activities is the best way to keep or regain control.	Slowing down the pace of one's activities often helps regain a sense of control.
Being perfectionistic is the best way to ensure high quality achievements.	Setting challenging but reasonable goals helps promote high quality achievements.
Openly expressing anger and hostility makes other people pay for getting in my way.	When feeling angry and hostile, I'm the one who pays.

Source: Thurman, C. W. (1984). Cognitive-behavioral interventions with type A faculty. *The Personnel and Guidance Journal*, 62, 358–362.

link; the importance of moderate exercise and good health habits; and the importance of social support networks both on and off the job.

For Type C and Type A modification and rehabilitation, Eysenck and Grossarth-Maticek advocate a form of CBT with suggestive relaxation training which they have called "Creation Novation Behaviour Therapy" (Grossarth-Maticek & Eysenck, 1991; Eysenck & Grossarth-Maticek, 1991). In the latter program and in other similar "combination programs" designed to help Type C clients, the content issues which are dealt with commonly include one or more of the following: anxiety, depression, and anger management; the importance of autonomous behavior; the importance of the mind-body-behavior "well-being" link; the usefulness of asserting one's own needs and feelings; and the importance of healthy versus overly dependent social support networking.

Grossarth-Maticek and Eysenck are convinced that their Creation Novation Behavior Therapy works well in the moderation and rehabilitation of pronounced Type A and Type C patterning. To give clinicians insights as to how their treatment program works, these experts described their procedures in two academic papers on the topic (Grossarth-Maticek & Eysenck, 1991; Eysenck & Grossarth-Maticek, 1991). In one of these papers, the case history of a Type C-predisposed client who sought Creative Novation Behavior Therapy is described. Because this minicase illustrates well the kind of irrational beliefs that can drive Type Cs to become mentally and physically ill, it will be shared with participants.

The case is of Mrs. D, a woman who was chronically depressed, declared unfit for work by her employer, and pensioned. When she appeared for treatment, Mrs. D had been suffering for the previous two years from a rapidly metastasizing mastocarcinoma (i.e., a form of cancer), a sore left arm, and repeat bouts of depression. Besides seeking medical treatment for her physiological discomforts, Mrs. D made several attempts at psychotherapeutic treatment to relieve her emotional pain. After the latter treatment attempts failed to bring her pain and depression relief, Mrs. D requested Creation Novation Behavior Therapy. Grossarth-Maticek and Eysenck describe the situation of Mrs. D as follows:

She came to see us after being through various psychotherapeutic treatments. Her first psychoanalytic treatment took place when she was 23, but was broken off after a year. The reason for analysis was separation from her boyfriend who had suddenly left her. She developed severe depression and had expected behavioural direction and speedy help from the therapist.

When she found no improvement in her condition after this period, she broke off therapy. After telling the therapist that her depression had actually gotten worse, the therapist insisted that she was therapy-resistant and was not prepared to work hard enough. While she was in therapy she had particularly felt the therapist did not accept her and was convinced that the depression got worse during this time. Mrs. D. suffered from torturing feelings of inferiority, just because she is a woman. In her family the three sons were always preferred and she was pushed aside with the argument that she was "only a woman."

Because of this she felt dependent on her mother and her father, because both of them were interested only in the sons. When her boyfriend left her suddenly when she was 23 and entered into a homosexual relationship, she had her conviction that she counted for nothing as a woman reinforced. After unsuccessful psychoanalysis, she buried herself in an intensive period of study and concluded it with very good marks. During this time she had no relationships with men, and after this she fell in love with a female friend. . . . In this relationship she felt herself to be masculine, and was secure, and experienced satisfied feelings of great emotional meaning. Her woman friend . . . left her in the same way, very suddenly to go to a male friend. After this she experienced even more severe depression than after the first separation. During [one primal scream therapy session], the memory came back vividly, that when she was a child and was naughty her parents often said, "Be good, because without us you are nothing." She experienced sudden panic and anxiety at the idea that the parents would abandon her, and reacted for several days with persecution mania. "I feel that everyone is coming up behind me, in order to point a finger and show that I am inferior and unfit to live." . . .

She described her most important psychic difficulties as follows: "(a) I cannot stop thinking, and the thoughts go round and round on the one theme, That as a woman I am rejected and worthless; (b) I have longed during my whole life to be close to my parents, my boyfriend and my woman friend, but have never achieved this, and for this reason I become depressed and still more convinced that I am worthless as a woman. I can visualize now, in my illness, how the metastases spread, but not how I can become even partly healthy, either physically or mentally." (1991, p. 10)

Grossarth-Maticek and Eysenck noted that after the successful completion of Creative Novation Behaviour Therapy, Mrs. D joined a fundamentalist Christian religion and felt so well when praying that she left her therapy sessions with a farewell letter of thanks. In her letter, she said that through Creative Novation Behaviour Therapy she had learned for the first time in her life the feeling of complete happiness by "inactivating" negative thoughts. Not only was the pain in her left arm relieved, but Mrs. D lived for three years after "autonomy training" in a state of emotional stability.

CONCLUSION

This session's objective was intended to give participants useful feedback on their personality predispositions, so that they could appraise their placement along a health-disease continuum. While attention in this session focused very much on the usefulness of such information to organizational members, mention was also made of the usefulness of such information to clinicians in planning treatment interventions for clients.

STRESS-COPING SUMMARY POINTS

1. Before finalizing their decisions about seeking professional advice for mental or physical ill-health, organizational members might want to obtain their readings on a health-disease continuum by completing the inventories provided in the Appendix of this chapter.

2. Before deciding the best approach for modifying clients' disease-proneness and for formulating treatment interventions, clinicians might want to collect five-factor model data on their clients using the NEO-PI inventory.

Appendix 8.1
Slocum and Hellriegel's Short Inventory on "Type"

Instructions: Please respond to the following questions. There are no right or wrong answers, so please be as honest as you can when answering. Simply CIRCLE the response in each pair that more accurately reflects how you feel.

1. Are you more careful about: A. people's feelings B. their rights	10. Which word appeals to you more: A. compassion B. foresight
2. Do you usually get on better with: A. imaginative people B. realistic people	11. Which word appeals to you more: A. justice B. mercy
3. Which of these two is the higher compliment: A. a person has real feeling B. a person is consistently reasonable	12. Which word appeals to you more: A. production B. design
4. In doing something with many other people, does it appeal more to you: A. to do it in the accepted way B. to invent a way of your own	13. Which word appeals to you more: A. gentle B. firm
5. Do you get more annoyed at: A. fancy theories B. people who don't like theories	14. Which word appeals to you more: A. uncritical B. critical
6. It is higher praise to call someone: A. a person of vision B. a person of common sense	15. Which word appeals to you more: A. literal B. figurative
7. Do you more often let: A. your heart rule your head B. your head rule your heart	16. Which word appeals to you more: A. imaginative B. matter-of-fact
8. Do you think it a worse fault: A. to show too much warmth B. to be unsympathetic	
9. If you were a teacher, would you rather teach: A. courses involving theory B. fact courses	

Source: Slocum, J. W., Jr., & Hellriegel, D. (1983). A look at how managers' minds work. *Business Horizons*, (July–August), 58–68.

Appendix 8.2
The Five-Factor Model Personality "Type"

Do you see yourself as:

1. Calm	Worrying
2. Even-tempered	Temperamental
3. Reserved	Affectionate
4. Loner	Joiner
5. Down-to-earth	Imaginative
6. Uncreative	Creative
7. Ruthless	Soft-hearted
8. Suspicious	Trusting
9. Negligent	Conscientious
10. Lazy	Hard-working
11. Self-satisfied	Self-pitying
12. Comfortable	Self-conscious
13. Quiet	Talkative
14. Passive	Active
15. Conventional	Original
16. Prefer routine	Prefer variety
17. Stingy	Generous
18. Antagonistic	Acquiescent
19. Disorganized	Well-organized
20. Late	Punctual
21. Unemotional	Emotional
22. Hardy	Vulnerable
23. Sober	Fun-loving
24. Unfeeling	Passionate
25. Uncurious	Curious
26. Conservative	Liberal
27. Critical	Lenient
28. Irritable	Good-natured
29. Aimless	Ambitious
30. Quitting	Persevering

Instructions: For the 70 item statements below, please place an X in the "Yes" Column if you agree with the statement or place an X in the "No" column if you disagree with the statement. Please be as honest as you.

Since these items were translated from German into English, a few of the expressions may at first seem different from what you are used to. You may, therefore, want to read each statement over several times before responding.

	YES	NO
1. I find it very difficult to stand up for myself.		
2. I have been complaining for years about various unfavourable conditions, but I am not able to change them.		
3. I am mainly concerned with my own well-being.		
4. I am usually content and happy with my daily activities.		
5. I can express my feelings only when there are good reasons for them.		
6. I don't believe in social rules and don't pay much attention to other people's expectations or the obligations I may have towards them.		
7. I cannot live happily and contentedly with or without a particular person.		
8. I prefer to agree with others rather than assert my own views.		
9. Certain people are the most important causes of my personal misfortunes.		
10. I alternate to a great degree between the positive and negative evaluation of people and conditions.		
11. When I cannot achieve closeness with someone who is emotionally important to me, I have no difficulties in letting them go.		
12. I have difficulties in showing my emotions because for every positive emotion there is a negative one.		
13. My behaviour towards other people alters from being very friendly and good-natured to being very hostile and aggressive.		
14. I cannot live happily and contentedly in the presence of the absence of certain states or conditions; e.g., I need my work but am unhappy doing it.		
15. I tend to act more to fulfill the expectations of people close to me rather than look after my own needs.		
16. Certain conditions or situations are the most important cause of my personal misfortunes.		

	YES	NO
17. With people I love, I keep changing from keeping them at a great distance to stifling dependence, and from stifling dependence to excessive distancing.		
18. I can usually arrange things so that people who are emotionally important to me are as close to or as distant from me as I wish.		
19. Reason, rather than emotion, guides my behavior.		
20. I often expect others to fulfill agreements very strictly but do not believe in doing so myself.		
21. I often have thoughts which terrify me and make me unhappy.		
22. I tend to give in and abandon my own aims in order to achieve harmony with other people.		
23. I feel helpless against people or conditions which cause great unhappiness for me, because I cannot change them.		
24. When I am in a situation which I experience as threatening, I immediately try to get other people to help and support me.		
25. When I fail to achieve my objectives, I can easily change tack.		
26. When people make emotional demands on me, I usually react only rationally, never emotionally.		
27. I usually act in a spontaneous manner, following my immediate feelings without considering the actual consequences.		
28. Relations with certain people are always pretty unsatisfactory, but there is nothing I can do about it.		
29. I am unable to express my feelings and needs openly to other people.		
30. I always seem to be confronted with the undesirable aspects of people and conditions.		
31. When someone who is emotionally important to me hurts me ever so slightly, I immediately dissociate myself from that person.		
32. I can manage to live fairly contentedly with or without someone who is emotionally important to me.		
33. I am quite unable to allow myself to be guided by emotional considerations.		
34. I often feel like attacking other people and crushing them.		

	YES	NO
35. Certain situations and states (e.g., at my place of work) tend to make me unhappy, but there is nothing I can do to alter things.		
36. I tend to accept conditions which work against my personal interests without being able to protest.		
37. Certain people keep interfering with my personal development.		
38. I expect others to live up to the highest moral standards but do not feel that these are binding on myself.		
39. I can usually change my behaviour to suit conditions.		
40. My actions are never influenced by emotions to the degree that they might appear irrational.		
41. When my partner demonstrates love towards me, I sometimes become particularly aggressive.		
42. Certain bodily conditions (e.g., being overweight) make me unhappy, but I feel unable to do anything about them.		
43. I often feel inhibited when it comes to openly showing negative feelings such as hatred, aggression, or anger.		
44. Certain conditions keep interfering with my personal development.		
45. I seek satisfaction of my own needs and desires first, regardless of the needs and rights of others.		
46. I am usually capable of finding new points of view and successful, sometimes surprising, solutions for problems.		
47. I always try to do what is rational and logically correct.		
48. When I feel like attacking someone physically, I have no inhibitions about doing this at all.		
49. I can relax bodily and mentally only very rarely; most of the time I am very tense.		
50. I am inclined not to be demonstrative when emotional shocks upset me.		
51. I cannot control excitement or stress in my life because this is dependent on the actions of other people.		
52. When I make emotional demands on another person, I require immediate satisfaction.		
53. I am independent in what I do and do not depend on other people when this works to my disadvantage.		

	YES	NO
54. I always try to express my needs and desires in a rational and reasonable manner.		
55. I have no inhibitions in hurting myself physically if I feel like doing so.		
56. I have great difficulties in entering into happy and contented relations with people.		
57. When I feel emotionally let down, I tend to be paralysed and inhibited.		
58. I cannot control excitement or stress in my life because this depends on conditions over which I have no control.		
59. I usually find fulfillment in everyday situations which are NOT subject to ordinary rules, regulations, and expectations.		
60. When things don't work out, this does not make me give up but rather makes me change my way of doing things.		
61. I try to solve my problems in light of relevant and rational consideration.		
62. I resent all moral obligations because they hamper and inhibit me.		
63. I am helpless when confronted with emotional shocks, depression, or anxiety.		
64. When something terrible happens to me, such as the death of a loved one, I am quite unable to express my emotions and desires.		
65. I can express my aims and desires clearly but feel that it is quite impossible to achieve them.		
66. As soon as someone becomes emotionally important for me, I tend to place contradictory demands upon them, such as "Don't ever leave me" or "Get away from me."		
67. When things lead to harmful results for me, I have no trouble in changing my behaviour to make for success.		
68. I only believe in things which can be proven scientifically and logically.		
69. When it benefits me, I have no hesitation in lying and pretending.		
70. I am seldom able to feel enthusiasm for anything.		

Source: Grossarth-Maticek, R., & Eysenck, H. J. (1990). Personality, stress and disease: Description and validation of a new inventory. *Psychological Reports, 66,* 355–373.

Scoring Appendix 8.1

Instructions: To get your preferences for Sensation (S), Intuition (N) Thinking (T), and Feeling (F), count one mark for each response of yours that matches the answers in the four columns below. Then, total your marks for each of the four columns.			
Sensation (S):	Intuition (N):	Thinking (T):	Feeling (F):
2.b	2.a	1.b	1.a
4.a	4.b	3.b	3.a
5.a	5.b	7.b	7.a
6.b	6.a	8.a	8.b
9.b	9.a	10.b	10.a
12.á	12.b	11.a	11.b
15.a	15.b	13.b	13.a
16.b	16.a	14.b	14.a
Total: _____	Total: _____	Total: _____	Total: _____

Source: Slocum, J. W., Jr., & Hellriegel, D. (1983). A look at how managers' minds work. *Business Horizons*, (July–August), 58–68.

Scoring Appendix 8.2

Instructions: To receive your scores based on The Five-Factor Model of Personality, count one mark for each response of yours that matches the answers in the five columns below. Then total your marks for each of the five columns.				
Neuroticism (N)	Extraversion (E)	Openness (O)	Agreeableness (A)	Conscientious (C)
1 Worry	3 Affectionate	5 Imaginative	7 Soft-hearted	9 Conscientious
2 Temperamental	4 Joiner	6 Creative	8 Trusting	10 Hard-working
11 Self-pitying	13 Talkative	15 Original	17 Generous	19 Well-organized
12 Self-conscious	14 Active	16 Prefer variety	18 Acquiescent	20 Punctual
21 Emotional	23 Fun-loving	25 Curious	27 Lenient	29 Ambitious
22 Vulnerable	24 Passionate	26 Liberal	28 Good-natured	30 Persevering
Total: _____	Total: _____	Total: _____	Total: _____	Total: _____

Scoring Appendix 8.3

<table>
<tr><td colspan="6">Instructions: You will get your scoring on six personality Types. Type 4a and Type 4b are two different measures of the same Type. Your strongest personality predisposition is your highest score. Your secondary predisposition is your second highest score. A "tie" score on two Types indicates "equal" predispositions.</td></tr>
<tr>
<td>Type 1
Add your "yes" answers to questions:
1 8 15 22
29 36 43 50
57 64</td>
<td>Type 2
Add your "yes" answers to questions:
2 9 16 23 30
37 44 51 58
65</td>
<td>Type 3
Add your "yes" answers to questions:
3 10 17 24
31 38 45 52
59 66</td>
<td>Type 4a
Add your "yes" answers to questions:
4 11 18 25
32 39 46 53
60 67

Type 4b
Add your "no" answers to questions:
7 14 21 28
35 42 49 56
63 70</td>
<td>Type 5
Add your "yes" answers to questions:
5 12 19 26
33 40 47 54
61 68</td>
<td>Type 6
Add your "yes" answers to questions:
6 13 20 27
34 41 48 55
62 69</td>
</tr>
</table>

Source: Grossarth-Maticek, R., & Eysenck, H. J. (1990). Personality, stress and disease: Description and validation of a new inventory. *Psychological Reports, 66*, 355–373.

REFERENCES

Bortner, R. A. (1969). A short rating scale as a potential measure of Pattern A behavior. *Journal of Chronic Disorders*, 22, 87–91.

Briggs, K. C., & Myers, I. B. (1976). *The Myers-Briggs Type Indicator, Form F.* Palo Alto, CA: Consulting Psychologists Press.

Byrne, D. G., Rosenman, R. H., Schiller, E., & Chesney, M. A. (1985). Consistency and validation among instruments purporting to measure the Type A behavior pattern. *Psychosomatic Medicine*, 47, 242–259.

Deszca, G., & Burke, R. J. (1981). Changing Type A behavior. *Canadian Psychology*, 22, 173–187.

Eysenck, H. J. (1987). Personality as a predictor of cancer and cardiovascular disease, and the application of behavior therapy in prophylaxis. *The European Journal of Psychiatry*, 1, 29–41.

Eysenck, H. J., & Grossarth-Maticek, R. (1991). Creative novation behaviour therapy as a prophylactic treatment for cancer and coronary heart disease: Part II—Effects of treatment. *Behavioral Research Therapy*, 29, 17–31.

Friedman, M. (1978). Modifying the Type A behavior in heart attack patients. *Primary Cardiology*, 4, 9–13.

Friedman, C., Thoreson, C., & Gill, J. (1981). Type A behavior: Its possible role, detection, and alteration in patients with ischemic heart disease. In J. Hurst (Ed.), *Update V: The Heart*. New York: McGraw-Hill, 81–100.

Grossarth-Maticek, R., & Eysenck, H. J. (1990). Personality, stress and disease: Description and validation of a new inventory. *Psychological Reports*, 66, 355–373.

Grossarth-Maticek, R., & Eysenck, H. J. (1991). Creative novation behaviour therapy as a prophylactic treatment for cancer and coronary heart disease: Part I—Description of treatment. *Behavioral Research Therapy*, 19, 1–16.

Grossarth-Maticek, R., Eysenck, H. J., & Vetter, H. (1988). Personality type, smoking habits and their interaction on predictors of cancer and coronary heart disease. *Personality and Individual Differences*, 9, 479–495.

Haynes, S., Levine, S., Scotch, N., Feinleib, M., & Kannel, W. (1978). The relationship of psychosocial factors to coronary heart disease in the Framingham Study: Methods and risk factors. *American Journal of Epidemiology*, 107, 362–383.

Jenkins, C., Rosenman, R., & Zyzanski, S. (1974). Prediction of clinical coronary heart disease by a test for the coronary-prone behavior pattern. *New England Journal of Medicine*, 290, 1271–1275.

Jenkins, C., Zyzanski, S. J., & Rosenman, R. H. (1979). *Jenkins Activity Survey. Form C. JAS Manual.* New York: The Psychological Corporation.

Levenkron, J. C., Cohen, J. D., Mueller, H. S., & Fisher, E. P., Jr. (1983). Modifying the Type A coronary-prone behavior pattern. *Journal of Consulting and Clinical Psychology*, 51, 192–204.

Linton, P. H., Kuechenmeister, C. A., & Kuechenmeister, S. B. (1986). Personality type and psychiatric formation. *Research Communications in Psychology, Psychiatry, and Behavior*, 11, 37–49.

MacDougall, J., Dembroski, T., & Musante, L. (1979). The structured interview and questionnaire methods of assessing coronary-prone behavior in male and female college students. *Journal of Behavioral Medicine*, 2, 71–92.

McCrae, R. R. (1991). The five-factor model and its assessment in clinical settings. *Journal of Personality Assessment, 57,* 399–414.

Miller, T. R. (1991). The psychotherapeutic utility of the five-factor model of personality: A clinician's experience. *Journal of Personality Assessment, 57,* 415–433.

Muten, E. (1991). Self-reports, spouse ratings, and psychophysiological assessment in a behavioral medicine program: An application of the five-factor model. *Journal of Personality Assessment, 57,* 449–464.

Myers, I. B. (1962). *Manual: The Myers-Briggs Type Indicator.* Palo Alto, CA: Consulting Psychologists Press.

Rosenman, R. H., Friedman, M., Straus, R., Wurm, M., Kositchek, R., Hahn, W., & Werthessen, N. T. (1964). A predictive study of coronary heart disease. *Journal of the American Medical Association, 189,* 15–22.

Roskies, E. (1980). Considerations in developing a treatment program for the coronary-prone (Type A) behavior pattern. In P. O. Davidson & S. M. Davidson (Eds.), *Behavioral Medicine: Changing Health Life Styles.* New York: Brunner/Mazel, 299–333.

Roskies, E., Spevack, M., Surkis, A., Cohen, C., & Gilman, S. (1978). Changing the coronary prone (Type A) behavior pattern in a nonclinical population. *Journal of Behavioral Medicine, 1,* 201–216.

Slocum, J. W., Jr., & Hellriegel, D. (1983). A look at how managers' minds work. *Business Horizons* (July–August), 58-68.

Suinn, R. M. (1982). Intervention with Type A behaviors. *Journal of Consulting and Clinical Psychology, 50,* 933–949.

Thurman, C. W. (1984). Cognitive-behavioral interventions with Type A faculty. *The Personnel and Guidance Journal,62,* 358–362.

Wheelwright, J. B., Wheelwright, J. H., & Buehler, H. A. (1964). *Jungian Type Survey: The Gray-Wheelwright Test* (16th revision). San Francisco: Society of Jungian Analysts of Northern California.

Part V

The Energy Expenditure and Energy Returns Issue

Chapter 9

Assessing One's Own Energy-Balance Effectiveness

A CASE IN POINT

William Bartell, Human Resource Manager for Wyler Industries Limited, knew that the stress-empowerment sessions had been very successful, but they were about to come to an end. In a few minutes, he would be entering the *Energy* expenditures/returns session, the fourth and final element in the C-O-P-*E* model. By now, participants had a pretty good idea about whether they were good stress managers or not. This last set of sessions would complete the picture by verifying for participants whether they were expending their finite life energy "critically intelligently" or "imprudently."

THE OPENING ADDRESS: TO BURN OUT OR NOT TO BURN OUT; THAT IS THE QUESTION

William began his first session on energy expenditures and energy returns:

We are moving into the "last leg" of our stress-empowerment sessions. This session and the one to follow deal with the final and critical issue of energy expenditures and energy returns. This session's objective is to allow participants to take a critical look at their own energy expenditure patterns. The next session's objective is to assess how companies contribute to organizational members' energy-refueling.

To set the backdrop for this session, I'd like to share a minicase with you that appeared in a piece by Oliver Niehouse in *Business Horizons* in 1984—at the height of The Burnout-Identification Era (described earlier in Chapter 4). It was appropriately titled, "Controlling Burnout: A Leadership Guide for Managers," and the case went like this:

"I told you not to do it that way," shouted Frank Halpern, a product manager at a major electronics firm. He was directing his annoyance at his design engineer, Jerry.

At thirty-three, Jerry Rasmussen seemed well on the road to success and personal happiness. A graduate of M.I.T., he began his career with a small New England company so that, as he said, "I wouldn't be hassled by big business bureaucracies." He got married about a year later and was able to put a down payment on a house just one hour's drive from the White Mountains of New Hampshire, where he and his wife enjoyed camping and fishing on weekends. He designed various electronic components at work and was instrumental in the design of a breakthrough product, which brought him to the attention of a major firm in Dallas.

The Dallas firm made Jerry a generous offer, which he agonized over but ultimately accepted. Jerry consequently sold his house and moved his family, which then included a son, to Texas.

Initially, Frank Halpern, Jerry's boss, was all smiles and enthusiastic at having a talented engineer "join my team." That quickly faded as Jerry learned the meaning of Frank's reference to "my team." Within fifteen months, Frank was constantly shouting at Jerry.

"Yes, but look at the results," retorted Jerry.

"No buts! Just do it the way I said."

Over time, similar scenes led Jerry to give up trying. Frustrated, Jerry did consider taking his talents elsewhere, preferably to a small company once again. However, he saw that as a career move backwards since smaller firms could not match his present salary, and not that many firms were hiring during the current recession. Further complicating the matter was the newest addition to his family, a daughter, and the fact that the family were really happy with their new home and Texas lifestyle. He, alone, longed for the White Mountains. Time passed slowly. Frustration became cynicism at work and outbursts of irritability at home. He began to wake up tired and to dread the drive to work.

Obviously, Jerry is burning out. The question is, what can he do to prevent further energy exhaustion and further deterioration? To burn out or not to burn out; that is the question. This session's objective is to supply some answers.

So as not to bias your responses to the inventories you are about to complete, *I would ask that you please turn to the appendixes for this session* (i.e., Chapter 9 Appendixes) *and complete as honestly as you can the inventory items that appear before you. Please do not score these inventory items until asked to do so. After you have finished responding, please join us for further discussions of this material.*

BURNOUT: HOW IT IS DEFINED AND MEASURED

Defining Burnout

As noted in an earlier session, the term "burnout" was introduced by Freudenberger in 1974 to refer to a phenomenon which he had observed in his coworkers in the free-clinic movement. The work environment of free clinics was characterized as demanding long hours of service and presenting emotionally draining encounters with clients, yet offering low pay to organizational members as well as meager resources for doing what had to be done. The shortfall in resources, Freudenberger noted, was bridged by the dedication and camaraderie among the clinic's staff members.

Freudenberger suggested that since there were few rewards for the staff members working in this macroenvironment, the energy that drove most of the organizational members could best be described as "youthful enthusiasm" for doing the job well. But as youthful enthusiasm is finite (recall Selye's warning), many staff members, chronically overworked and unacknowledged, had more energy "going out" than they had "coming in." They were in a state of energy imbalance. Freudenberger (1974) labeled these "walking wounded" among the clinic staff as "burnt out." He defined "burn out" as "to fail, wear out, or become exhausted by making excessive demands on [one's] energy, strength, or resources." For this expert, the syndrome of failing, wearing out, and becoming exhausted was attributed to the unceasing pressures of staff members' working with emotionally needy and demanding clients—with few resources and with few perceived "returns" on their energy investments.

In the 1970s, experts noted that Freudenberger's definition of burnout is not all that different from Selye's definition of "exhaustion," the major point in both conceptualizations being that the burned-out or exhausted individual runs "low on" or "out of" finite life energy, depending on the degree of burnout presenting. Unlike Selye, Freudenberger linked exhaustion or burnout to a particular occupational group—the helping professions.

Thus, in the 1980s, experts began to look more closely at burnout in health professionals to get a clearer understanding of what traits manifest when individuals say that they are "burned out." As a result of this search, two widely accepted delineations surfaced in the literature: one by Maslach (1982) and Maslach and Jackson (1985) and another by Pines and Aronson (1981).

Maslach (1982) and Maslach and Jackson (1985) said that "burnout" is characterized, in varying degrees, by three major presentations:

- *Emotional exhaustion*, whereby an organizational member's emotional "resources" are depleted and the feeling that he or she has nothing left to give to others at a psychological level prevails;
- *Depersonalization*, whereby an organizational member develops cold and callous attitudes about his or her coworkers or clients; and
- *Personal accomplishment decreases*, whereby an organizational member develops a negative evaluation of his or her task accomplishments.

Maslach (1982) and Maslach and Jackson (1985) further warned that the seriousness of burnout as a social and organizational problem lies in its links to turnover, absenteeism, poor job performance, and various types of personal dysfunction.

Pines and Aronson (1981) referred to "burnout" simply as "all-encompassing physical, emotional, and mental exhaustion." The major consequence of this malady, they noted, is the apparent lessening of burned-out health professionals' willingness to help or nurture others, thus defeating the purpose of the so-called "helping professions."

By the late 1980s, other experts' work revealed that organizational members in other occupations besides the health professions can become victimized by "burnout." Executives, too, were reported to become "burned out," whereas health-care organizational members had a reduced willingness to help others or turned callous, burned-out executives had a combined feeling of emotional exhaustion/depersonalization and a marked lessening of their will to excel or achieve (Garden, 1989; Levinson, 1981; Evans, 1989). What's more, experts noted, when executives "burned out," their fellow organizational members suffered nearly as much as they did.

Now in the 1990s, experts report that no occupation is left unscathed by burnout if the "right" conditions prevail; namely, limited organizational resources, high organizational task demands, and low perceived returns on the energy investments by organizational members. It is little wonder, therefore, that burned-out organizational members have been reported in task-demanding occupations—some requiring high people interactions and others requiring high technical skills—such as human services (Shinn et al., 1984), teaching (Russell, Altmaier, & Velzen, 1987), library media specialists (Fimian, Benedict, & Johnson, 1989), information system managers (Weiss, 1983), and software development teams (Sonnentag et al., 1994).

As a result of recent research, "burnout" in organizations seems to be low in macrosystem environments where there is a high degree of personal control appraised by organizational members (i.e., where there is empowerment), where the required jobs/tasks are appraised by organizational members as being "challenging" but not "life- or safety-threatening," and where organizational members perceive that their achievements are recognized by their bosses, peers, and society in general (Gaines & Jermier, 1983; Landsbergis, 1988; Friesen & Sarros, 1989). In macrosystems where group or team interactions are required, cohesive and socially supportive work group climates deter burnout up to a certain critical point (Etzion, 1984; Himle, Jayaratne, & Thyness, 1989; Leiter, 1988). After this point, the group climate can actually become "too highly cohesive"; thus, it produces chronic distress for group members and can lead to "burned-out" group members. Essentially, burnout results because group members feel that their individual opinions will be censored by the group prematurely, or that group-think (whereby group members keep quiet and go along with the "tight-knit" group's decisions rather than voicing their own opinions) will

Table 9.1
Golembiewski's Proposed Stages of Progressive Burnout (From I to VIII)

MBI Dimension	Phase I	Phase II	Phase III	Phase IV	Phase V	Phase VI	Phase VI	Phase VIII
Depersonalizing	Lo	Hi	Lo	Hi	Lo	Hi	Lo	Hi
Diminished Personal Accomplishment	Lo	Lo	Hi	Hi	Lo	Lo	Hi	Hi
Emotional Exhaustion	Lo	Lo	Lo	Lo	Hi	Hi	Hi	Hi

Source: Golembiewski, R. T. (1989). A note on Leiter's study: Highlighting two models of burnout. *Group and Organizational Studies,* 14, 5–13.

prevent their individual points of view from being shared altogether (Bois-joly, 1993; Sonnentag et al., 1994).

Measuring Burnout and Its Various "Degrees of"

The Maslach Burnout Inventory (MBI), developed by Maslach and Jackson (1981), is probably the most widely used self-report instrument for assessing the various degrees of burnout. The MBI consists of 22 items and gives participants indicators of low-, moderate-, or high-burnout risk on each of the three burnout dimensions: emotional exhaustion, depersonalization, and lack of personal accomplishment.

There is little question among experts that emotional exhaustion is the critical element in the burnout phenomenon. Experts have conjectured that individuals on the way to "full-blown burnout" typically depersonalize others or reduce their task accomplishments as a means of preserving dwindling energy and preventing (they hope) emotional exhaustion. The question is, where along the "degrees of" continuum do these three burnout dimensions place? The latter question has produced quite a debate between two academic "teams," in particular.

Golembiewski, Munzenrider, and Stevenson (1988), on the one hand, suggest that depersonalization and reduction in personal accomplishments occur at the earlier stages of burnout, and that once emotional exhaustion is experienced, the organizational member is at the high end of the health-disease continuum. The stages of burnout proposed by Golembiewski's team (1989, p. 7) are outlined in Table 9.1. Several independent research teams (Golembiewski, 1989) have assessed the external or concurrent validity of this "phase model" in at least a dozen populations. The developers of the model report that these study results have been quite uniform; in virtually all of the cases studied, the phases of burnout progressed, as outlined in Table 9.1, from stage I through stage VIII.

Leiter (1991a), as a one-person team, has taken exception to the rigidity of the eight stages proposed by Goliembiewski and his colleagues and to the manner in which clients' MBI scores are reduced from a continuous scale with all of its richness of information to a "lo" or "hi" state. Unlike the former research team's model of phased burnout, Leiter's work is based on a "process model" of burnout. Two hypotheses have been associated with Leiter's (1991a) process model:

1. The three components of burnout (i.e., emotional exhaustion, depersonalization, and diminished personal accomplishment) influence one another as they develop over time; and

2. The three components have distinct relationships that result from the unique individual-environmental *interactions* that occur within various organizations and within occupational groups.

Thus, Leiter suggests, unlike Golembiewski and his colleagues, that the process of burnout can vary from occupation to occupation and from organization to organization because prevailing organizational member environmental conditions vary. Leiter's (1991b) more recent empirical work using structural equation modeling (rather than stage delineation) indicates that his approach not only lets researchers explore a process model of burnout for various occupations using the MBI's three-factor structure but allows researchers to do so utilizing the richness of the three "continuous" MBI scales. Structural equation modeling also allows for the study of one dimension's impact on the other two—in specific organizations and in specific occupational groups (Leiter, 1989).

Although it seems premature to reach a conclusion on which research team's approach is more appropriate or useful at this stage of development, Leiter's approach seems to take into serious consideration organizational, occupational, and organizational member differences and allows for full utilization of the MBI model scales. In short, Leiter's approach seems to be consistent with that taken by us in our stress-empowerment sessions.

PERSONAL FEEDBACK: ARE YOU AT RISK FOR BURNOUT?

Participants can now receive feedback on their risk for full-blown burnout. *Please now score your responses to the energy expenditure inventory* (in Appendix 9.1).

Participants should now have three scores before them: one for emotional exhaustion, one for depersonalization, and one for lack of personal accomplishment. Using Leiter's approach, how many of your scores are approaching "the ceiling" on each of the three burnout dimensions? Using

Golembiewski's approach, how many of your scores were "hi" (let's say, exceeded the "half-way mark") on each of the three dimensions, and how many of your scores were "lo" (let's say, fell below the "half-way mark") on each of the three dimensions? If your colleagues who work closely with you were to complete the MBI, how do you think that they would score on these three MBI dimensions?

Participants should now be able to conclude:

• If their inventory scores indicate that they are at high risk for burnout; and
• If their colleagues' inventory scores would likely indicate that they are at high risk for burnout.

OTHER MIND-BODY-BEHAVIOR SYMPTOMS OF BURNOUT

Besides the three dimensions described by Maslach, experts have reported other mind-body-behavior symptoms associated with burnout. Einsiedel and Tully (1981) listed 84 burnout symptoms collated from several sources and Carroll and White (1982) listed 47 symptoms. There are dozens more in the literature, notes Kahill (1988), including practically any sign of psychological distress imaginable. Having reviewed the burnout literature from 1974 to 1984, when the bulk of research was being conducted on the topic, Kahill concluded that burnout includes the following mind-body-behavioral "outward signs" of distress (Kahill, 1988):

Mind Symptoms: Burnout is, without a doubt, related to depression (as manifested by Jerry in the case described earlier). The data regarding most other emotional symptoms—guilt, anxiety, nervousness, and irritability—although suggestive, are insufficient to permit firm conclusions at this time.

Body Symptoms: There is substantial evidence that burnout is related to poor physical health. In a number of studies, organizational members have complained of fatigue and physical exhaustion, sleep difficulties, and specific somatic problems such as headaches, gastrointestinal disturbances, colds, and flu. Individuals complaining of burnout often have high scores on symptom checklists like the SCL and the GHQ (discussed in Chapter 5). Although ulcers, gallbladder disease, and cardiovascular disorders have been linked to burnout, the relationship of this syndrome to major illness has not been consistently demonstrated.

Behavioral Symptoms: Burnout is related to a number of unproductive behaviors on the job. Turnover has been clearly linked to burnout, and the findings with regard to excessive use of alcohol and drugs are suggestive. Burnout also seems to be related to poor interpersonal behavior and social dysfunction. Burned-out organizational members tend to communicate with clients and coworkers in impersonal, stereotyped ways, finding it very difficult to concentrate on clients', coworkers', or their own problems.

Burned-out organizational members often withdraw from others (as Jerry did in the case described earlier). Other negative behaviors manifested range from irritability (as admitted by Jerry in the case described earlier) to pronounced verbal and behavioral violence toward coworkers, clients, and family members. At home, burned-out members seem to distance themselves from family members (as Jerry did in the case described earlier), at a time when good communication links with trusted significant others are essential for de-stressing.

COGNITIONS AND STRESS-COPING BEHAVIORS ASSOCIATED WITH BURNOUT

Individual cognition and stress-coping behavioral differences are important when it comes to burnout risk. Although earlier studies showed females to be more at risk for full-blown burnout than males, present-day studies indicate that there are no gender differences, and that earlier gender differences were likely a function of the female-predominant health and teaching occupations being studied (Maslach & Jackson, 1985).

Cognitions

Meier (1983) maintains that individuals' negative cognitions can place them at risk for burnout. "Deep information processors," Meier suggests, are less at risk for burnout than "shallow information processors." It is possible that deep information processors—who can remember both their positive and negative life experiences—are actually low-neurotic, high-intuitive (N) Types; because of their recall of positive experiences, deep information processors seem to be more immune to burning out. It is possible that shallow information processors—who can remember only painful, negative life experiences—are actually high-neurotic, high-sensing Types; because of their predisposition to dwell on what's real and negative, shallow information processors seem to be at high risk for burnout.

Meier (1983) suggests that burnout-prone individuals maintain three self-destructive cognitions, in particular:

• Low expectations regarding the presence of positive reinforcement and high expectations regarding the presence of punishment in the work environment;
• Low expectations regarding ways of controlling the reinforcers that are present in the work environment; and
• Low expectations for personal competence in performing the behaviors necessary to control the reinforcement.

(Note that Jerry in the case described earlier seemed to have all three cognitions; thus, he, increasingly, became withdrawn and depressed, feeling hopeless and helpless that things would improve in his present work situation.)

Stress-Coping Behaviors

Leiter (1991b) has found that organizational members who utilize predominantly "escapist" stress-coping behaviors rather than "control" strategies place themselves at high risk for burnout. A combination of escapist coping with a lack of asserting one's own needs is especially damaging. Escapist coping/unassertive behavior is particularly ineffective for avoiding burnout because instead of resolving organizational problems to the suitability of the parties concerned (i.e., witness Jerry and his boss in the case described earlier), this combination consumes precious finite life energy but rarely, if ever, brings a perceived adequate return on the unassertive individual's energy investment. A control-coping/assertive behavior combination, on the other hand, appears to be incompatible with burnout. To the extent that organizational members employ control-coping with assertive behaviors, notes Leiter, they will find themselves reporting low scores on all three aspects of burnout.

TREATMENT INTERVENTIONS FOR BURNED-OUT ORGANIZATIONAL MEMBERS

As Leiter (1991a) and other experts warn, to develop burnout strategies for organizational members without altering a "poisoned" macrosystem is like healing a patient suffering from some infectious disease and then sending him/her back into the disease-infested area. Accepting this point, experts have found that certain measures can be taken to help organizational members improve their chances of staying "in control" (and reducing their chances of burnout) in a hostile environment.

First, as noted by Leiter, organizational members need to develop and heavily rely on control-coping strategies rather than to develop and heavily rely on escapist-coping strategies.

Second, say Kipnis and Schmidt (1988), organizational members can learn to improve their "upward-influence styles" by first, learning what their influence style is like and, second, by trying to move toward a style that is interpersonal-skill broad-based as well as reasonable. In Kipnis and Schmidt's studies of blue-collar, supervisory, and chief executive officer organizational members, they found that the degree of stress (and burnout) experienced by organizational members was, in large part, a function of the way that they attempted to influence their bosses and others of influence in the organization. In short, reduced stress on the job, higher salaries, and positive performance evaluations were most likely to be reported by men utilizing a tactician style of influence, followed by a bystander style of influence, followed by an ingratiator style of influence, followed by a shotgun style of influence. Kipnis and Schmidt (1988) described these four styles of interpersonal influence as follows:

- *Tactitioners* (like the assertive, autonomous Type Bs) have high scores on reason and logic and have average scores on "friendliness," "assertiveness," "bargaining," "going to higher authority figures," and "forming coalitions with others" in order to influence upwardly;
- *Bystanders* have low scores on all of the interpersonal influence styles just cited;
- *Ingratiators* (like Type Cs?) score high on the "friendliness" influence strategy and have average scores on the remaining strategies; and
- *Shotguns* (like pronounced Type As) have high scores on all six influence strategies—especially "assertiveness"—suggesting that not only do they engage in nonjudicious selection of their influence strategies but that they will "try almost anything" to gain control of their work environment and of others in it.

Third, as is obvious from both Leiter's and Kipnis and Schmidt's work, organizational members need to assert themselves in order for their needs and their points of view to be heard—both on and off the job. If other assertive or aggressive people in the organizational and/or home environment unilaterally determine "whose needs" are going to be met (as seems to be the case, increasingly, in Jerry's work and home environments), then the nonassertive individual's chances for refueling and for thwarting burnout are not very good. Individuals (like Jerry) who experience a lot of anxiety asserting themselves in either the work or home environment could use a course in assertiveness training. In just six or eight sessions with a professional facilitator, formerly unassertive individuals can become "healthily" assertive (Gambrill & Richey, 1975).

Fourth, organizational members have to be wise about saving some energy for the job, some for personal creative pursuits (like painting, woodworking, or engaging in leisure-time activities), and some for intimate and emotionally refueling family and friend relationships. Experts Friedman and Rosenman, in their popular book *Type A Behavior and Your Heart*, provided some philosophical guidelines for changing Type A behavior patterns. These guidelines were so well done that clinicians have found them to be useful in rehabilitating "burned-out" clients as well. These guidelines are summarized as follows:

- *Retrieve your total personality* by spending time communicating with people on topics of interest to *you*—art, music, drama, nature, or spiritual matters.
- *Establish life goals*, which include realistic energy expenditure and energy return objectives for both on the job and off the job.
- *Make some gestures toward myth, ritual, and traditions* that formerly brought

you peace of mind and harmony (such as visiting relatives for Sunday dinners and attending religious activities of your choice).

- *Stop using your right hand to do the work your left hand should be doing;* that is, devote less energy to "left-handed" activities that require less vigilance or should be delegated to someone else to do and devote more energy to "right-handed" activities that require greater personal attention from you as well as your unique talents.

- *Let your means justify your ends;* that is, stop trying to excuse "daily errors of living" by looking toward some great end, because each day and each activity should be valued for its own sake. Before you retire at night (or in the morning if you are on shift-work), remind yourself of all the good things that you have accomplished in the previous eight hours.

- *Remember that a successful life always involves "unfinishedness,"* for life is structured on and consists of primarily uncompleted processes, tasks, and events—and only a corpse is completely finished! Therefore, it is okay to put off until tomorrow what cannot be safely and competently completed today. (Friedman & Rosenman, 1974, pp. 214–233)

PERSONAL FEEDBACK: IS LACK OF ASSERTIVENESS TAKING YOU DOWN THE PATH TO BURNOUT?

Participants can now receive feedback on their assertive predispositions. *Please now score your responses to the Gambrill and Richey inventory on interpersonal behavior* (in Appendix 9.2).

Participants should now have two scores before them: a "discomfort score" (ranging from 40 to 200) and a "response probability score" (also ranging from 40 to 200). Taking these two scores and looking at the chart displayed on the scoring instructions, participants can now determine if their interpersonal predispositions place in the "unassertive," "don't care," "anxious-performer," or "assertive" range. That is, cell one includes scores for individuals with an assertion problem—high discomfort coupled with low assertion. Cell two includes scores for individuals who tend to exhibit assertive behavior in spite of high discomfort, and are thus labeled "anxious-performers." Cell three includes scores for individuals who report low discomfort as well as low response probability; such individuals may not be concerned about expressing themselves assertively or may see assertion as futile—thus, the "why bother" label. Cell four includes scores for individuals who are appropriately assertive; that is, they have low discomfort and a high response probability.

In which cell do your two scores lie? Do you think that your scores reflect an appropriately assertive person, or do you think that you could use some assertiveness training sessions? Participants should be able to conclude:

- If they are "appropriately assertive" in interpersonal situations.

CONCLUSION

This session began with the case of Jerry, an engineer who was on the road to burnout. The bulk of this session detailed the symptoms of burnout, the cognitions and behaviors associated with it, and interventions that can help deter or reduce burnout. By the end of this session, it became obvious to many of you, I would think, that Jerry could move off the path of burnout and move back on the road of health—if he made conscientious efforts to do so. However, a "do nothing" escapist strategy would likely make Jerry's situation worse, leading him further down the path to "full-blown burnout."

STRESS-COPING SUMMARY POINTS

1. To assess whether they are getting good returns on their energy investments as a means of preventing exhaustion and burnout, individuals need to regularly monitor their "energy-balances." The Maslach Burnout Inventory—a version of which appears in the Appendix 9.1—is particularly helpful in this regard.

2. If organizational members perceive that they may be at risk for burnout, control-coping strategies can be tried. However, if members find themselves "exhausted and burning out fast," they should seek professional assistance immediately. Once things are brought back "in order," assertiveness training is often a useful treatment intervention for those wanting to avoid relapses.

Appendix 9.1
Energy Expenditure Inventory

Instructions: For the 22 statements below, please put an X in the "True" or "false" Column, depending on how you really feel. Please be honest.		
Statement	True	False
1. I feel emotionally drained from my work.		
2. I feel "used up" at the end of the workday.		
3. I feel fatigued when I get up in the morning and have to face another day.		
4. I can easily understand how my clients or coworkers feel about things.		
5. I feel I treat some clients or coworkers as if they were impersonal objects.		
6. Working with people all day is really a strain for me.		
7. I deal effectively with the problems of my clients or coworkers.		
8. I feel "burned out" from my work.		
9. I feel I'm positively influencing other people's lives through my work.		
10. I've become more callous toward people since I took this job.		
11. I worry that this job is hardening me emotionally.		
12. I feel very energetic.		

Appendix 9.1 (continued)

13. I feel frustrated by my job.		
14. I feel I'm working too hard on my job.		
15. I don't really care what happens to some clients or coworkers.		
16. Working with people directly puts too much stress on me.		
17. I can easily create a relaxed atmosphere with my clients or coworkers.		
18. I feel exhilarated after working closely with my clients or coworkers.		
19. I have accomplished many worthwhile things in this job.		
20. I feel like I'm at the end of my rope.		
21. In my work, I deal with emotional problems very calmly.		
22. I feel that clients or coworkers blame me for some of their problems.		

Source: Maslach, C., & Jackson, S. E. (1981). The measurement of experienced burnout. *Journal of Occupational Behaviour, 2,* 99–113.

Appendix 9.2
Gambrill and Richey's Inventory on Interpersonal Behavior

Instructions: Many people experience difficulty in handling interpersonal situations requiring them to assert themselves in some way, for example, turning down a request, asking a friend for a favor, giving someone a compliment, expressing disapproval or approval, and so on.

Please indicate your degree of discomfort or anxiety in the space provided BEFORE each situation listed below. Use the following scale to indicate your **degree of discomfort**:
1=none; 2=a little; 3=a fair amount; 4=much; 5=very much.

Then, go over the list a second time and indicate AFTER each item the probability or likelihood of your displaying the behavior if actually presented with the situation. For example, if you rarely apologize when you are at fault, you would mark a "4" AFTER that item. Use the following scale to indicate **response probability**:
1=always do it; 2=usually do it; 3=do it about half the time; 4=rarely do it; 5=never do it.

Degree of Discomfort	Situation	Response Probability
	1. Turn down a request to borrow your car.	
	2. Compliment a friend.	
	3. Ask a favor of someone.	
	4. Resist sales pressure.	
	5. Apologize when you are at fault.	
	6. Turn down a request for a meeting or date.	
	7. Admit fear and request consideration.	
	8. Tell a person you are intimately involved with when he/she says or does something that bothers you.	
	9. Ask for a raise.	
	10. Admit ignorance in some area.	

11. Turn down a request to borrow money.	
12. Ask personal questions.	
13. Turn off a talkative friend.	
14. Ask for constructive criticism.	
15. Initiate a conversation with a stranger.	
16. Compliment a person you are romantically involved with or interested in.	
17. Request a meeting or a date with a person.	
18. Your initial request for a meeting is turned down and you ask the person again at a later time.	
19. Admit confusion about a point under discussion and ask for clarification.	
20. Apply for a job.	
21. Ask whether you have offended someone.	
22. Tell someone that you like them.	
23. Request expected service when such is not forthcoming; e.g., in a restaurant.	
24. Discuss openly with the person his/her criticism of your behavior.	
25. Return defective items; e.g., store or restaurant.	
26. Express an opinion that differs from that of the person you are talking to.	
27. Resist sexual overtones when you are not interested.	

	28. Tell the person when you feel he/she has done something that is unfair to you.	
	29. Accept a date.	
	30. Tell someone good news about yourself.	
	31. Resist pressure to drink.	
	32. Resist a significant person's unfair demand.	
	33. Quit a job.	
	34. Resist pressure to "turn on."	
	35. Discuss openly with the person his/her criticism of your work.	
	36. Request the return of borrowed items.	
	37. Receive compliments.	
	38. Continue to converse with someone who disagrees with you.	
	39. Tell a friend or someone with whom you work when he/she says or does something that bothers you.	
	40. Ask a person who is annoying you in a public situation to stop.	

Source: Gambrill, E. D., & Richey, C. A. (1975). An assertion inventory for use in assessment and research. *Behavior Therapy, 6,* 550–561.

Scoring Appendix 9.1

Instructions: You will be getting three scores from this exercise: One for emotional exhaustion, one for depersonalization, and one for lack of personal accomplishment. In each column, give yourself one mark for each of your responses that matches those listed. Then, total your marks for each column.

Emotional Exhaustion:	Depersonalization:	Lack of Personal Accomplishment:
Item 1 true	Item 5 true	Item 4 false
Item 2 true	Item 10 true	Item 7 false
Item 3 true	Item 11 true	Item 9 false
Item 6 true	Item 15 true	Item 12 false
Item 8 true	Item 22 true	Item 17 false
Item 13 true		Item 18 false
Item 14 true		Item 19 false
Item 16 true		Item 21 false
Item 20 true		
Total: _____/9	Total: _____/5	Total: _____/8

Source: Maslach, C., & Jackson, S. E. (1981). The measurement of experienced burnout. *Journal of Occupational Behaviour, 2,* 99–113.

Scoring Appendix 9.2

Instructions: (1) Total your marks for the left-hand column of Appendix 9.2. This is your Discomfort score. Mark it here: _____
(2) Total your marks for the right-hand column of Appendix 9.2. This is your Response Probability score. Mark it here: _____.
(3) In which cell range do your Discomfort and Response Probability scores place you (see chart below)--in the unassertive, don't care, anxious performer, or assertive range?

Discomfort Score	Response Probability Score Greater than 105	Response Probability Score Less than 104
Greater than 96	Unassertive	Anxious-performer
Less than 95	Don't care	Assertive

Source: Gambrill, E. D., & Richey, C. A. (1975). An assertion inventory for use in assessment and research. *Behavior Therapy, 6,* 550–561.

REFERENCES

Boisjoly, R. M. (1993). Personal integrity and accountability. *Accounting Horizons*, 7, 59–69.

Carroll, J. F., & White, W. L. (1982). Theory building: Integrating individual and environmental factors within an ecological framework. In W. S. Paine (Ed.), *Job Stress and Burnout: Research, Theory, and Intervention Perspectives*. Beverly Hills, CA: Sage Publications, 41–60.

Evans, B. K. (1989). *The Structure and Antecedents of Burnout: A Causal Modelling Approach*. Unpublished Doctoral Dissertation, University of Saskatchewan.

Einsiedel, A. A., Jr., & Tully, H. A. (1981). Methodological considerations in studying the burnout phenomenon. In J. W. Jones (Ed.), *The Burnout Syndrome: Current Research, Theory, Interventions*. Park Ridge, IL: London House Press, 89–106.

Etzion, D. (1984). Moderating effect of social support on the stress-burnout relationship. *Journal of Applied Psychology*, 69, 615–622.

Fimian, M. J., Benedict, S. A., & Johnson, S. (1989). The measure of occupational stress and burnout among library media specialists. *Library and Information Science Research*, 11, 3–9.

Freudenberger, H. J. (1974). Staff burnout. *Journal of Social Issues*, 30, 159–165.

Friedman, M., & Rosenman, R. H. (1974). *Type A Behavior and Your Heart*. New York: Fawcett Crest.

Friesen, D., & Sarros, J. C. (1989). Sources of burnout among educators. *Journal of Organizational Behavior*, 10, 179–188.

Gaines, J., & Jermier, J. M. (1983). Emotional exhaustion in a high stress organization. *Academy of Management Journal*, 26, 567–586.

Gambrill, E. D., & Richey, C. A. (1975). An assertion inventory for use in assessment and research. *Behavior Therapy*, 6, 550–561.

Garden, A.-M. (1989). Burnout: The effect of psychological type on research findings. *Journal of Occupational Psychology*, 62, 223–234.

Golembiewski, R. T. (1989). A note on Leiter's study. *Group and Organizational Studies*, 14, 5–13.

Golembiewski, R. T., Munzenrider, R. F., & Stevenson, G. (1988). *Stress in Organizations*. New York: Praeger.

Himle, D. P., Jayaratne, S., & Thyness, P. (1989). The effects of emotional support on burnout, work stress, and mental health among Norwegian and American social workers. *Journal of Social Science Research*, 13, 27–45.

Kahill, S. (1988). Symptoms of professional burnout: A review of the empirical evidence. *Canadian Psychology*, 29, 284–297.

Kipnis, D., & Schmidt, S. M. (1988). Upward-influence styles: Relationship with performance, evaluations, salary, and stress. *Administrative Science Quarterly*, 33, 528–542.

Landsbergis, P. A. (1988). Occupational stress among health care workers: A test of the job demands-control model. *Journal of Organizational Behavior*, 9, 217–239.

Leiter, M. P. (1988). Burnout as a function of communication patterns: A study of a multidisciplinary mental health team. *Group and Organization Studies*, 13, 111–128.

Leiter, M. P. (1989). Conceptual implication of two models of burnout. *Group and Organizational Studies*, 14, 15–22.

Leiter, M. (1991a). The dream denied: Professional burnout and the constraints of human service organizations. *Canadian Psychology*, 32, 547–555.

Leiter, M. P. (1991b). Coping patterns as predictors of burnout: The function of control and escapist coping patterns. *Journal of Organizational Behavior*, 12, 123–144.

Levinson, H. (1981). When executives burnout. *Harvard Business Review*, (May–June), 73–81.

Maslach, C. (1982). *Burnout, The Cost of Caring*. Englewood Cliffs, NJ: Prentice-Hall.

Maslach, C., & Jackson, S. E. (1981). The measurement of experienced burnout. *Journal of Occupational Behaviour*, 2, 99–113.

Maslach, C., & Jackson, S. E. (1985). The role of sex and family variables in burnout. *Sex Roles*, 12, 837–851.

Meier, S. T. (1983). Toward a theory of burnout. *Human Relations*, 36, 899–910.

Niehouse, O. I. (1984). Controlling burnout: A leadership guide for managers. *Business Horizons*, 27, 80–85.

Pines, A., & Aronson, E. (1981). *Burnout: From Tedium to Personal Growth*. New York: Free Press.

Russell, D. W., Altmaier, E., & Velzen, D. (1987). Job-related stress, social support, and burnout among classroom teachers. *Journal of Applied Psychology*, 72, 269–274.

Shinn, M., Rosario, M., Morch, H., & Chestnur, D. E. (1984). Coping with job stress and burnout in the human services. *Journal of Personality and Social Psychology*, 46, 854–876.

Sonnentag, S., Brodbeck, F. C., Heinbokel, T., and Stolte, W. (1994). Stressor-burnout relationship in software development teams. *Journal of Occupational and Organizational Psychology*, 67, 327–341.

Weiss, M. (1983). Effects of work stress and social support on information systems managers. *MIS Quarterly*, 7, 29–43.

Chapter 10

Understanding the Organization's Function in Promoting Energy Balance

A CASE IN POINT

William Bartell, Human Resource Manager for Wyler Industries Limited, was relieved. His first group of stress-empowerment volunteers was about to be graduated, hopefully paving the way for new recruits in upcoming sessions. This last session, the fourth element in the C-O-P-E model, was to close with the participants' rating their organization on its promotion of Energy-balance in organizational members. He wondered if Wyler Industries would rate as a "10"—either now or in the near future.

THE OPENING ADDRESS: THE ORGANIZATION'S FUNCTION IN PROMOTING ENERGY BALANCE IN ORGANIZATIONAL MEMBERS

William began his last session on stress-empowerment and energy balance:

In a few minutes, we will be at the end of our C-O-P-E sessions. But before we leave, we need to consider the macrosystem's role in preventing burnout and in promoting energy-balance in organizational members.

We started our sessions with the case of Warren Potts, realizing that Wyler Industries had a way to go to reduce pathological levels of job stress and to promote energy balance in organizational members. Thus, we embarked on these stress-empowerment sessions, utilizing the C-O-P-E Model as we proceeded and realizing that organizational members need to regularly assess:

- Whether they are "in control";
- Whether they are showing outward signs of distress;
- Whether their personality predispositions are escalating or deescalating stress situations; and
- Whether they are maintaining energy balances.

By this final stage of the program, participants likely have a good idea of the macrosystem's role in preventing pathological levels of job stress and burnout for its members. But before we summarize for the last time the macrosystem factors that have made it on the "Top Ten Macrosystem Burnout-Prevention Strategies List," I would like to share with you one final case about some organizational members who are feeling highly stressed and burned out.

I read this case in *The Globe and Mail* about a year ago and decided to save it in case Wyler Industries elected to move ahead with its stress-empowerment program. Entitled, "For a nervous breakdown, please press 1," this fascinating case reads as follows:

Sweatshops. The word conjures visions of dishevelled women running frantically between clamouring machines of the industrial revolution. Or tired, grey women walking slowly in the evening twilight, dragging bone-weary children home for meagre dinners of thin soup and crusts of stale bread. Hardship and physical exhaustion were endemic to work. In today's sweatshops, a reversal is taking place. Now people are physically pampered, but their mental and emotional forces are savaged by the fierce pace of work. At least that's the way it is in the telephone sweatshops.

Although I left my position as an "inside salesperson" several months ago, I am still grappling with the question of why handling 60 to 80 telephone calls a day is so difficult. The surroundings are pleasant enough: comfortable chairs, carpeted floors, brightly painted walls hung with framed prints. Our small cubicles have lots of desk space and some of the telephones have headsets. These help to make you more efficient on the computer keyboard. It's just that headsets remind me of horses in halters tied to their stalls.

Our purpose in life is to handle orders and keep the customers satisfied. We are invariably courteous, pleasant and upbeat as the customer calls rain in upon us. You never know what the next call will bring. Sometimes customers are angry because a part hasn't arrived. Sometimes the part sent will not do the job it's intended for. Sometimes someone needs a quote before 5 o'clock because the boss is going away and wants to take the information with her.

Phone mail increases the volume of calls. It is not uncommon to get off the telephone after a short conversation with one customer, only to discover three new messages waiting for attention. Sometimes the volume of calls coming in is so great that customers leave two and three messages asking why their original call has not been returned.

There are heroes among us. My friend, Donald, who does the inside sales for the company's major account, handled up to 140 calls a day. At least once a week the outside sales person on the account would heap sarcastic comments and criticism on Donald's head. We call this outside rep "Toxic Tony" because of his poisonous attitude toward all those who support his efforts. Don continues to hang on to his job, but now I get calls that go like this:

"Hi. It's me. I'm still at work."

"It's 9 o'clock at night. Why are you still there?"

"Big month . . . you know how it is. The pressure's on and the pay's okay."

"Yeah, but is it worth shortening your life?"

"Do you think I am?"

"Well, you know the symptoms . . . high heart rate, locked knees, tightness in the neck and shoulders—and you're losing your hair!" (Don, when he has time, is on the prowl for a girlfriend; he believes the right woman will need a man with a full head of hair.) If you were 15 years older, I bet they'd be carrying you out on a stretcher with a massive heart attack. It's only age that's protecting you. Look at yourself, Don. You used to have a sense of humour."

"I did, didn't I? . . . I went to a bar last night and this really good-looking girl came up and I couldn't even make her laugh. Everything I said was flat. *I feel flat.* It's like there are no highs or lows any more, just this monotonous static hum of numbed-out emotions. What do you think I should do?"

"Get out of that job and take that trip you've been planning." . . . telephone sales/customer service does provide work, that's true, but those who do this work frequently burn out within a year to 18 months.

Telemarketers and customer-support representatives endure a relentless hail of incoming calls, over which they have no control. The work is the equivalent of being a white rat on an electronic grid that delivers shocks at an uncontrollable and unpredictable rate. Psychologists and biologists have proven that such a state is harmful, yet this knowledge is not transferred into the workplace.

As far as I know, there are no companies that regularly cycle their inside sales/customer service people into less-stressful positions. Nor do they willingly grant stress leave. A mental-health day is often viewed as unacceptable sloth or as letting down the team.

Yet recent changes to the Unemployment Insurance Act mean that when employees in a phone sweatshop recognize that they are totally stressed-out, nuked, and emotionally void and in danger of exploding over the phone to some cherished customer, they can't quit to save their sanity, their reputation and family life.

In these economically frigid times, the exploitation of people's psychological health will continue. The Victorian sweatshop is alive and well, and it has gone hi-tech. (Stewart, 1994, p. A26)

Take five minutes, please, and jot down ten macrosystem factors that you think are creating energy imbalances for Don and the other telemarketers. After you have done this, *I would ask that you please turn to the appendix (i.e., Chapter 10 Appendix) and complete as honestly as you can the inventory items that appear before you. Please do not score these inventory items until asked to do so. After you have finished responding, please join us for further discussions of this material.*

ORGANIZATIONAL FEEDBACK: DOES YOUR ORGANIZATION PROMOTE ENERGY BALANCE IN ORGANIZATIONAL MEMBERS?

Participants can now receive feedback on whether they think that their organization promotes energy balance in its organizational members. *Please now score your responses to the "work environment scale"* (Appendix 10.1), an instrument used widely by organizational development (OD) experts to identify macrosystem factors causing pathological distress and burnout for organizational members (Golembiewski, Hilles, & Daly, 1987).

After completing Appendix 10.1, participants should have one "average rating score" ranging from 1 to 10. The higher the rating score, the more participants perceive that their work environment promotes energy balance in its organizational members.

Where did your score place on this 1–10 continuum? If all organizational members were to rate your organization, where on this continuum, do you perceive the broader "average score" would place?

Given their responses to these questions, participants should be able to conclude:

- If their organization is promoting energy balances in organizational members; and
- If not, what targets for change should be forwarded to upper management and to the Human Resource Department?

CONCLUSION

This final session using the C-O-P-E model had one simple objective: to give participants time to consider whether their organizations are promoting energy balances in organizational members. This short session started with the case of burned-out telemarketers and ended with some introspection and an open question for participants.

STRESS-COPING SUMMARY POINTS

1. To assess whether organizations are promoting energy balances in their organizational members, members throughout the organization should be asked to anonymously complete the Work Environment Scale, a version of which appears in the Appendix.

2. If the organizational "average score" is low, upper management needs to seriously consider—with the help of organizational members throughout the organization—how they can improve the work environment so as to reduce pathological levels of job stress and to promote energy balances in their organizational members.

Appendix 10.1
Work Environment Scale: Is Your Organization a "10"?

Instructions: Please rate your organization on the ten Work Environment Scales shown below. In the right-hand column, rate your organization from 1 to 10 on each scale, where 1 means that your organization "has none" of this trait and where 10 means that your organization "has full representation" of this trait.	
1. **Autonomy and Personal Control**: Organizational members are encouraged to be self-sufficient and to make their own decisions.	**RATING (from 1 - 10)**
2. **Task Orientation**: The organizational climate emphasizes good planning and efficiency and encourages organizational members to "get the job done"--safely.	
3. **Involvement**: The extent to which organizational members are concerned about and committed to their jobs.	
4. **Peer Cohesion**: The extent to which organizational members are friendly and supportive of each other--but not to the degree that "group-think" exists.	
5. **Staff Support**: The extent to which management is supportive of organizational members and encourages members to be supportive of each other.	

6. **Work Pressure:** The extent to which moderated work pressures prevail.	
7. **Clarity:** The extent to which organizational members know what to expect in their daily routines, and the provisions made for quality communications by unions and management regarding company policies and rules.	
8. **Accountability:** The extent to which organizational members throughout the organization are held accountable for abiding by company policies and rules.	
9. **Innovation:** The extent to which "healthy amounts" of variety, change, and new approaches are emphasized in the work environment.	
10. **Physical, Emotional, and Behavioral Comfort:** The amount of physical, emotional, and behavioral comfort and well-being allowed by the organizational environment.	

Source: Golembiewski, R. T., Hilles, R., & Daly, R. (1987). Some effects of multiple OD interventions on burnout and work site features. *The Journal of Applied Behavioral Science*, 23, 295–313.

Scoring Appendix 10.1

REFERENCES

Golembiewski, R. T., Hilles, R., & Daly, R. (1987). Some effects of multiple OD interventions on burnout and work site features. *The Journal of Applied Behavioral Science*, 23, 295–313.

Rosenthal, D., Tague, M., Retish, P., West, J., & Vessell, R. (1983). The relationship between work environment attributes and burnout. *Journal of Leisure Research*, 15, 125–135.

Stewart, A. M. (1994). For a nervous breakdown, please press 1. *The Globe and Mail*, June 1, p. A26.

Selected Annotated Bibliography

For those who are interested in reading further on the topics discussed in *A Self-Diagnostic Approach to Understanding Organizational and Personal Stressors*, an annotated bibliography of "classic" books cited follows.

Beck, A. T., Emery, G., & Greenberg, R. L. (1985). *Anxiety Disorders and Phobias*. New York: Basic Books. Technical in nature, this book, written by leading experts in the depression and anxiety fields, gives excellent insights into anxiety disorders and phobias.

Bradburn, N. M. (1969). *The Structure of Psychological Well-Being*. Chicago: Aldine. Like the former, this book details the notion of psychological well-being.

Cannon, W. G. (1929). *Bodily Changes in Pain, Hunger, Fear and Rage: An Account of Recent Researches into the Function of Emotional Excitement*. 2d ed. New York: Appleton. Rather technical in nature, this early classic by one of the two founding fathers of stress theory, Walter Cannon, provides a look at the physiological changes that occur with pain, hunger, fear, and anger.

Cascio, W. F. (1991). *Costing Human Resources: The Financial Impact of Behavior in Organizations*. 3d ed. Boston: PWS-Kent. A must for human resource managers, this book covers the difficult area of assessing the financial impact of behavior in organizations.

Cooper, C. L. (1983). *Stress Research*. Chichester: Wiley. An excellent collection of chapters written by leading stress experts from around the world, this important book includes Selye's "The stress concept: Past, present, future" and Chesney and Rosenman's "Specificity in stress models: Examples drawn from Type A behavior."

Davidson, P. O., & Davidson, S. M. (1980) *Behavioral Medicine: Changing Health*

Life Styles. New York: Brunner/Mazel. An excellent look at how to change health lifestyles from not-so-good to good, this book includes Roskies's excellent piece entitled, "Considerations in developing a treatment program for the coronary-prone (Type A) behavior pattern."

The Diagnostic and Statistical Manual of Mental Disorders. (1987). Rev. 3d ed. Washington, DC: American Psychiatric Association. Technical in nature, this book is an excellent reference text for human resource managers wanting to become more informed about the mental disorder terminology used by experts and lawyers in stress claim cases.

Friedman, H. S. (1991). *The Self-healing Personality: Why Some People Achieve Health While Others Succumb to Illness*. New York: Holt. A rather new addition to the personality literature family, this book gives an excellent description of the self-healing personality.

Friedman, M., & Rosenman, R. H. (1974). *Type A Behavior and Your Heart*. New York: Fawcett Crest. Written by the developers of Type A theory, this easy-to-read book describes the causes and effects of Type A behavior patterning.

Golembiewski, R. T., Munzenrider, R. F., & Stevenson, G. (1988). *Stress in Organizations*. New York: Praeger. One of the few books that details the progression of burnout, it gives insights into the critical relationship between organizational environments and burnout development in organizational members.

Hackman, J. R., & Oldham, C. R. (1980). *Work Redesign*. Reading, MA: Addison-Wesley. An organizational behavior favorite from the 1980s, this book describes the notion of Person-Environmental (P-E) fit and provides normative data across occupational groups for the Job Diagnostic Survey (JDS).

Hawton, K., Salkovskis, P., Kirk, J., & Clark, D. M. (1989). *Cognitive Behavior Therapy for Psychiatric Problems: A Practical Guide*. Oxford: Oxford University Press. Technical in nature, this book details cognitive behavior therapies (CBT) for psychiatric problems and includes an excellent chapter by D. M. Clark on anxiety and panic states (pp. 53–96).

Herzberg, F. (1966). *Work and the Nature of Man*. Chicago: World Publishing Company. Known to experts in the organizational behavior field, this book delineates the important interactive relationship between work and organizational members' needs.

Hurst, J. (1981) *Update V: The Heart*. New York: McGraw-Hill. A more recent account of what keeps the heart healthy, this book includes an excellent piece by Friedman, Thoreson, and Gill, entitled, "Type A behavior: Its possible role, detection, and alteration in patients with ischemic heart disease."

Jahoda, M. (1958). *Current Concepts of Positive Mental Health*. New York: Basic Books. This book gives a good description of positive mental health, a label which has since become known in the psychological liturature as Positive Affect predominance, or PA.

Kahn, R., Wolfe, D., Quinn, R., Snoek, J., & Rosenthal, R. (1964). *Organizational Stress: Studies in Role Conflict and Ambiguity*. New York: Wiley. An organizational behavior favorite from the 1960s Role Stress Era, this book provides a comprehensive look at experts' views on role stressors.

Lazarus, R. S. (1966). *Psychological Stress and the Coping Process*. New York:

McGraw-Hill. A book familiar to experts in the stress field, this book details the importance of individuals' unique appraisals of stressors.

Maslach, C. (1982). *Burnout, The Cost of Caring.* Englewood Cliffs, NJ: Prentice-Hall. A contribution from the Burnout Prevention Era, this book, written by the developer of the Maslach Burnout Inventory, describes the causes and effects of burnout.

Maslow, A. H. (1973). *The Farther Reaches of Human Nature.* London: Penguin. Familiar to most in the organizational behavior field, this book builds on the notion of Maslow's Hierarchy of Needs and details the important role of self-actualization in human development.

Novaco, R. W. (1975). *Anger Control: The Development and Evaluation of an Experimental Treatment.* Lexington, MA: Lexington Books. An international award winner, this book, written by one of the world's leading experts on anger management, describes the healthy and unhealthy sides of anger, the important role of anger provocation, and the intervention strategies for controlling anger.

Paine, W. S. (1982), *Job Stress and Burnout: Research, Theory, and Intervention Perspectives.* Beverly Hills, CA: Sage Publications. A comprehensive look at job stress and burnout, this excellent book includes Carroll's and White's piece entitled, "Theory building: Integrating individual and environmental factors within an ecological framework."

Pines, A., & Aronson, E. (1981). *Burnout: From Tedium to Personal Growth.* New York: Free Press. Another contribution from the Burnout Prevention Era, this book not only describes burnout but details how it can be beaten.

Piotrkowski, C. S. (1978). *Work and the Family System.* New York: Free Press. For those wanting to know more about negative carryover, this book describes the importance of two-way healthy interactions between the work environment and the family system.

Price, V. A. (1982). *Type A Behavior: A Model for Research and Practice.* New York: Academic Press. A recent and comprehensive text on the Type A personality, this excellent book details the psychological, behavioral, and physiological changes accompanying the Type A predisposition and suggests intervention strategies for reducing the destructiveness of this pattern.

Selye, H. (1950). *The Physiology and Pathology of Exposure to Stress.* Montreal: Acta. Rather technical in nature, this early classic provides a detailed look at the physiological changes that occur in living creatures exposed to uncontrollable stressors.

Selye, H. (1974). *Stress without Distress.* Philadelphia: Lippincott. A must for anybody's stress bookshelf, this book is written by one of the two founding fathers of stress theory, Hans Selye, and details the difference between positive stress (i.e., eustress) and negative stress (i.e., distress).

Index

About the Author

BERNADETTE H. SCHELL is a Professor in the School of Administration at Laurentian University in Ontario. Dr. Schell is President of her own human resource management consulting firm, is an active stress-management and industrial consultant, has served as a consulting editor for *Psychology and Marketing*, and has published many journal articles in the human resource area.